"Nevada's Enterprises" by
Gene and Adele Malott

Produced in cooperation with
the State of Nevada Commission
on Economic Development

Windsor Publications, Inc.
Chatsworth, California

NEVADA

Golden Challenge in the Silver State

A Contemporary Portrait by Guy Shipler

Windsor Publications, Inc.—Book Division
Managing Editor: Karen Story
Design Director: Alexander D'Anca
Photo Director: Susan L. Wells
Executive Editor: Pamela Schroeder

Staff for *Nevada: Golden Challenge in the Silver State*
Manuscript Editor: Doreen Nakakihara
Photo Editor: Larry Molmud
Production Editor, Text: Susan M. Pahle
Senior Editor, Corporate Profiles: Judith L. Hunter
Production Editor, Corporate Profiles: Albert Polito
Customer Service Manager: Phyllis Feldman-Schroeder
Editorial Assistants: Kim Kievman, Michael Nugwynne, Michele
Oakley, Kathy B. Peyser, Susan Schlanger, Theresa J. Solis
Publisher's Representative, Corporate Profiles: Bev Cornell
Layout Artist, Corporate Profiles: Bonnie Felt
Layout Artists: Michael Burg, Christina Rosepapa
Designer: Christina Rosepapa

Library of Congress Cataloging-in-Publication Data
Shipler, Guy, 1913-
Nevada : golden challenge in the silver state : a contemporary
portrait / by Guy Shipler.—1st ed.
p. 352 cm. 23 x 31
Includes bibliographical references.
ISBN 0-89781-348-0
1. Nevada—Economic conditions. I. Title.
HC107.N3S45 1990
330.9793'033—dc20   89-48655
                                                          CIP

Windsor Publications, Inc.
Elliot Martin, Chairman of the Board
James L. Fish III, Chief Operating Officer
Michele Sylvestro, Vice President/Sales-Marketing
Mac Buhler, Vice President/Sponsor Acquisitions

Title Spread: Photo by Tom Campbell

This Spread: Night settles in on the Lake Tahoe shoreline
at Lake Tahoe State Park. Photo by Tom Campbell

● The spine of a classic sand dune formation seemingly undulates into infinity in Amorgosa Valley. Photo by Tom Campbell

CONTENTS

PREFACE

The research for any book about Nevada can cover an area as vast as the state itself. What appears to be a barren wasteland at first appraisal turns out with each succeeding discovery to be a landscape teeming with so many of the elements of creation and survival as to be a microcosm of the universe. The covers of a single volume can contain only a broad overview of this phenomenon; the whole spectrum requires an encyclopedia.

Facts and figures always form the foundation of even a brief panorama such as this one. But in doing the research for this book, I found the tones and textures that illustrate meaning and character to have a more subtle source. They come from countless personal contacts across the years, from brief encounters to long friendships, from chance conversations to deep discussions. Their bits of color meld into a kaleidoscope of the good and the bad, the beautiful and the ugly, the wise and the ignorant, the rich and the poor. The faces, the words, and even the names of most of them may be lost in the shadows of time, but the marks they have left in passing have guided and defined the panorama.

Yet it would not have been possible to bring all that together into what I hope is a logical pattern without a solid foundation of fact and figure. If I have succeeded, much credit must go to a special group of people whose names and faces and words do indeed remain sharp and clear. They willingly gave their time and their invaluable expertise and professionalism to the sometimes monotonous research into everything from Kit Carson to the atom bomb. I am in awe of their knowledge and their perserverance, and deeply indebted to them for their help.

Jean Towne, then an associate with the Commission on Economic Development, started me off in the right direction with her insight into the commission's goal and purposes. She backed up her knowledge by digging out many of the economic facts and figures which appear in this book.

Nevada State Librarian Joan Kerschner allowed me constant access to her remarkably efficient staff; I became an almost daily visitor. It didn't matter how obscure or strange the information I sought, any staffer I asked always found it in some seemingly inaccessible recess.

I am especially indebted to Allison Cowgill, the library's Head of Reference Services. She got stuck with the brunt of my requests, some of which (like boxing) completely turned her off personally. But she always pursued them relentlessly, with accurate results, no matter how boring or distasteful the job may have been.

When Allison was not available, I confidently turned to Joyce Lee, Assistant State Librarian. Somehow she was able, without blinking, to add one of my off-the-wall requests to the myriad other duties she was juggling without dropping any of them—and see that I had the right answer quickly.

A great assist on historical accuracy, especially in separating the facts from some of the legends about Carson City, came from State Archivist Guy Louis Rocha, who seems to have such detail literally at his fingertips.

And then there were the innumerable issues of *Nevada* magazine, whose editors allowed me to peruse them freely to help bring the general theme into focus through the vast information about Nevada in their articles over the years.

My editor at Windsor Publications, Doreen Nakakihara, has my undying gratitude for her guidance, suggestions, and encouragement—and most of all, for her eagle eye that has caught most of those exasperating glitches that always manage to hide like land mines in every manuscript. By long distance, she has managed to hold the reins gently but firmly, somehow knowing where it was all going to go, and in the end making sure it would go that way.

● The Strip is most alive at night in this view of Las Vegas Boulevard. Photo by Tom Campbell

● It's easy to see how Elephant Rock
got its name. Photo by Tom Campbell

VALLEY BANK
Harrah's

Photo by Tom Campbell

.1.

The Taming Of A Wilderness

◆◆◆◆

The earliest explorers of Nevada
entered the "Northern Mystery,"
as the area was referred to,
with fear and trepidation.
But their discoveries eventually
put Nevada on the long road
to statehood.

◆◆◆◆

● Some present-day explorers probe the interior of Lehman Cave in Great Basin National Park. Photo by Tom Campbell

March 17, 1953. The first faint light of dawn breaks over Yucca Flat. A detachment of soldiers waits in shallow trenches, shivering in the sharp chill typical of the Nevada desert at night.

The public address system crackles to life and a metallic voice jars the brooding silence, sounding as unreal as the situation itself.

"Attention all personnel! . . . Repeat, all personnel! . . . Turn your eyes 180 degrees from the tower—immediately! Turn away immediately!"

The disembodied voice stops. Silence again, deeper now. The men turn their backs on a tower some 2,000 yards away.

Suddenly a light brighter than the sun itself shatters the gloom, but still no sound shatters the silence.

Then, as the soldiers turn back to become the official witnesses to the first public demonstration of an atomic explosion, they see that everything has changed.

The tower has disappeared into a huge, boiling cauldron of sand and debris, churning up into the eerie glow of a mushroom cloud reaching toward the sky. Without warning, the unseen wind of the shock wave hits, staggering the soldiers and rumbling across the desert floor, overwhelming the silence in a gigantic roar.

It is as if the primordial, raw elements of the universe have let loose to reenact the Creation itself . . .

Ever since that day, the Nevada Test Site has symbolized the extremes, the contrasts, and the contradictions which have been the soul and sinew of Nevada since the beginning of time. The some 600 atomic blasts that have since been set off there have provided a striking example of Nevada's unique history of combining the prehistoric with the future—and, in a meaningful sense, the Old West with the New West.

The existence of the site has always been a source of controversy. But over its 40-odd years of existence, it has proved to be more than just a safe place for massive explosions. Its 850,000 acres of stark, forbidding desert wilderness have become one of the world's largest and most advanced outdoor laboratories. It involves hundreds of millions of dollars of capital investment in elaborate equipment and installations, and the Department of Energy currently spends a total of about $425 million a year on the site's payroll and services.

That money goes to some 8,000 employees who work daily on key defense projects, ranging from underground nuclear tests to rocket development. For more than a quarter of a century, it has been one of the state's most important industries.

By contrast to this highly sophisticated operation, the land it occupies remains untamed and unconquered, still reflecting the harsh environment of its origin. And by further contrast, many of the employees who work on that ancient land can be home, in a completely different world, within an hour's drive on a four-lane highway. They live in Las Vegas, only 65 miles away from their workplace in distance but a million years away in time.

It puzzles some outsiders to learn that anyone at all would live in Las Vegas by choice. They know it only as the gambling and entertainment capital of the world, a desert hot spot that entirely lives up to its carefully fostered reputation as a glitzy, lusty playground for carefree Americans and wealthy foreigners of the late twentieth century.

What those outsiders usually don't know (and really don't want to believe) is that Las Vegas also functions as a modern community for its more than a quarter of a million permanent residents, who live and work in much the same fashion as their counterparts in Chicago or Dubuque.

A contradiction? Of course. It would probably make no sense anywhere else for a city of such a cosmopolitan and worldly nature to exist next door to a primitive and other-worldly neighbor. But even outsiders feel that it makes sense in Nevada—note that both the Nevada Test Site and Las Vegas enjoy precisely the same degree of worldwide fame (or notoriety), but for completely opposite reasons.

Such extremes have been woven through the whole fabric of Nevada, reaching back deep into the darkness of prehistory and stretching toward the everlasting hope of a bright tomorrow. Even its geological birth 500 million years ago was catastrophic compared to that of most other states—Illinois, for example, grew only one inch a year out of dust and mud that settled peacefully onto fairly level ground.

But for millions of years, the area from which Nevada would one day emerge went through one of the most extensive periods of upheaval, change, and confusion that has ever taken place on this planet. When it finally settled down, the resulting area was so

▼ This early scene was captured at the gateway to the University of Nevada, Reno. Courtesy, Nevada Historical Society

▶ The Washo Indian tribe were among the few people who found the rugged land of early Nevada even remotely habitable. They survived at a minimal level; without reliable water sources, they were unable to cultivate regular crops even though much of the land was rich and fertile. Courtesy, Nevada Historical Society

huge that it would occupy one-sixth of the land in the United States. And half of that would become the State of Nevada.

Early during its period of creation, some awful cataclysm blasted and tore at the gigantic mountains which had long towered over the land, sinking them beneath the surface of the ocean. Eons later, the massive interior forces of the earth erupted in a new cataclysm and pushed the sunken land back up above the seas. That didn't last either—violent earthquakes and flaming volcanoes rocked and battered the land again, this time covering most of it with a vast inland sea.

Finally, in one last gigantic upheaval, it rose once more to a high, wild desert country. Laced with the chains of rugged mountains and dry, sweeping valleys, the whole area that went through that tortuous beginning now covers more than 220,000 square miles. It stretches from the Wasatch Range of the Rocky Mountains in the east to the Sierra Nevada Range in the west, from the Columbia River Basin in the north to the Colorado River Basin in the south.

For centuries it lay nameless and virtually untouched by human beings. Stark, severe, and forbidding, it was regarded as too dangerous to explore, and it turned away all but a handful of white men until the early nineteenth century. It was finally named in 1844, thanks to one of its brave explorers. Brevet Captain John C. Frémont called it the "Great Basin" because, even though he had seen only a small part of it, he thought the vast wilderness resembled a huge bowl.

He was wrong. Rather than a single large bowl, the Great Basin (as it is still known today) consists of many bowls intermingled with mountain ranges and peaks up to 13,000 feet high. All cover a large, elevated plateau that slopes gradually from an average altitude in the north of about 5,000 feet above sea level to almost 300 feet below sea level in the south, in what is now Death Valley.

Although the Great Basin covers portions of six states, Nevada's total area of 110,540 square miles takes up a little more than half of it. Rugged mountain ranges, running north and south and forested only at the high elevations, are separated by long, flat valleys. Because the land and sea changed places so often during its long and violent history of development, the shells of crustaceans still lie at the tops of many high mountain peaks.

But by an ironic geological contradiction, and despite all those millions of square miles of water that washed over it to such depths, Nevada today is the driest of any of the 50 states, averaging only nine inches of precipitation a year.

The little water that remains behaves differently here than it does anywhere else in the country. The Great Basin is the only one of the 12 drainage areas within the United States whose waters do not flow into oceans. Instead, its few rivers and streams—all of them small—flow into the equally few existing lakes, or into "sinks" (former lakes that have dried up into alkaline flats). The water from the sinks then disappears into the ground or into the air. The air itself is so dry that it can evaporate from 7 to 19 times the amount of water that falls as rain. Some Nevada valleys see no rain at all for a year and a half or more.

▶ One of the first white men to cross the breadth of what would become Nevada, Jedediah Smith was fascinated by the mystical attraction of the American West. Courtesy, Nevada Historical Society

For centuries, the only people who found this raw land even remotely habitable were the Paiute, Shoshone, and Washo Indian tribes. They survived at a minimal level; without adequate and reliable water sources, they could not cultivate many crops even though much of the land was unusually rich and fertile. Like their ancestors for millenia before them, they had to learn how to subsist on such nourishment as ground-up mesquite pods, grasshoppers, and crickets.

No outside visitors came to share that unappetizing fare until many years after white men began exploring the rest of the continental wilderness. Those who had an urge to pioneer the West had concentrated on more benign climates and landscapes. That had turned out to be tough enough; they saw no need to risk life and limb on the greater challenge of an area known only for its dangers. Even the bold Spaniards, who as early as the seventeenth century had started to settle the Southwest and finally extended their presidios up the Pacific Coast to San Francisco, would not venture into the unknown, unnamed land. They called it the "Northern Mystery."

The white men who finally did make the first cautious probings in the early 1880s confirmed that the stories and rumors they had heard were true. One of the bravest of these early pioneers was a pious New Englander named Jedediah Smith. Fascinated by the mystical attraction of the American West that later would become so widespread, he set out in 1827 into that "Northern Mystery" and became the first white man to cross the full breadth of what would someday be Nevada.

As it would be to thousands who followed him, the experience of mastering the rugged desert mountains, and surviving the broad, parched valleys of sand and glaring white alkaline flats and salt beds, became an almost unbearable ordeal.

Wrote Smith in his diary: "We frequently travel without water sometimes for two days over sandy deserts, where there was no sign of vegetation."

Between Smith's arduous trip and 1844, an occasional band of trappers and hunters ventured into the area. Many of them died of hunger or thirst, and those who lived felt lucky to survive at all. A trapper named Milton Sublette, who led a party into northeastern Nevada in 1832, later described the typical experience:

The men, though tough and seasoned frontiersmen, had their troubles . . . Their stock of food ran low. Hunters found little game [although they were in an area which today is favored by hunters]. Beaver were available, but were judged inedible because they had been eating poisonous wild carrot. The horses lost weight. Water was hard to find. Men bled mules and made a soup of the blood.

On New Year's Day 1844, a party of 25 frontiersmen, heading south from Oregon, stood on the edge of what would become known as Nevada's Black Rock Desert. Led by John C. Frémont, the men were making the first official government exploration of the still little-known wilderness, the last of what would become the lower 48 United States to be penetrated by the white man. No stranger himself to exploring unknown land, Frémont had chosen as members of his party several highly experienced frontiersmen and mountain men, including such noted veterans of the Rocky Mountain fur brigades as Thomas "Broken Hand" Fitzpatrick and Christopher "Kit" Carson.

All had seen more than their

◀ Kit Carson was one of a party of frontiersmen led by John C. Frémont who would penetrate the unknown wilderness that would eventually become Nevada. Courtesy, Nevada Historical Society

♦♦♦

KIT CARSON'S NAMESAKE

♦♦♦

It had taken months for John C. Frémont and his handpicked party of 25 frontiersmen and mountain men to reach the valley at the western edge of the rugged, high desert wilderness. They had made it largely because of the expertise of their guide and scout, a veteran of the Rocky Mountain fur brigades named Christopher "Kit" Carson.

Frémont had chosen Carson carefully. As leader of the first official government exploration of the vast, unknown wilderness west of the Rocky Mountains, Frémont figured he had to have the best. Kit Carson was the candidate whose reputation fit that requirement.

Carson had demonstrated his expertise and sure knowledge as a scout during the long months spent crossing the Great Basin's harsh landscape. Now, close by the Sierra Nevada foothills, he had found a verdant valley, nourished by a river that flowed from the towering mountain range, where the party could rest for a while. The contrast to the desert filled the weary travelers with such gratitude that Frémont named the welcome river for the man who had gotten them there. It has officially been the Carson River ever since.

But it wasn't until seven years later, in 1851, that the first white settlers established a trading post near the river. Needing a name for their post, they nailed the feathers of a large eagle over the door and called it Eagle Station.

By 1858 the trading post had expanded into a community. Since it was now larger than a trading post, the local citizens decided to change its name. Eagle Station became Eagle Valley, and the community became Carson City, named after the nearby river and the legendary scout.

But Kit Carson never saw the town. His only recorded visit to the area after the 1844 Frémont expedition came in 1853, when he passed through during a sheep drive from New Mexico to Sacramento. All he saw was a trading post named Eagle Station.

The 1859 discovery of gold and silver on the Comstock Lode, only 17 miles away in Virginia City, gave Carson City a boost toward becoming a thriving commercial and industrial center. That gave it enough political clout to be named the capital city of the Territory of Nevada and the seat of the newly created Ormsby County— but not enough for it to automatically become the state capital.

In fact, it very nearly lost out in that quest. During the state constitutional convention in 1864, a heated debate took place over Section 1 of Article XVI of the proposed constitution, which read: "The seat of government shall be Carson City, but no appropriation for the erection or purchase of capitol buildings shall be made during the next three years."

No sooner had the secretary finished reading it than J.H. Warwick, a delegate from Lander County, jumped up and proclaimed: "I move to amend the section by striking out the words, 'at Carson City,' and inserting the words, 'wherever the Legislature may prescribe' [because] at the present time the capital is situated on the extreme western border of the Territory, and the business and population is steadily going over on the other side."

J. Neely Johnson, president of the convention and, it so happened, a delegate from Ormsby County, rose to say that in spite of the possible sense of "impropriety" he would defend the choice of Carson City. He said he was sure the representatives "do not want this matter left in such a condition as to place the state capital upon wheels, and let it go traveling around from one place to another."

To support his argument, Johnson cited that California had gone through "various removals of the capital." He added, "Year after year the seat of government was changed, greatly to the perplexity and bewilderment of the people [of that state who] were agitated with the all-important question, not alone of where the capital should be, but where it really was."

Johnson's argument carried the day, and Carson City has been the capital for the 125 years of Nevada's statehood. But not everyone remains happy with that choice. In recent years, as the Las Vegas area has experienced unprecedented population growth, area loyalists have argued that the capital should be moved there.

However, such a drastic change appears unlikely in the foreseeable future, if at all. As the longest continuously incorporated city in the state, Carson City began establishing deep roots as Nevada's historic and cultural center right from the start. In the beginning it had stood at the heart of the Nevada economy as well.

For instance, Nevada's first short-line railroad, the Virginia & Truckee, was completed in 1870 to carry the rich ore from the Comstock mines to the mills along the Carson River for processing. An extension of the track two years later connected it to the transcontinental Central Pacific Railroad in Reno. Maintenance shops and an engine house were its headquarters in Carson City until the V&T was abandoned in 1950.

Early commercial and industrial development came about through the efforts of Abraham Curry, a pioneer who arrived in Eagle Valley in July 1858. Certain that Carson City would become the state capital, in September of that year the visionary Curry surveyed and platted 10 acres of land expressly for the construction of a capitol building. He worked to establish a branch of the United States Mint in Carson City, and succeeded in 1866.

As the branch's first superintendent, Curry supervised the production of gold and silver coins from Comstock bullion starting in 1870. The building operated as a mint and assay office until 1933, was sold to the State of Nevada in 1939, and became the Nevada State Museum in 1941.

Two blocks away, the four-story, brick federal building opened in 1891 to house the district court, land office, weather bureau, and post office. The only federal building of its architectural style still standing in the western United States, it has operated since the post office left it in 1970 as the home of the Nevada State Library.

The other major federal project in Carson City, the former Stewart Indian School at the south end of town, was opened in 1890. A gracious complex of stone buildings, it served as a federal training school for Native Americans for 90 years, and is now used by the state for government offices.

Meanwhile, local entrepreneurs built their homes on the west side of town, an area that has become the largest historical residential district of its kind in Nevada. When Orion Clemens served as secretary for the Nevada Territory, he and his brother, Mark Twain, lived there in a house which still exists. The Abe Curry house and the home of George Ferris, Sr., whose son invented the Ferris wheel, still stand. The governor's mansion, completed in 1909, has been acclaimed as one of the finest such structures in the country. In all, 22 historic sites and buildings are so marked in Carson City.

THE WORLD'S CHA
HEAVY WEIGHT —— USES EXCLUS
Ratsch Peerless ATHLET
GOO
CHICAGO SPORTING GOODS

share of rugged country but this spot looked more like something on the moon, causing them "considerable unease," as Frémont later reported. In the distance they saw the vapor plumes of hot springs, but the trail they blazed down a creek went through ice and snow and salty soil "amid formidable burnt scenery that looked like monumental heaps of coal and cinders."

Two days later the expedition found itself in fog so dense no one could see 100 yards ahead. Yet when one of the party climbed a hill, he suddenly found himself in brilliant sunshine. Wrote Frémont in his report: "The appearance of the country was so forbidding that I was afraid to enter it."

But he entered it anyway, walking southward with his party into a completely unknown and incredibly dry land. Suddenly, totally unexpectedly, they came upon a huge,

ION

MADE
BY

CO.

◄ With the discovery of a wealth of natural resources came a huge influx of people and their pastimes. This bout was captured at Rick's Resort Training Camp near the turn of the century. Courtesy, Nevada Historical Society

green-blue lake some 30 miles long and from 4 to 11 miles wide. "It broke on our eyes like an ocean," wrote Frémont. It lay in striking contradiction between barren, rugged ranges of russet brown, with a triangular rock rising high above the surface of the lake. Wrote Samuel G. Houghton in *The Great Basin Story*: "Frémont observed it . . . offshore about midway along his passage, and likened it to the Great Pyramid of Cheops, which structure dates from about 5,000 years ago and is 481 feet high, comparable in size if not precisely in shape. The natural one is of course many times the age of the Egyptians'."

Naturally Frémont named this seemingly out-of-place inland body of water Pyramid Lake. Lying in its mysterious and prehistoric beauty 30 miles northeast of the twentieth-century city of Reno, it still belongs to the Paiute Indian tribe as it did for centuries before its "discovery" by Frémont. But in addition to being the headquarters of the Paiutes' reservation, it has also become a prime example for present-day tourists enchanted by the primitive nature of the land.

Only some 50 miles to the southwest, Frémont became the first white man to see the breathtaking sight of another spectacular lake, this one high in the Sierra Nevada Mountains. Here again the explorers saw one of the striking contradictions so typical of the area. Except for being roughly the same size, this body of water was totally different from the harsh desert hills and shores of Pyramid Lake. Instead, dramatic snowcapped peaks and thick pine forests surrounded the lake, which itself was some 22 miles long and 15 miles wide. Intensely blue under the usually brilliant blue skies, its surface lay some 6,225 feet above sea level.

Lake Tahoe, as it would later be named, is bisected by the border between California and Nevada, with two-thirds of it on the California side. It was destined to become one of the nation's natural wonders, an attraction for tourists from all over the world.

Few explorers had seen more unusual landscapes than John C. Frémont before he ever came to the Great Basin. But the deeper he penetrated it, the less formidable it became, especially after he had set eyes on that spectacular Sierra lake. His 1845 report of his first visit to the territory revealed the impact the variety of the landscape was having on him:

The whole idea of such a desert is a novelty in our country, and excites Asiatic, not American ideas. Interior basins, with their own system of lakes and rivers, and often sterile, are common enough in Asia . . . but in America such things are new and strange, unknown and unsuspected, and discredited when related . . .

Throughout this nakedness of sand and gravel were many beautiful plants and flowering shrubs, which occurred in many new species, and with greater variety than we had been accustomed to see in the most luxuriant prairie countries; this was a peculiarity of this desert. Even where no grass would take root, the naked sand would bloom with some rich and rare flower, which found its appropriate home in the arid and barren spot.

But it would take years for such attractions to convince any but the most adventurous Easterners that this would be a good place to come and settle. They lived in more placid places, and only the stories of the trials and tribulations of the pioneers stuck in their minds. To them the Great Basin, by then part of the Utah Territory, was a frightening and capricious land. That apprehension kept hordes of them away . . . until the news came of the 1848 discovery in California of wealth beyond anyone's wildest dreams.

Gold became the magic word. A year later, a flood of fortune seekers put aside any fears of the "Northern Mystery"; some 30,000 of them stampeded in from the East, making the Forty-niners the first large group of non-Indians to come into—and go through—the area. Simple geography told them that this was the shortest route to their shining goal, and their eagerness made them willing to put up with any hardship.

The journey turned out to be worse than they anticipated. Few of the Forty-niners had the training, the stamina, or the experience of the frontiersmen who themselves had approached the area with trepidation. Yet they had to cross the land which Frémont himself had said in the beginning he was afraid to enter.

"Unfortunately," wrote historian Richard G. Lillard, "the golden news from California started an impetuous mass migration before the desert lore of the pathfinders had become general knowledge. Needless death and suffering resulted, but Nevada could no more stop the stampede than it could stop the wheels of destiny.

"The rush of '49 was a crucial episode in American history, one of the great mid-century events that changed the map and the civilization of the country. To participants it was an experience to record, to recall. Hundreds of men and women kept diaries and journals or later penned reminiscences. As a result the crossing to California is the most documented mass movement in history."

It was also one of the most important. One historian, Bayard Taylor, put it at the top of the list:

The story of 30,000 souls accomplishing a journey of more than 2,000 miles through a savage and but partially explored wilderness, crossing on their way two mountain chains equal to the Alps in height and asperity, besides broad tracts of burning desert, and plains of nearly equal desolation, where a few patches of stunted shrubs and springs of brackish water were their only stay, has in it so much of heroism, of daring and sublime endurance, that we may vainly question the records of any age for its equal.

The worst of all was an infamous area known as the Forty-Mile Desert. This stretch of soft sand runs between the Humboldt and Carson rivers, but its only water was steaming hot or poisonous, all of it seemingly diabolically placed to taunt tongues thick with thirst.

Wagons foundered in the sand. To lighten loads, the emigrants had to dump priceless possessions they had brought all the way across the prairies and the Rockies. Oxen and cattle died in such numbers that one diarist wrote that a man could walk almost the length of the desert on their bodies without ever stepping on the ground. "Every mile the evidence of panic increased," he wrote. "Dead animals lay in front of the wagons . . . a man counted a thousand abandoned wagons in 42 miles . . . It was a dryland Sargossa Sea, a graveyard of overland schooners."

Yet the place held some mystical attraction for others, even after such horror stories. They came on foot, on horseback, in covered wagons, by stagecoach. Individuals who might have been outcasts at home and families with little children braved the hard journey to settle on the desert and in the mountains. They found lush valleys, thick with tall grass, hidden in canyons and nourished by streams from the snowpacks in the mountains above. They built cabins in them and spread out into farms, and later into sheep and cattle ranches.

They found, to their surprise, that the soil was remarkably rich despite the lack of adequate water. They applied their ingenuity to bring water from the hills for irrigation. Combined with a climate with an average of 300 days a year of sunshine, they learned that they could grow abundant crops, especially hay. It seemed to grow almost automatically, and it was remarkably nutritious. Men were beginning to learn that they could make a living from this supposed wasteland.

Not all the settlers came to farm. Among them were mining men who, with their special instinct, could look at the hills and tell that somewhere beneath their russet surfaces lay mineral wealth.

They turned out to be right, early in the game. In 1859, high in the desert mountains above a river named for the great explorer, Kit Carson, the big strike that every mining man dreamed about materialized—the Comstock Lode. Its mines turned out to be the richest in precious metals ever to be discovered in the U.S., their veins so deep and extensive that they gave more permanence than the California placer camps, or most of the hard-rock camps Nevada itself would ever know.

But the location of the Comstock Lode presented an awesome challenge. Because it lay 6,200 feet above sea level, far from any community that could be called civilized even in those pioneer days, it took the most ingenious engineering to get the fabulously rich ore out of the ground. The mining camp atop it was named Virginia City, a town which would at its peak number nearly 30,000 souls. But it had one major drawback—there was no water supply within 20 miles. The solution was a wooden flume built from Marlette Lake, high in the Sierra to the west. The flume wound down the canyons to a low point at about 5,000 feet above sea level, then syphoned up to a small lake built just above the town.

Likewise, with no timber on the sagebrush-covered Virginia range, lumber essential for the mines had to be brought from the Sierra. It was floated down flumes to mills in the valleys, then wagons carried the timbers up the tortuous, steep roads to the Comstock. The demand grew as the mines got deeper. But as the underground rooms got larger, a serious problem developed—the mines began to collapse.

One of the greatest mining booms in history might have ended prematurely except for another key bit of ingenuity. Philip Deidesheimer, a German immigrant and a mining expert, invented a method of timbering the mines called the "square set," which was a system of supports built in a honeycombed fashion to contain the loose ore. It not only ended the mine collapse, but is now used the world over.

More importantly for the future of the Great Basin, this invention made it possible for the miners to spread the tunneling through the huge deposit and take the fabulously rich silver ore out of vein after vein over a more than 20-year period. So fabulous was the production of silver from beneath that colorful and violent land that it not only gave Nevada its first major nonagricultural industry, but in the process, it changed the course of history.

The major change came in 1864. Only 20 years after Frémont first set foot in it, more than half of the "Northern Mystery" became the State of Nevada—an official part of the United States of America, number 36 in the roll call. This did not come about because the landscape might somehow have been transformed from its inherent wilderness nature into a latter-day Garden of Eden; it had not changed one iota in that respect. Instead, this sudden recognition that despite a rather uncouth background it might qualify as a legitimate resident of the civilized world rested on the old-fashioned combination of money and politics.

The first part of that equation was, of course, the fabulous wealth coming from the rich silver-bearing ore being taken from the mines beneath the town of Virginia City. Standing alone, that would hardly be an acceptable reason for bestowing statehood on any large piece of land, much less on a crude, remote desert whose only claim to fame was the silver under a shanty town in the Wild West. Even the wheelers and dealers in Washington, D.C., would not go that far.

True, the politicians knew that some men were getting fabulously rich from the produce beneath that shanty town, and that made them sound a little more respectable in the effete East—especially since their wealth was helping to build the gracious and sophisticated city of San Francisco in nearby California. But that wouldn't be enough in itself, either.

It was politics and perfect timing that tipped the scale: a combination of the Comstock Lode riches and the Civil War led to an internal struggle between the North and the South. Nobody on either side really wanted the place, but this neat coincidence suddenly had everybody on both sides trying to obtain it—a familiar situation for this land with its history of contrasts, contradictions, and extremes.

The first side to start wooing Nevada to join its cause in the early 1860s was the Confederacy, already desperately short of funds. As soon as its president, Jefferson Davis, learned of the rich mines in the distant wilderness, he figured that if he could make a deal it would go a long way toward solving his financial problems. He wasted no time. Off went a proposal to the territorial government; he would make the area a Confederate state in return for its silver.

But Davis was up against a population of individualists, people who had risked life and limb to establish themselves in a still-unconquered land. They had a fierce desire for stability. A deal with Davis meant secession, and a gamble that the attempt to establish a Confederate government would be successful.

That looked much too uncertain. If they were going to join anybody, the Union looked a lot more substantial, especially since its Congress had already paved the way for statehood by creating the Nevada Territory in 1861.

The local folk fully realized that this move by Congress came not because of any affection for their territory. The Union wanted to keep those fabulous mines out of Confederate hands. But Abraham Lincoln made it clear that he would not grant statehood for Nevada unless he could get something else out of the bargain—a promise that the new

● There was an enormous wealth coming from the rich, silver-bearing ore being taken from the mines beneath the town of Virginia City. Many came to the desert territory, not yet the 36th state, to work in the mines or to stake their own claims. Courtesy, Nevada Historical Society

◄ A group of rugged miners pose outside their boarding house in 1901. Courtesy, Nevada Historical Society

state would cast its three votes in Congress to assure passage of the Thirteenth Amendment. That amendment was essential to making permanent the freedom of the slaves, and thus vital to giving meaning to the president's cause.

But passage of the amendment had also become a key military necessity. As Lincoln said to Charles A. Dana, Assistant Secretary of War: "If we don't carry this vote, then we will be compelled to raise another million, and I don't know how many more, men and fight no one knows how long. It's easier to admit Nevada than to raise another million soldiers."

And so on October 31, 1864, this undeveloped frontier became the 36th member of the refined family of states, 48 years before Arizona, its next-door neighbor to the south, would enjoy such a distinction.

But the rest of the family didn't exactly receive the newcomer with open arms. In fact, they generally regarded Nevada as a black-sheep member who had to eat in the kitchen when company came to dinner. Right from the start, it seemed so much of a maverick that indignant editorials demanding its ouster from the Union became a favorite topic for many years.

Nevada remains a maverick, still carrying many of the characteristics of the freewheeling Old West. It takes fierce pride in living by what most of its citizens regard as a realistic view of human nature. They argue that their acceptance of liberal marriage and divorce laws, controlled legalized gambling, and the independence of the individual are far less hypocritical—and less immoral—than denying the existence of these aspects of life as most other states still do.

And they are grateful, from a purely economic point of view, that outsiders find all this so horrifying that their states have refused to go along with that attitude. For it is the outsiders who come to Nevada to take advantage of these freedoms that make the state's economy flourish. Every year an average of 25 million people visit Nevada as tourists. That is about 25 times the permanent population, and is more than the number of visitors received by either Washington, D.C, or Florida.

And what of the future? Will the easing of antigambling sentiment elsewhere adversely affect the major ingredient of Nevada's tourism economy?

All current signs indicate no such problem on the horizon. Even though Atlantic City has had directly competing casino gambling since 1978, and even though more and more states have full-blown lotteries (which, by the way, are unconstitutional in Nevada), gaming continues to boom here. Especially in the state's major gaming centers—Las Vegas, Laughlin, Reno, and Lake Tahoe—the gaming business has been a growth industry almost steadily since gambling was legalized more than half a century ago. The communities involved face only a positive problem: how to plan building and licensing regulations to serve continued growth without straining local resources.

But there have long been strong efforts to avoid keeping all the economic eggs in one basket. Especially during the past six years, the state has taken major, concrete steps toward diversification of industry. In 1983 the Nevada Legislature approved Governor

▶ Gaming and stage-shows remain at the heart of tourism, the state's number-one industry. Courtesy, Nevada Historical Society

Richard Bryan's proposal to create a Commission on Economic Development to expand and revitalize the 28-year-old State Department of Economic Development. Its main goal has been to promote Nevada among out-of-state businesses and industries, and encourage them to relocate here. The results have been impressive so far: Governor Bryan announced in 1988 that 6,258 new firms have located in Nevada since the commission was created.

But diversification does not mean substitution. Gaming remains the heart of tourism, the state's number one industry. Like economic development, tourism has received its own added boost through the governor's recommendation: the legislature also established a Commission on Tourism for that purpose. It engages in national advertising of everything from hunting and fishing in the state's still pristine, undisturbed natural environment to skiing in some of the world's most spectacular country. And it is directly or indirectly involved in promoting everything from the top stage shows in hotel casinos to rodeos, from air races to camel races.

In less than 150 years, a relative handful of adventurous and independent people have not only tamed an awesomely challenging wilderness but have made it attractive to so many others that Nevada has become one of the nation's fastest-growing states. Those who come and stay learn that the sharp contrasts and contradictions that seemed so fearsome to the early pioneers hold strong but benign subtleties of serenity and beauty. Most see it toward the end of their first day, when the bold profiles of rugged desert peaks in the distance become a tapestry of delicate pastels in the soft evening.

▼ This group of relaxed cowhands posed outside the WM Stock Ranch in Paradise Valley, Nevada. Courtesy, Nevada Historical Society

▲ As this post-World War II photo shows, Reno had become quite a thriving metropolis. Courtesy, Nevada Historical Society

.2.

THE BLOOMING OF THE DESERT

◆◆◆◆

Mining and ranching have long been mainstays of Nevada's economy—helping to create a viable system of commerce for the Silver State.

◆◆◆◆

● A steady stream of visitors and commerce flows in and out of Nevada's major population centers, day and night. This is U.S. 95 heading into downtown Las Vegas. Photo by Tom Campbell

Nevada has been a sovereign state of the Union for more than 125 years. But nearly 87 percent of its land is still under the ownership or control of the federal government, just as it has been since the area first became a U.S. territory.

Most residents resent it. Periodically they campaign—to no avail—for freedom from what they feel is the government yoke. Even official efforts don't work. In 1979 the Nevada Legislature passed a resolution which led to the so-called "Sagebrush Rebellion." In effect, it demanded that the federal government turn over most of its lands to the state.

It didn't, of course, and it won't for a long time to come.

But as yokes go, federal control is really not unbearable. Like states which own most of their land, Nevada has autonomy over its own political structure. It established 17 counties, which cover all of the state's 110,540 square miles. Each county has its own commission and other local elected officials. Its voters send assemblymen and senators to represent them in the state legislature, which meets in Carson City, the state capital, every two years.

And, although the state cannot collect taxes from that federal land, it gets proportionately large funds from Washington for projects ranging from military installations to huge reclamation programs. Moreover, for relatively low costs, residents and visitors alike can use the public lands for their livelihoods: prospectors stake claims and mine its precious metals, ranchers send their livestock across the endless miles of sagebrush-covered range to feed on whatever browse is available, and the recreation industry flourishes on the lakes, mountains, and streams that offer everything from boating and skiing to hunting and fishing.

So the average Nevadan finds his fierce sense of independence torn. He is loyal, on the one hand, to his conviction that freedom to use the land is not the same thing as the freedom to own it. On the other, he would hate to see those federal funds disappear . . .

For more than half a century after its discovery in 1859, the Comstock Lode poured out its wealth of precious metal. Gold and silver—especially the latter—flowed in such a rich, heavy stream that no one thought it could ever be matched again, at least not in Nevada.

There was good reason for such confidence. Before the mines were exhausted in 1921, $336,339,720 in silver and $164,023,917 in gold—both staggering sums in those days—came out of the Comstock. To those who worked so hard to extract it, and who made huge fortunes in the process, this had to be the bonanza to end all bonanzas. And they made the most of it.

As soon as it became clear that the rich strike was no flash in the pan, they set about turning the boomtown mining camp on the rugged terrain above the mines into Nevada's first real city. Within five years the tents and jerry-built shacks that had mushroomed at the time of the discovery began to disappear into a community of permanent buildings. Virginia City, spreading over the ever-deepening mines, developed a pattern of urban life; it even had straight, regular streets just like more civilized towns. The land along them was quickly subdivided into expensive lots—preferred frontages of 40 or 50 feet sold for between $10,000 and $20,000.

That was chicken feed to the suddenly affluent mining officials and local merchants. They not only snapped up the land, but then spent astronomical sums to build plush houses. Since Virginia City was perched precariously on a mountain slope some 6,200 feet above sea level, all building supplies, tools, equipment, and furnishings had to be brought in from 20 to 100 miles away, and hauled up from the valleys at horrendous cost. Between what was needed to shore up the mines

◀ Samuel Clemens, also known as Mark Twain, worked as a staff reporter for Virginia City's flamboyant local newspaper, the *Territorial Enterprise*. Courtesy, Nevada Historical Society

and build the new housing, there was as much lumber in and under the virtually treeless desert community of Virginia City as there was in the whole city of Chicago.

Lavish spending became the Virginia City norm. The residents tried to outdo one another by living the way they had heard the gentry of Europe lived. They threw elaborate banquets, heavily featuring caviar and champagne—not because they particularly liked either one, but because that was the way rich people lived.

They also knew that rich people promoted such elegant activities as the theater and the opera, so they decided to emulate them in that field, too. Because most of the residents came from crude backgrounds and had little education and no experience in the social graces, they entered this unknown field somewhat self-consciously. Most had come from an environment where just staying alive was a daily challenge, but now they had to deal with the strange luxury of something called culture.

Their role was simple: Provide money. Since they had it in abundance, theaters soon blossomed to a point where Virginia City offered some of the best entertainment in the nation. The most popular, the most famous, and the most adored actors, opera singers, and musicians of the day, from Edwin Booth to Maude Adams, performed on the local stages.

And there was a young man from Missouri who started a writing career that would make him world famous.

The reason Samuel Clemens had come to the state was to pay a short visit to his brother, Orion Clemens, who had been made Secretary of the Territory of Nevada when it was separated from the Territory of Utah in 1861. The booming excitement intrigued Sam and he decided to stick around awhile—especially after discovering Virginia City's flamboyant local newspaper, the *Territorial Enterprise*. Being of a flamboyant nature himself, Sam figured he would fit in nicely on the staff, and he managed to get a job as a reporter for the paper.

Fortunately for Sam's literary future, the paper took a rather lax attitude toward

▶ Orion Clemens, brother of writer Mark Twain, had been made the secretary of the Territory of Nevada when it was separated from the Territory of Utah in 1861. Courtesy, Nevada Historical Society

facts. Clemens took full advantage of that wide-open perception of freedom of the press by keeping much of his "reporting" to light, humorous stories that came out of his head.

A biographer of Clemens, Albert Bigelow Paine, later explained that the the paper's co-owner and editor, Joseph T. Goodman, "let his staff write and print, with almost no restraint . . . Some of the sketches were indeed fancy. Sam Clemens wrote a number of hoaxes that not only fooled readers, but many papers along the coast."

But the Clemens stories, usually in the form of letters, were unsigned. "They were easily identified with one another," wrote Paine, "but not with a personality. To build a reputation it was necessary to have a name.

"Clemens reflected upon the matter, trying to hit upon something brief, crisp and unforgettable." Reaching back to his youthful memories of the Mississippi River, he found something that "would give a new meaning in this faraway land." He went to Goodman with the idea, telling him he wanted to sign his articles so he could be identified to a wider audience. When Goodman asked what name he wanted to use, Clemens said, according to Paine:

I want to sign them "Mark Twain." It is an old river term, a leadsman's call, signifying two fathoms—twelve feet. It has a richness about it; it was always a pleasant sound for a pilot to hear on a dark night; it meant safe water.

Paine reports that the pen name "was first signed to an *Enterprise* letter on Feb. 2, 1863, and from that time was attached to all of Samuel Clemens' work."

Yet neither the genius of Mark Twain, nor the gourmet banquets of the rich and famous, nor the self-conscious preoccupation with culture could turn Virginia City into what passed even then as a civilized community. It remained a raw, frontier town; none of these things could hide the overwhelming number of more earthly pursuits which made this the most famous, the toughest, and the most lively of all the mining camps in the West.

True, the place did have its share of staid and upright citizens who tried to give the impression that its skirts were both clean and proper by boasting that it had six churches. But that was hardly enough to offset the louder boasts from others that Virginia City also had 110 saloons, 5 breweries, and 10 wholesale liquor stores. One record claims that in

◄ Much of Nevada retains a raw and wild character that has become an integral part of its charm. This is "The Bottle House" in Rhyolite, constructed of 30,000 individual glass containers. Photo by Kerrick James/New West Images

● This is all that remains of a silver mining town that was thriving in Hamilton, Nevada, in the middle of the last century. Photos by Kerrick James/New West Images

a two-year period, gunfights took the lives of 400 people.

Nevertheless, for all its crudeness, pretensions, and wildness, Virginia City signaled the establishment of mining as Nevada's first major industry, and did so in spectacular fashion. But it turned out to be just a prelude to an even greater bonanza that would take place a century later, this time with no end in sight.

In November 1987 a story in *Forbes* magazine noted the contrast between the new bonanza and that of its famed predecessor this way:

Not even the state's great silver rush of over a hundred years ago comes close to matching the current gold mining boom in Nevada's barren hills and valleys . . . The improvements made since 1979 in recovery processes . . . have made pay dirt of once-uneconomic ore. Today ore that contains as little as 0.015 ounces of gold per ton can be profitable. Just eight years ago you needed ore seven times as rich.

Unlike most mining booms this one seems almost certain to continue well into the 1990s, barring an unexpected and disastrous drop in the price of gold. By the end of 1988, according to the Nevada Bureau of Mines and Geology, Nevada was leading all other states, with 60 percent of the nation's gold production. And of the 25 leading gold-producing mines in the United States, 14 were in Nevada.

"Gold is now mined in every county in Nevada except Carson City," the Nevada Employ-

▼ Nevada has been a key factor in making the United States the world's third-largest gold producer. This is the Newmont Gold Mine in Carlin, Nevada. Photo by Tom Campbell

ment Security Department reported in March 1988. "More than 10 substantial new mines were opened in 1986 and 1987, and others are under construction. All of these mines have reserves that won't be exhausted for 15 years or more."

Nevada has been a key factor in making the United States the world's third-largest gold producer, after South Africa and the Soviet Union.

Why this sudden surge? And why didn't it take place long ago?

The main answer lies in recent high-technology developments that have made it possible to recover "invisible gold," which is spread so finely through ore bodies that it is submicroscopic, its average size measured in microns.

The process used is called "heap leaching," discovered in the 1920s but not widely used until recently. It involves piling a flat plateau of low-grade ore on a pad and spraying it with a sprinkler system like that used for lawns. But instead of using water, the system sprays the pile with a cyanide solution, which absorbs the gold as it drains through the pile. An impermeable substance at the bottom of the pile funnels the gold-filled cyanide to collection areas.

This system permits the recovery of gold from ore that is so low-grade that it used to be nothing but waste; in some cases up to 30 tons of rock must be processed to recover one ounce of gold. In the days before these high-tech procedures, it simply could not be done profitably.

But even with the new techniques, it could not be done profitably without the booming price of gold. Modern technology has made the maximum cost of gold recovery about $250 an ounce in open-pit operations, and $325 an ounce in subsurface operations. With the price of gold running well above that (in late 1989 it was selling at around $375 an ounce), it can drop drastically and still allow the mining companies to operate profitably.

The 17 largest mines are located in the northern two-thirds of the state, and all of them are far enough away from the major urban areas to be of huge benefit to the rural communities nearby. In 1986 alone, for example, the dozen or so new mines that opened, combined with the expansion of existing operations, provided about 2,000 new jobs in rural Nevada. By early 1988 it had become all but impossible to find a motel room in towns like Elko, in eastern Nevada, because of the influx of miners from all over the West. A big reason is money: the Employment Security Department says that in 1988 the average annual wages stood at more than $29,000 per worker.

But a few have hit an even bigger jackpot. Among them are Roy Ash and the heirs of the late Charles "Tex" Thornton. *Forbes* magazine reported:

In the early 1960s, Ash and Thornton each paid $1.25 million for the T Lazy S, a 223,000-acre cattle ranch stretching from Battle Mountain to Carlin, Nev. As these things go, the ranch was a good tax shelter. Better yet, the investment turned out years later to be sitting atop the Gold Quarry deposit, where Newmont Mining Corp. was extensively exploring.

The ranch and certain mineral rights were sold to Newmont in 1982 for $35 million—plus an unusually large 16.2 percent gross revenue royalty on all minerals produced . . .

In 1988 a little under 600,000 ounces will be produced from Gold Quarry, entitling the royalty holders to at least $25 million. Ash and Thornton's heirs could realize about $300 million to $350 million in royalties from Gold Quarry over the next 15 years.

But the ground beneath Nevada's rugged hills and valleys is not only rich in the two precious metals of gold and silver. More than 25 industrial minerals and 3 important energy sources—petroleum, coal, and geothermal steam—have been located in Nevada.

They range from huge copper deposits to exotic minerals with special industrial capabilities. For instance there is diatomite, a product with scores of uses including the filtering of beverages and swimming pools. And Nevada has the largest deposit in the world of magnesite, an industrial mineral used in the manufacture of refractory bricks and other

◄ This snake-like apparition in the desert is the Geothermal Steam Plant in Stillwater, Nevada. Photos by Tom Campbell

shapes used in high-temperature situations, such as iron ore blast furnaces.

Except for petroleum and coal, Nevada is unusually rich in almost all metallic and nonmetallic minerals. And yet the history of mining any and all of them has followed that age-old Nevada characteristic of extremes and contradictions. Every one of these underground riches has had a roller-coaster existence, a lifetime of boom and bust, of bonanza and borasca.

Consider, for instance, that mineral production dropped from a peak of $46.7 million in 1877 to $2.5 million in 1900. By 1918, after the discovery of gold and silver at Tonopah and Goldfield, it soared to a new record of $48.6 million.

And by 1987, total mineral production in Nevada stood at between $700 million and $800 million.

● A great many of Nevada's natural resources, like diatomite and magnesite, are of high industrial value. Photos by Tom Campbell

The people who have contributed to the booms and suffered from the busts have ranged from the grizzled prospector far out in the lonely hills to giant corporations. Most of the strikes across the years have been small, sparkling briefly for the pick-and-shovel men who sweated to get enough out of the ground for a decent assay. Their tiny workings would disappear quickly, leaving little more evidence than a deep hole.

Sometimes the find would be big and promising, and a mining camp would spring up and soon get a name of its own—colorful handles like Bullfrog, Seven Troughs, Wonder, and Searchlight. But within months, even the most thriving of these communities would disappear, their legacy only a few abandoned buildings graying under the blazing sun, the only sound created by the soft, hot breeze swinging a sagging door on a creaking hinge.

The dream so often ended that way that Nevada has more than 575 ghost towns—communities and settlements that either have been entirely abandoned or have dwindled to a handful of die-hard residents. There have been a few exceptions, the most notable being Virginia City, which today flourishes as a major tourist attraction under the slogan, "The Liveliest Ghost Town in the West."

But most lost their usefulness so completely that they disappeared. They included stage stops, railroad stations, and military posts; but by far the great majority were the mines which had so briefly produced their untold riches. They played to roaring, bustling crowds then; now their crumbling ruins play host only to the occasional curious tourist, the lonely rockhound, or, sometimes, the even lonelier prospector who still hopes and dreams that maybe, just maybe, something precious was left behind.

The trouble with mining has always been its uncertainty. Both that lonely prospector and the giant corporation sooner or later seem to be at the mercy of the boom-and-bust nature of the business. And nowhere has that been truer than in Nevada, the land that has always had a corner on contrasts, contradictions, and extremes. What it has needed right from the start has been a nice, stable offset, an industry that could be relied on to last awhile.

Oddly enough, it turned out to be the most unlikely industry one would imagine for the driest area in the nation—agriculture. Not only that, it had existed long before any inhabitant had even heard of mining.

The earliest people known to have had the ingenuity to figure out how to make anything edible grow in the desert were the Basket Maker Indians who, around 1000 B.C., learned to raise corn in what are now the Moapa and Virgin valleys in southern Nevada.

After that there is a blank until sometime during the first 500 years of the Christian era, when Pueblo Indians migrated to the area from the south. They developed extensive irrigation systems to cultivate much of the lower Moapa Valley, raising not only corn but beans, squash, and cotton. But all this disappeared into the mists of time around

▶ Even though the majority of the resources in Nevada are extracted by larger concerns, some rugged individuals still practice more traditional methods of mining technology. Photo by Tom Campbell

◆ ◆ ◆

THE GHOSTS OF THE DESERT

◆ ◆ ◆

Most of the mining camps sprang to life in the middle of nowhere to live the quick, short lives of mushrooms. What usually got them started was the lone prospector working on a grubstake, seeking and finally finding a promising outcropping of ore. If the samples he had assayed indicated it might indeed be a good strike, the word spread like wildfire, and the rush was on. More often than not the boom it produced was short-lived, and another ghost town was born.

It happened all across Nevada, beginning with the first discovery of gold near Dayton in 1850 in the north and the big silver mining operations at Potosi, 25 miles southwest of Las Vegas, that started in 1861. No matter where they were, most of the hundreds of strikes took on the traditional character of the Wild West in those early days, including having their share of gunfights.

Men flocked to the promised land, oblivious of however remote it was from any established community, no matter how hard it was to get there. They came on horseback or mules, by buggy or wagon—even on foot, pushing the wheelbarrows they hoped to fill with the gold or silver they had heard was so plentiful.

On their heels came the saloon-keepers and the merchants, ready to set up business in tents. More than that the towns especially tempted the swindlers and the card cheats and

the fast-talking promoters, all more than ready to cash in on the irrational euphoria. There were the slick operators who bought up mining sites for further development or resale through brand new, jerry-built stock companies. A real estate broker could be counted on to show up to plat a townsite and begin selling sagebrush lots. The whole scene became a confusion of continuous noise and raucous excitement.

The more prosperous the strike, the more substantial the town it produced. What started as a community of tents began to give way to wood-frame buildings. In most camps these were little more than shanties, hastily put up on the theory that even the rich mines would play out relatively soon because of the frantic efforts of the first arrivals to gobble it up as fast as they could.

It was a different matter with the big bonanzas, such as the fabulous Comstock Lode. The mining camp above it, Virginia City, proved to be so opulent that it moved quickly from tents to shanties to the most elaborate mansions as the big operators raked in untold wealth.

But in the end, even the greatest silver mining center of the nineteenth century quieted after the fabulous outpourings from beneath it were exhausted. Technically that made it a ghost town. Yet its history had been so remarkable, and the tremendous wealth it produced had given it such

▶ ▶ The flavor and memories of the Old West are preserved throughout Nevada in even the most modern, commercial settings. Photo by Tom Campbell

▶ More often than not, the various booms that historically fueled the growth of Nevada invariably produced a plethora of ghost towns. Photo by Tom Campbell

▲ Now eerily quiet, an old movie theatre stands as a relic of Nevada's rustic past. Photo by Bo Richards

permanence, that Virginia City thrives today as a major Western tourist attraction. Visitors from all over the world find much of it still in its original form, from the bars and gambling halls to many of the mansions which vividly portray the opulence of those earlier times.

Most of the hundreds of other Nevada towns had no such future. When the ore bodies played out altogether or, more likely, simply could no longer produce a profit, the towns were abandoned. Word of new finds in distant ranges lured the inhabitants away so quickly that they left their bulkier possessions behind.

"Merchants closed their doors leaving stock on the shelves," wrote well-known Nevada historian Stanley W. Paher. "Furniture was left in hotels

and cabins, billiard balls and cues lay where they had been dropped on saloon pool tables, and tools and machinery were abandoned beside mills and furnaces.

"With the passing of time the graded streets were lost to the encroaching desert growth; sagebrush pushed its way up through rotting floor planks and extended along crumbling walls; and tall imposing smoke-stacks stood alone near shambles of mills."

But the dry desert climate treats decay kindly. However far off the beaten track and however crumbled they may be, the old ruins somehow convey the feeling that their occupants left only yesterday, not 100 years ago. That's the fascination that makes the ghost towns live on.

A.D. 800. Archaeologists still don't know why, but assume that some disasters like flood, drought, or invasion by hostile tribes drove the highly skilled Pueblos from the area.

Farming and livestock production by the white man didn't begin on any consistent scale until almost 1,200 years later. In the spring of 1851, Colonel John Reese and a crew of 17 men trudged their way across the Great Basin from Salt Lake City. Sent out by their Mormon leader, Brigham Young, they built a two-story log hotel on the Overland Trail at the eastern foot of the Sierra Nevada Mountains. Reese called the place Mormon Station (now Genoa).

Lying in a lush, green valley, fed by streams from the adjacent mountains, Mormon Station not only became Nevada's first town of any kind but its first boomtown—not because of mining, but because of agriculture. Colonel Reese had brought with him seeds, grain, and livestock. He laid out a ranch next to the station, constructed a canal, cleared 30 acres of sagebrush, and plowed the land for crops. In 1852—one year after his arrival—barley, wheat, turnips, and watermelons were harvested to bring top prices from California-bound emigrants. News of that success enticed more adventurous types not only to Mormon Station, but to the fertile area around it. Named Carson Valley after Frémont's famous pathfinder, Kit Carson, it spread far enough for the newcomers to start their own ranching and farming operations. Similar valleys nearby and along the eastern slope of the Sierra Nevadas also benefited from the runoff of winter snows and were settled by still more pioneer ranchers.

By the time the Comstock Lode hit its population peak, Nevada farmers and ranchers were producing not only fruits and vegetables, but hay and grain for horses and dairy cattle. The annual production of potatoes ran to about 300,000 bushels; barley, more than 500,000 bushels; oats, 75,000 bushels; and wheat, 76,000 bushels. And there was enough milk, butter, and cheese coming off the ranches to supply all the local mining centers.

A combination of ingenuity and irrigation made it possible for crops to be grown in an increasing number of areas. Desert or no, the land had an inherent fertility that matched the rich mineral deposits beneath it. During the 1890s there was much talk of building storage dams in the Sierras to bring the great desert valleys under cultivation. The state had no resources to undertake such a huge project, but Nevada's U.S. Senator William M. Stewart headed a congressional committee that raised national interest in reclamation projects in general.

As a result another Nevada senator, Francis G. Newlands, fashioned the National Reclamation Act and saw it become law in 1902. And in 1908, Nevada was chosen for the first reclamation project in the United States. It involved a series of diversion dams and canals to store water from the Carson and Truckee rivers. It would reclaim 100,000 acres of desert in Churchill and Lyon counties, some 60 miles east of the Sierras.

In 1905 there had been 72 farms in Churchill County; by the fall of 1908, 400 farms were under cultivation. So great has been its success, sustained and amplified since then, that its original name, the "Truckee-Carson Project," was changed long ago to "The Newlands Project."

● Oddly enough, one of the most stable and successful industries in the driest area of the nation is agriculture. Photo by Tom Campbell

But despite these remarkably successful efforts to raise crops, the vast majority of Nevada land remains desert, making the state unable to compete in terms of volume with its much more fertile neighboring states. As a result Nevada farmers and ranchers have concentrated on livestock, mainly cattle and sheep.

"Beef is still king in Nevada, and always has been," wrote Dale W. Bohmont, dean of the University of Nevada's Max C. Fleischmann College of Agriculture, in 1964. "Those long-established and highly successful ranches along every remote stream have remained the backbone of Nevada's agriculture industry for the past 75 years."

Colonel Reese had brought cattle with him in 1851, for both dairy and meat production. He found the demand for both unusually high; others who followed brought more and more cattle; and it soon became clear that in Nevada it was a lot easier to raise livestock than vegetables. Cattle, sheep, and horses could withstand the desert and its climate better than vegetables, which were at the mercy of drought and frost.

Nevada is the seventh-largest state in the Union in area, but so much of it is unreclaimable desert that it ranks 49th in terms of the value of farm products it sends to market. But despite frost and drought, feed for livestock grows so well that 90 percent of the harvested crop acreage is used for raising hay and grain.

Yet even that has not been enough to feed the growing herds of cattle year-round. Ranchers must overcome the lack on the open range: public land where cattle can find enough forage on the sagebrush-covered landscape to supplement what can be grown at home. But edible feed on a desert range is sparse, so it takes anywhere from 10 to 50 acres a month, depending on the area, to feed one animal.

The cattle population expanded rapidly throughout western Nevada in the early 1860s to take care of the growing mining-camp markets. Despite the decline of the bonanza period, it got greater impetus in 1869, the year the Central Pacific Railroad was completed. That transcontinental line, which ran across the center of the state, was followed by a series of narrow-gauge lines. These great leaps in transportation and communication put the ranches within sensible cattle-driving distances to shipping points. Over the next few years stockmen were sending carloads of their animals by rail to Omaha and San Francisco. During the mid-1870s, for example, San Francisco was purchasing half its beef

▼ The rugged terrain of Nevada is more accommodating to livestock than to crops, which are always at the mercy of drought and frost. Photo by Bo Richards

supply from Nevada—80,000 head per year.

Experienced cattlemen in Texas and elsewhere in the West heard of these successes and moved into Nevada with their herds. They wanted to settle near the railroads, too, so it was in central Nevada that the livestock industry had its greatest expansion.

That led to an inevitable problem—overgrazing on the sparse open range. Ranchers were not prepared for it, and in the winter of 1879-80, at least one-third of the livestock in Nevada died of cold and starvation. It was as if this rugged land was reminding the industry that it was still master, still unconquered. The lesson has stuck with the ranchers ever since: Treat both rangeland and livestock with care.

By long tradition the job of taking care of the open range has fallen to the best-known romantic symbol of the American West—the cowboy. It still does. Although four-wheel-drive vehicles, two-way radios, and other sophisticated equipment have modernized the job considerably, the vast areas that the rangeland covers in Nevada have only allowed

▲ Work is no easier now than 100 years ago for the "buckaroos," or cowboys of Nevada. Photo by Tom Campbell

the basic job to change very little. So common are the rugged canyons, steep cliffs, and other difficult terrain characteristics that even today only a man on horseback can move the cattle—or sometimes even find them.

In Nevada cowboys are usually called "buckaroos." Most authorities believe the word is derived from "vaquero," which the Spanish ranchers used in California when it was still owned by Mexico. It was the preferred word in northern Nevada in the early days, and was finally corrupted to buckaroo.

Wages for cowboys vary according to both area and season, but generally they run from $5,000 to $7,500 a year, plus room and board. The work is not much easier now than it was 100 years ago. Despite all the modern equipment, ranching still has no set hours and no time clocks; hay harvest at the ranch and roundups out on the range still have to go nonstop. The "room" the cowboy gets as part of his pay as often as not is still a bedroll of some blankets and a big piece of heavy canvas laid out under the stars.

Even lonelier than the cowboy's life in the hills is that of the sheepherder. Cowboys generally work in teams or small groups, but the sheepherder must stay by himself for days, weeks, or months literally without seeing another person.

The late Clel Georgetta, a Nevada district judge who once owned and operated the Tri-une Ranch, a sheep outfit in eastern Nevada, understood that loneliness. He wrote in 1972:

This is no job for a gregarious man who must have the companionship of other human beings. For company the sheepherder has only his dog, his burro and the sheep—those dumb speechless things. The dog shows love, affection and admiration . . . The burro nudges the herder with its nose for a feed of grain . . . The sheep—those cussed things—all they do for him is to leave the bedground too early in the morning, or get him up during the night, or refuse to go where he directs them, get lost, or get themselves killed by coyotes or bobcats. They give him no love or affection, but he gives his life to the sheep. Their welfare is his main concern in all this world.

It takes a special breed of men to live that kind of dedicated life, and they have always been hard to find. In the early days, even before there were ranches in Nevada, a good many herders were Scots, but other nationalities quickly followed. In 1869 there was a big influx of herders from among the hordes of Chinese who had worked on the building of the Central Pacific Railroad, but afterward were out of jobs and far from home. Until the 1890s, they predominated the sheepherding business.

That was when the French and Spanish Basques came from the Pyrenees to dominate what was becoming a major industry. Even today in Nevada, most sheepherders are Basque, and they are still regarded as the best.

"They and their ancestors had been herding sheep in rough mountain country for many generations—hundreds of years," wrote Georgetta. "A 'feeling' for sheep is bred in the bones of a Basque. They proved to be the best herders of all. A Basque, more than any other nationality of man, is able to guess right what a sheep will do next . . ."

◀ Wages for cowboys vary according to both area and season, but generally run from $5,000 to $7,500 a year, plus room and board. Photo by Tom Campbell

But the cattlemen knew the major thing the sheep did, and resented it enough to become violent on occasion. Sheep graze on the same public land used by cattle. In a desert state like Nevada feed is limited to begin with, which in itself makes the competition fierce. But in addition, sheep bite the grass almost down to the roots, leaving nothing for cattle to eat because they cannot bite the grass off that close to the ground. Georgetta wrote:

The early cattleman hated sheep so much he had little trouble soothing his conscience when he resorted to violence to rid his range of the detested, destructive animals. "Range wars" flared in many parts of the West . . . Sheepherders were shot or clubbed to death . . . Thousands of sheep were killed by poisoning the range with blue vitriol and saltpeter which would kill sheep but not cattle.

The problem intensified geometrically with the increasing numbers of cattle and sheep sharing the open range. There was just not enough grass and water for the animals of both cattlemen and sheepherders. The free open range had gotten out of hand by the 1930s, to a point where intervention by the federal government became the only solution.

In 1934 Congress passed the Taylor Grazing Act into law. It partly solved the range war problem by limiting the number of animals that could be grazed on the open range. Neither the cattlemen nor the sheepherders liked the idea. But by then the situation had gotten to a point where only a drastic measure such as government regulation could prevent chaos.

When the Taylor Grazing Act first went into effect, ranchers paid only a minimal fee to the federal government to run their livestock on the open range. But like everything else, grazing fees have risen over the years. By mid-1988 cattlemen, for example, were paying grazing fees of $1.54 per cow per month, or $138.48 per year for every 10 cows.

Partly as a result of such increases, livestock populations have steadily dwindled in Nevada. The range wars have diminished to a point where ranchers now raise both sheep and cattle, but they raise fewer of both. The boom times had come at the end of the nineteenth century, when more than 1.5 million head of cattle and 2.5 million head of sheep roamed the Nevada landscape.

By January 1, 1985, the total number of cattle and calves in Nevada stood at 620,000 head, down 6 percent from the year before. Sheep and lambs on the same date numbered only 100,000 head, as contrasted with a twentieth-century peak level of more than 1.3 million in 1920.

But agriculture is far from dead in Nevada. Its more than 2,500 500-acre farms and ranches still play a vital, ongoing part in the state's economy; on the whole they have weathered well the shifting factors which have plagued agriculture throughout the nation. But the economic burden will be lessened because of dramatic developments in other industries during the twentieth century. They have made it possible for Nevada to expand into new fields which are not so dependent on the land for economic welfare. That expansion started with one of the largest construction projects in the history of the world: the Hoover Dam.

▶ A large influx of French and Spanish Basques came from the Pyrenees to dominate the sheepherding business. Photo by Tom Campbell

.3.

The Wild West Goes Modern

◆◆◆◆

A great dam was built and
an area sprang to life . . .
Gaming became legal in Nevada,
and the state has never stopped
to look back.

◆◆◆◆

● Much of the architecture in even the most modern environs of Nevada contains definite elements of its Old West heritage. Photo by Tom Campbell

▶ President Franklin D. Roosevelt called the Boulder Dam "an engineering victory of the first order, another great achievement of American resourcefulness, skill and determination." Photo by Tom Campbell

For thousands of years the river asserted its awesome power. Along a 1,400-mile course from the Rocky Mountains to the Gulf of California, it defied every natural obstacle in its path, virtually rebuilding the landscape. Before it reached the high plateaus of northern Arizona to create the mile-deep magnificence of the Grand Canyon, the Colorado River used its tremendous energy to gouge great gorges out of the Black Mountains.

It was in one of those gorges, deep and strong enough to contain it, that man decided to take the dare to tame one of the world's most treacherous rivers for his own use. He would build a dam between the sheer walls of Black Canyon, even though he knew it would require a structure of such mammoth dimensions that it would surpass anything of its kind.

The cost would be tremendous, but if it came out as planned, the project would provide flood control, water storage, and the generation of electrical energy for the fast-growing area of the Southwest. And so on December 21, 1928, President Calvin Coolidge signed the Boulder Canyon Project Act, which would provide the construction of a dam and appurtenant works at a total cost not to exceed $165 million.

From the start it was clear the job would be so enormous that there wasn't a construction company in the country that could handle it alone. But half a dozen large contractors decided that if they joined forces, they could do the job together. As Six Companies, Inc., they submitted a bid to the U.S. Department of Interior's Bureau of Reclamation. It awarded the unusual consortium the contract, and they went to work. In 1935, five years after they started and two years ahead of schedule, Six Companies completed Boulder Dam (later renamed Hoover Dam), declared by many to be the engineering feat of the age. The professionals in the business officially recognized it as such years later, when the American Society of Civil Engineers named it one of the nation's Seven Modern Engineering Wonders.

Laymen also stood in awe. Wrote Richard G. Lillard in 1942: "Boulder Dam is to Americans what Chartres Cathedral was to medieval Europeans, what the Temple at Karnak was to ancient Egyptians. The clean functional lines, the colossal beauty, and impersonal mass and strength of the dam itself are as symbolic as real. The dam is a symbol of how physical science, guided by enlightened social principles, can turn desolation into green valleys and thriving cities."

Boulder Canyon, also known as Black Canyon, lies on the short stretch of the Colorado River that serves as Nevada's southern boundary with Arizona. High, sheer cliffs rise straight up from both sides of the river, and rugged hills sweep back from them to add to the difficulty of even reaching the bottom of the canyon, much less working there. Moreover, this site on the river that was technically ideal for a dam had nothing to offer as a place to live. For one thing, it was in the middle of nowhere—the nearest settlement was the sleepy desert town of Las Vegas, 30 miles to the northwest. With a population of less than 5,000, Las Vegas had no way of supplying anything needed for the largest construction project ever undertaken in the United States—including housing for the nearly 6,000

► This interior view of Hoover Dam shows its massive hydroelectric generators. Photo by Tom Campbell

workers for the dam.

Besides, Las Vegas was too far away from the site, so the federal government built Boulder City on the nearest flat piece of desert wasteland, eight miles to the west of the dam. It started out like the early mining camps. Tents housed everything from company offices to workers' quarters until plywood houses could be built. Within a year the town grew into a community of a thousand homes, a dozen dormitories, four churches, a grade school, shops, stores, restaurants, garages, a 700-seat theater, tourist camps, and even a hotel.

Buses took everyone involved to and from the project down the treacherous mountain road that was the only access to the canyon. Once there the workers found themselves in "an environment as close to hell as you can get," as one of them described his tour of duty. That was especially true in the summertime, when 100-plus-degree days are routine in that part of southern Nevada. At the bottom of the dam at the riverbed, the highest temperature recorded during construction was 130 degrees.

Even an official government report on the extreme difficulties encountered during the building of the dam waxed unusually eloquent, calling the achievement "the victory of man over the desert's summer sun, the vagaries of the most treacherous river, and the extreme hazards of great heights on the chasm's sheer walls." And in his speech dedicating the dam in 1935, President Franklin D. Roosevelt called the dam "an engineering victory of the first order, another great achievement of American resourcefulness, skill and determination."

The statistics give only an inkling of why a mere dam received such adulation. Into the 726-foot-high structure went 3.25 million yards of concrete, a larger volume than all the material in the Great Pyramid of Egypt. Its base is 660 feet thick; its top is 45 feet thick and 1,244 feet long. It can hold back two years' worth of water in Lake Mead, the reservoir it created—a body of water 115 miles long with a maximum depth of 589 feet, with 29.8 million acre feet of capacity, and covering 163,000 acres.

All this development did far more than make a radical change in the landscape. During the more than half a century of its existence, Hoover Dam has made equally radical changes in the whole economy of the Southwest. For example, since 1935 the water it has stored in Lake Mead has irrigated more than 1.25 million acres of land in the United States and Mexico, all of which can be farmed without fear of flooding. At the same time that huge reservoir has supplemented the water needs and recreational demands of more than 10 million area residents. And every

◄ Nevada was the first state to realize the possibilities of divorce as a business investment. Photo by Tom Campbell

year the dam's power plant generates 4.5 billion kilowatt hours of hydroelectric energy to provide power to a vast area of the Southwest.

About the time the Boulder Canyon Project was getting started in earnest, the Great Depression began to take its toll. Although there would be a healthy boost to the local economy during the years of the dam's actual construction, the state of Nevada recognized the need for new long-term business incentives.

But since it had not lost its fierce sense of Old West independence, Nevada sought those incentives in areas and in ways that no other state had dared. In March 1931 the Nevada Legislature passed two bills that shocked the nation. One legalized casino gambling throughout the state. The other reduced the residency requirement for divorce from three months to six weeks.

There had not been much direct competition from other states when it came to legal gaming; it was generally limited to horse racing, and no other state had approved casinos. But there had been competition on the divorce front.

In 1906 Nevada became the first state to recognize the possibilities of divorce as a business investment, thanks to the wife of a Pittsburgh millionaire. Mrs. William Ellis Corey learned that Nevada had a residency requirement of only six months, far shorter than Pennsylvania, so she moved to Reno to divorce her husband. When she revealed that he had been paying undue attention to a young actress, such behavior was regarded as so sensational that it got worldwide publicity.

So did Reno. In a matter of weeks, the sleepy little community of fewer than 8,000 residents found itself having to cope with a sprightly new business. The reason was that it had more than just a short residency to offer those who felt chained more by the bonds of state law than by the bonds of matrimony. At least as important was an old Nevada law which had remarkably lenient grounds for divorce. Written back in 1861 by the Territorial Legislature, the law permitted divorce to be granted on a whole spectrum of grounds, including desertion, cruelty, nonsupport, drunkenness, impotence, imprisonment, and adultery.

By 1910 these advantages combined to give Reno a well-publicized "Divorce Colony." A transient group with a steady turnover of membership, it provided Reno lawyers with a nice flow of handsome fees and provided an equally nice revolving income to the operators of local hotels and area dude ranches (they would be called "guest ranches" during the later heyday of Nevada divorce). Most of its members were wealthy and demanded the best in style and entertainment. Their hosts quickly learned how best to provide both, giving the desert community an unaccustomed air of sophistication.

The tone took on an even more solid quality in 1920. Movie actress Mary Pickford, "America's Sweetheart," spent her six-month residency in Minden, 45 miles south of Reno. She was there to divorce Owen Moore so she could marry the famous, swashbuckling Hollywood star, Douglas Fairbanks. Her presence alone did enough to give the Nevada divorce business such a first-class aura that a growing number of people—even from the straitlaced East—arrived to end their domestic difficulties under unexpectedly pleasant circumstances.

Until 1927 Nevada was the only state to offer such quick, tailored, and pleasantly catered relief. But all of a sudden a threat came from afar: both Mexico and France began talking about cutting their residency requirements to six months to attract some of the American divorce wealth.

Nevada was quick to respond. That year its legislature passed a bill that halved the residency requirement to three months. In 1931, however, both Idaho and Arkansas dropped their requirements from six months to three. Nevada had to act even faster this time—and it did: On March 19 of that same year, with little fanfare and almost no opposition, Nevada governor Fred B. Balzar signed the six-week residency bill into law.

The rush was on to both Reno and Las Vegas; that year alone, Nevada granted more than 4,000 decrees. An added incentive to the short time span was an easing of the law allowing an even more lenient and purposely vague ground for divorce—"mental cruelty."

This was elastic enough to cover just about any human behavior from A to Z—anything from the lack of a sense of humor to high-decibel snoring. (One woman got her decree after testifying that her husband had humiliated her by bouncing a tennis ball off her head in the presence of their friends.)

If the divorce was uncontested and a settlement had been reached between the two parties, the court proceedings lasted only a few minutes and the divorce was final immediately. By contrast, other states had strict, hard-to-prove grounds such as adultery or desertion, and delays of several years before the divorce became final.

All this stunned the nation's other jurisdictions—their long traditions of conservatism found this easy, "wide-open" divorce system offensive to say the least. But even as they shouted it down, an increasing number of their wealthy citizens arrived to take advantage of it. Business picked up as word got around among Easterners who were mesmerized by the prospect of enjoying the glamorous life of the dude ranch, where days were spent horseback riding and swimming and nights were spent dining and gambling at elegant casinos.

These things appealed especially to celebrities because the dude ranches operated under a policy of absolute security for their guests. The hosts became as adept as the CIA or the Secret Service at holding journalists and photographers at bay. Generally they were highly successful, so Hollywood stars and Eastern socialites alike felt comfortable in staying unseen and uninterviewed at such famous guest ranches as the Flying ME or Washoe Pines, 20 miles south of Reno; the Pyramid Lake Ranch at Sutcliffe, 30 miles to the north; the Donner Trail Ranch at Verdi, near the California border a dozen miles to the west; or at Glenbrook on the eastern shore of nearby Lake Tahoe.

These places (plus certain hotels and upscale boardinghouses in Reno and nearby towns) and their clientele gave Reno the undisputed title of "Divorce Capital of the World." But in 1939 Las Vegas got into the act when Ria Langham Gable got her divorce there from her Oscar-winning husband, Clark Gable.

That decree gave Las Vegas the publicity boost it desperately needed. The workers who built Hoover Dam had left the area in 1936, and legalized gambling had not yet taken hold well enough to take up the slack in the city of 8,000 residents. So when Ria showed up, the Las Vegas Chamber of Commerce learned about it from her lawyer, and the story spread from the local press across the nation. The media reported her boat rides on Lake Mead and her brief stint dealing craps and blackjack. And when it was over, the press quoted her as saying her six weeks had been "the finest and shortest vacation I ever had in my life."

Most important of all for Las Vegas, Ria's presence led to the opening that July of the city's first large-scale divorce operation, the Boulderado Dude Ranch. Others quickly followed, and by the end of the year 738 divorces had been granted in Las Vegas.

But Reno retained its rank as queen of the trade until laws in other states were relaxed, making divorce easier everywhere. By the mid-1970s most of the guest ranches had all but disappeared, and today divorce attracts neither the great number of Hollywood stars nor the national attention it did in its heyday as a scandalous but juicy social evil.

Meanwhile, the other industry which the state approved along with the divorce trade got an even stronger negative reception outside Nevada. The only thing that comforted its staunch critics was their firm belief that the chances of legalized gambling becoming an economic success were about one in 100. Tradition alone would doom it to failure;

● Initial resistance to installing gaming as a legitimate industry in Nevada was to prove shortsighted. Photos by Tom Campbell

▲ The highly evolved gaming industry in Nevada is both sophisticated and carefully regulated. This is the Colorado Belle Casino on the Colorado River in Laughlin, Nevada. Photo by Tom Campbell

the respectable elements of the Western world had long before ordained that gambling was by its very nature a vice so destructive that legalizing it could not make it a successful enterprise.

Just look at history, they argued, for proof that this basic instinct of mankind could not last in the staid and stately patterns of civilized society. In the past gambling had flourished on a large scale only when it operated in the illegal darkness of the underworld. Even some of the supporters of Nevada's bold experiment admitted there was nothing to suggest, much less guarantee, that gambling could gain any serious acceptance by trying to function in the legal daylight.

For a while it appeared that the skeptics might well be right. From the start, they didn't believe that the state could keep anywhere near a sharp-enough eye on the casinos to keep the underworld from ultimately taking complete charge. Indeed, the first "controls" were minimal—only a haphazard arrangement of local government units regulated the small gaming operations which sprang up during the first 10 years of legalization.

But by 1945 the industry had grown beyond a handful of small casinos. Clearly a stronger hand was needed; the state recognized that as the business increased, so would the attraction of undesirable elements. The state legislature gave the Nevada Tax Commission the power to regulate gaming and issue state licenses to its operators.

Behind this move lay the basic foundation on which the control system was built, and which has been strengthened over the years: gambling in Nevada is not a right, but a privilege. The state interpreted that to mean it could revoke that privilege for cause almost at will. It hoped that this virtual autocratic authority would be the key to handling the underworld's advances on the industry, but it worried about the challenges of its constitutionality—challenges that over the years would repeatedly be taken to both state and federal courts, and which would be consistently decided in favor of the state.

This tough, arbitrary law works because, from the time the state legislature legalized gambling in 1931, the state recognized that this unique adventure could succeed only if the authorities had the expertise to control it. But few, if any, Nevadans had such expertise. The problem was to find professionals who could teach both the state authorities and casino managements and operating personnel how to spot and outsmart the confidence men, hoods, shysters, and "crossroaders" (cheaters) that gambling of any kind always attracts.

But where was Nevada to get some really expert, on-the-job training? Every other state had outlawed casino gambling, so raiding them for teachers was out of the question. Like it or not, the only skilled veterans were professional gamblers who had spent years plying their trade illegally. Far better than anyone else, these seasoned players knew every trick of the trade that crossroaders would use to try to fleece the casinos' naive staff.

But the state had no intention of inviting anyone it knew to belong to such a questionable group to come and help. It didn't have to, of course—those expert gamblers came of their own accord, some of them to try to cheat the system, but many to apply for jobs in the embryonic industry.

Even the job-seekers among them were not welcomed with open arms, despite their expertise. However naive it may have been, the state still knew fully well it faced the constant danger of attempts by the mob to take over. The state undertook a rigid background screening process in an effort to license as gaming operators only those applicants who had no record of illegal activity other than a violation of gambling laws.

That was just a start. To keep the card sharps from straying from the garden path, the gaming authorities laid down extremely tough conditions of behavior for them to follow once licensed. Number one, of course, was that they must avoid any association with underworld figures. Beyond that, they would have to walk an unaccustomed legal tightrope without so much as starting to lose their balance. Let any one of them break any law more serious than a parking regulation and he would wind up in jail in Nevada as fast as he did back home.

On the other hand, if he behaved himself, the state would honor his gaming license and allow him to live as a reasonably respected member of the community.

This was an attractive situation for those who were tired of looking over their

shoulder for pursuing sheriffs. Being a respected citizen was so appealing that most of them did their best to retain that rare status by teaching the inexperienced neophytes all they knew about how to keep the dishonest gamblers from breaking the casino operators—and the state. Eventually, the "graduates" of these courses were able to replace their teachers as dealers, pit bosses, managers, and owners with the same level of expertise.

Naturally the students could not keep the criminal element out completely; there was some underworld casino control in the early days. But they did their jobs well enough to keep mob infiltration to a minimum. Indeed, if they hadn't, legalized gambling would have been outlawed in Nevada long ago.

Instead, it has grown and flourished. And because of its success as a legitimate enterprise in Nevada, casino gambling is being legalized in an increasing number of jurisdictions every year.

However, although the majority of the people who owned and worked in this highly sensitive industry were honest businesspeople, with normal families and living typical American lives, many outsiders believed in the beginning that the mob exercised a stronger influence on gambling than it actually did.

No one anticipated that suspicion more clearly than the state of Nevada itself. And no one knew better how vitally important it was that the state do everything in its power to make sure gaming operated with as little underworld influence as possible. The state government felt confident it could do so—even though it knew it could not easily overcome the ingrained reputation gaming had to the contrary. Its basic weapon against the underworld was the law that gave it almost unlimited power to investigate to the last detail the background of anyone who wanted a license.

But that wasn't enough. This would be a war between the "white hats" of the state and the "black hats" who were determined to take over what they perceived as too lucrative a market to pass up. Something more would have to be done.

Robbins Cahill had the job of figuring out what that "something" would be. The reason was that he had been appointed executive secretary of the Nevada Tax Commission in 1945. Since the job had been expanded to include oversight of the gaming laws, Cahill got stuck with having to break new ground.

He didn't have much to work with. The state had the power to grant, deny, or revoke gaming licenses, but the tools for implementing that power were almost nonexistent.

"I was sitting there with one man," Cahill recalled, "and all of a sudden we found out we were in the business of investigations, reading fingerprints, going into backgrounds with absolutely no experience or any real equipment to do it with."

Cahill solved that problem by fashioning his own tools. They included, first and foremost, his notifying any mobsters on the premises that he was the czar, but that if they cooperated he would not act like a tyrant—and they would not only stay out of jail, but would be able to keep their gambling licenses.

It was at about that time that the gaming industry began to expand rapidly. With it,

◀ Legalized gambling isn't the only reason tourists flock to Nevada in droves: opportunities to explore countless natural wonders abound. Photo by Tom Campbell

THE
BASHFUL
BILLIONAIRE

◆◆◆

◆◆◆

At dawn on November 27, 1966, an eastbound transcontinental passenger train pulled to a stop near the Las Vegas depot. One car was uncoupled and shunted onto a siding. A few minutes later the shadowy figure of a man stepped out of the car and into a waiting automobile, which took him directly to the Desert Inn on the Las Vegas Strip. He walked to an elevator without registering and rode to the hotel's ninth-floor penthouse suite.

For all anyone knows, Howard Robards Hughes did not leave that suite for four-and-a-half years.

Yet the presence of the eccentric billionaire turned out to be one of the most important developments in the history of Nevada's legalized gaming industry. It not only had a profound effect on the economy; it was the key factor in giving that industry a new legitimacy and integrity.

Howard Hughes' impact was the result of his purchase of seven casinos during the short period of his Nevada residency. That made him the state's largest employer, with 8,000 people on his payrolls. (At the time, the Nevada Test Site was employing only 6,300.) It also made him the holder of more gaming licenses than anyone else in Nevada, with properties accounting for 16 percent of the state's gross gambling revenues, or around $84 million a year. And finally, the $100 million worth of hotels, casinos, and motels made the invisible occupant of the Desert Inn penthouse the state's biggest property owner.

Hughes accomplished all this without facing a single state official, real estate agent, or anyone else except a tiny handful of trusted aides. In the process, he moved faster than any professional gambler before or since, collecting casinos like other people might collect old cars—or stamps.

He started by buying the Desert Inn itself. He quickly added the nearby Sands, the Castaways, and the Frontier. By 1970 he had bought two more Vegas casinos—the Landmark and the Silver Slipper—and had reached out to Reno to lease the world-famous Harolds Club.

At first most Nevadans welcomed

these unique developments with open arms. Even though Howard Hughes was already a man of mystery before his equally mysterious dawn arrival in Las Vegas, his spectacular and glamorous exploits in both aviation and Hollywood had given him an aura of being a business daredevil. Before he became a complete recluse, he had moved in a kind of swashbuckling fashion into a variety of enterprises, ranging from airplanes to the careers of movie stars and brilliant engineers. These exploits always seemed either to succeed or fail in a blaze of glory.

Mostly they succeeded. Hughes had a record of skilled, sound business acumen. The Nevada authorities found that a more impressive guideline to what he might contribute to the state than his eccentricities; they felt he based his innovative trends on careful study and analysis rather than on fly-by-night whims.

Most important of all for the state's image was the widespread conviction that Hughes had come by his great wealth honestly. Nevadans reasoned that Hughes was a gambler only in society's accepted ways, taking his risks in the "respectable" areas of commerce. Therefore his willingness to risk so much of his fortune on Nevada's legalized gambling would tell the world that he found it, too, respectable.

That made Hughes' arrival seem like a dream come true. It was not common knowledge that Nevada's gaming industry had progressed from the era of underworld influences over the years, and the state needed something to help demonstrate it. The state's control system had matured into a strong, virtually autocratic dual agency with beefed-up investigative, licensing, and enforcement powers—measures that had dramatically shifted the bulk of casino ownership into the hands of legitimate operators, sharply diminishing the industry's questionable aspects.

Yet Nevada's reputation remained tarnished. Statewide lotteries and other forms of legalized gambling had not yet proliferated as they have today, so the rest of the nation persisted in nurturing its suspicions of mob control. The fact that respectable elements had taken over most of the casino industry in Nevada had brightened the image only slightly.

The delighted authorities saw the advent of Howard Hughes as a sort of official stamp of approval which legalized gambling had not enjoyed before. But they had to convert that approval from theory to fact for it to really change the state's image—especially in the eyes of the federal government, which at the time kept Nevada under great pressure to clean up an act the state felt it had already cleaned up.

So the state gaming control authorities gave Hughes privileges no other licensee could get. When he moved to buy the Desert Inn as his first acquisition, they did everything to smooth his path, including making exceptions to iron-clad rules. One of those rules was that every prospective licensee be questioned in person by gaming authorities. They waived that requirement in deference to Hughes' insistence on absolute privacy, allowing him to apply through what they believed were his chosen representatives.

Further, they curtailed the mandatory background investigation which everyone else had to go through. The state rationalized that it had no reason not to take these shortcuts because of Hughes' reputation as an honest, upright, successful citizen.

This did not set well with the rest of the gaming industry. By that time many of its owners and operators had reputations at least as honest, upright, and successful, yet they had had to go through the lengthy, tortuous, and expensive routine of applying for licenses for often smaller and less economically important casinos than the Desert Inn.

Their resentment grew as the process proliferated across Hughes' acquisitions of six more casinos, with the gaming authorities granting him licenses on what seemed to be the spur of the moment. (In one case he is said to have got a license as a result of a single midnight phone call.) By contrast, even operators already licensed for one casino had to appear before the Gaming Control Board and the Gaming Commission to be approved and licensed whenever they acquired a new property.

So Howard Hughes' presence began to lose some of its appeal as the perfect bonanza. Local people became increasingly concerned that, being the eccentric he clearly was, the Bashful Billionaire might leave as mysteriously as he had arrived and let the whole thing die. They knew that if seven casinos all shut down, it would spell at least temporary economic disaster for Nevada.

It didn't turn out that way. Hughes' gaming interests, split among several new owners since his death, survive as legacies of a major contribution to Nevada's image.

◄ Millionaire aviator Howard Hughes is shown here at the Chicago Municipal Airport in 1936 preparing for a flight to Los Angeles, California. He hoped to set a new speed record. Courtesy, Bettmann Archives

▼ Howard Hughes poses in his new XF-11 in 1946. Shortly after this picture was taken, the ship crashed in Beverly Hills, California, seriously injuring Hughes. Courtesy, Bettmann Archives

Cahill's power increased and the parameters of the system he headed became more distinct, clear, and effective. Remarkably, even though the law was so tough that it seemed to go against the grain of free enterprise and certain other "inalienable rights," it made all those involved with legalized gaming sit up and take notice.

But Cahill faced serious challenges—and threats—from the underworld. That surprised no one, least of all Cahill, who stood ready and willing to combat them. He brooked no nonsense from anybody, including a particularly powerful underworld figure named Benjamin "Bugsy" Siegel. The builder and owner of the Flamingo Hotel, the Las Vegas Strip's first major resort-casino, Siegel was so dangerous that he was feared not only by ordinary people, but even by other gangsters. It was common knowledge, in and out of the mob, that anyone who dared to challenge him literally risked death.

So Siegel, who loved to wear a chip on his shoulder, had no qualms about defying the state authorities. When notices came for him to pay his gaming taxes, he simply ignored them. Certainly no one would make an issue of it, he figured, but even if anybody did, the fearsome Siegel would intimidate them into backing down. That would not be hard, because his operation was too important to Nevada's fledgling industry for the state to revoke his license.

He was wrong. To Robbins Cahill, no casino, no matter how important to the economy, could be allowed to violate the law and stay in business. When he learned of Siegel's chip-on-the-shoulder defiance, he regarded it as an inexcusable affront to the state—and to the industry. Shaking with anger, Cahill picked up the phone in his Carson City office and called the Flamingo.

"This is Robbins Cahill, head of the state's gaming control system," he told the operator. "I want to talk to Siegel right now. Get him. This is an emergency."

Since word had spread about Cahill's tough stance, he was talking to Bugsy Siegel in less than a minute.

"Listen, Siegel," Cahill shouted. "You get a check in the mail for those taxes today or we'll come down to Las Vegas and close your joint for good."

Cahill slammed down the phone. The next day he had a check for the full amount of the gambling taxes Siegel owed the state of Nevada.

That steel-hard approach has been the basis of the system ever since. Most of the long-time observers of Nevada's gaming history give full credit for it to Robbins Cahill. They say that those who worked with him and succeeded him in operating the unique policing system have used his guidance and direction to bring it to full maturity.

In 1959 during the governorship of Grant Sawyer, the Gaming Control Board, which had been established as an adjunct of the Tax Commission under Governor Charles Russell, became an autonomous agency. Its three full-time members are all appointed by the governor to four-year terms, and each is an expert in a specific field, defined by law.

The chairman (Sawyer appointed Cahill to that job) must have at least five years of sound administrative experience; a second member must have five years as a certified public accountant and be an expert in corporate financing and auditing; the third must

be fully trained and experienced in law enforcement or the law.

This board is the system's investigative and enforcement agency. Its staff checks in minute detail the personal, financial, and social backgrounds of everyone who applies for a gaming license, no matter how excellent a reputation he or she may have at the outset. (The single exception, of course, was Howard Hughes.) The applicants must pay all the costs of this investigation, which is so thorough that it can run up into many thousands of dollars. They get no refund, even if their application is turned down.

If approved, the licensee still can't shake the board. It has the responsibility of enforcing all gaming laws and regulations. Its agents have peace-officer authority to arrive unannounced, examine casino premises, seize equipment or supplies, and check out and audit all books, papers, and records.

At the same time the Gaming Control Board got this near-absolute authority, the legislature created the Nevada Gaming Commission. It is made up of five part-time members, also appointed by the governor for staggered four-year terms. It grants or denies licenses and can revoke, suspend, or condition licenses of existing operations. All these actions are based on Gaming Control Board recommendations, but the commission is independent of the board and can act however it sees fit.

Contrary to a common belief outside Nevada, this system has functioned well enough not only to prevent anything approaching a takeover of the industry by organized crime, but has kept infiltration to a minimum. The best proof that it has become a legitimate business, safe from serious criminal harm, lies in the fact that the control system

▲ The flavor of the Old West is preserved at many authentic attractions throughout the state, like this re-enactment of an old-style business transaction at Mt. Charleston, Nevada. Photo by Tom Campbell

▶ Legalized gambling moved into high gear after World War II. Photo by Tom Campbell

has gained the confidence of major out-of-state corporations. Without that confidence, the likes of Hilton, Holiday Inn, MGM, and Del Webb, for example, would not have taken what could have turned out to be an almost fatal risk in making investments of millions of dollars to buy and operate Nevada casinos.

Their confidence rests on Nevada's cold, realistic awareness that it must be eternally vigilant if it is to keep legalized gambling clean. It can do that only by constantly moving to stop the "crossroaders" and "mechanics" (cheaters and other professional crooks) who are always at work in casinos somewhere. Its agents work closely with the licensed operators to nip in the bud any attempts by the highly skilled criminals at such gimmicks as skimming (stealing profits before they are entered in the books) and slot-machine rejiggering. The enforcement agents match those skills well enough to catch just about everyone bent on cheating the house, the customer, or the state, so few licenses have to be revoked.

That capability has been the main reason Nevada has overcome the 100-to-1 odds that its great experiment in legalized gambling could never last. In 1981, the 50th anniversary year of the legalization of gaming, then-governor Robert List pointed out what the success had meant to the state economically:

The gaming industry has brought an end to the boom-and-bust cycles that had for so long characterized Nevada's economy, and transformed the state into the resort and entertainment capital of the world . . .

The phenomenal growth of gaming in Nevada can best be illustrated by annual gaming revenue. In 1946, the first year that the state levied a gaming tax, total gaming revenues were listed at $24.5 million.

By 1988 that figure had mushroomed to $3.7 billion for the state's 155 largest casinos. More than half of Nevada's employees either work directly for the gaming industry or in offshoots from it in tourist-oriented businesses. What Robert List said nearly 10 years ago in celebration of the 50th anniversary of legalization still applies today.

"Gaming is Nevada's lifeblood," he said. "While we are striving to diversify and strengthen our economic base, we have not lost sight of the fact that the gaming industry plays a leading role in maintaining the economic well-being of our state."

Ironically, that huge success has come from tourists from other states—most of them people who wouldn't dream of allowing legalized gambling at home on the grounds of morality. But they come to Nevada in enough numbers—an average of about 25 times the state's population every year—to have long since turned that 100-to-1 shot into a winner.

But even they wouldn't have come in droves if the early entrepreneurs of Nevada gambling hadn't come up with a revolutionary idea. It was, quite simply, to broaden the narrow base of gambling from the elite provinces of European royalty to the common man, to move it from the private precincts of Monte Carlo to Main Street, U.S.A. The operator generally credited with being the first to publicize this bold (and in some ways disrespectful) concept was Raymond I. "Pappy" Smith, an old-time carnival man from California.

With his son, Harold, Smith moved to Reno in the 1930s, opened Harolds Club, and used his professional carnival background to think up new ways to attract out-of-state tourists.

One thing he noticed was that most advertising for the early Nevada casinos was used for goodwill, not for promotion or marketing. Most of it, both in Reno and Las Vegas, consisted of little more than eight-inch, two-column ads in local newspapers. One exception was the Commercial Hotel in Elko, in the eastern part of the state, which launched Nevada's first big-name

◀ The rapid growth of densely populated centers of tourism and entertainment has, by necessity, stimulated other industries. Photo by Tom Campbell

entertainment in 1941. It promoted its show talent not only locally but in Salt Lake City.

World War II moved legalized gambling into high gear. Servicemen and servicewomen traveled the country and the world; they got a taste of things they had never seen back home. The casinos responded: the Flamingo in Las Vegas began using billboards on highways as far away as Hollywood.

Up in Reno, Pappy Smith decided that this was a bit too timid. He got his advertising agency to begin testing roadside signs in the 11 western states. He published ads in every newspaper in Nevada, was the first to put on a radio campaign in the West—and shortly had road signs across the nation with the slogan that soon became world famous: "Harolds Club or Bust." By the early 1950s more than 2,300 of the signs, with the slogan and humorous cartoon characters, were spread across the nation. His agency even posted signs in Antarctica, Alaska, and the Marshall Islands.

Smith's other innovations included breaking an age-old tradition by hiring women as dealers for his table games. He chartered planes to bring in players from California—a revolutionary idea that has long since been adopted by casinos statewide. He stressed the idea that the person with an average income could get as much entertainment out of gambling a few dollars—or a few coins—as the wealthy people did spending thousands at the tables in the exclusive clubs of Europe. He encouraged that idea by walking around his casino, doubling customers' bets at random and buying them drinks on the house.

Other casinos quickly followed suit. The average person, the small gambler, became the backbone of the industry's rapid growth. But that growth by no means excluded the wealthy: the "high rollers," the princes from abroad, and the millionaires at home. To entice them the industry offered far more attractions than they could find anywhere else in the world—including Monte Carlo.

As *Nevada* magazine boasted in its special 50th anniversary edition in 1981: "You can play roulette in Monaco, you can dine splendidly in Rome, but the best place on earth to do both is Nevada."

By that time the state was indeed attracting the great chefs of Europe, Africa, and Asia to provide haute cuisine not only in its outstanding restaurants, separate from the gaming areas, but in its elaborate showrooms which made the state the entertainment capital of the world. It was impossible to find any star who hadn't played Reno or Las Vegas or Lake Tahoe, the three biggest gaming areas in the state. Said *Nevada* magazine: "What New York was in the great days of the theatre, Hollywood in the palmy times of film, Nevada has become with the advent of international tourism and electronic entertainment: Gathering place of the superstars."

In effect, legalized gambling was the main vehicle that moved Nevada from the Wild West to a modern state. The momentum made Reno and Las Vegas the main centers of that industry and gave their surrounding rural areas the impetus to expand their economies—not only through small gaming operations but also through diverse industries that have nothing to do with gaming. That expansion through diversity has become a major project of the state of Nevada for the 1990s and beyond.

● A recent Great Reno Balloon Race filled the countryside with milling spectators and the sky with bright colors. Photos by Bo Richards and John Gale

.4.

CREATING
A DESERT
CIVILIZATION

◆◆◆◆

*Nevada offers some of the best
places to do business in the
United States. Its limited taxation,
prime locations, and industrious
work force are definite
advantages.*

◆◆◆◆

Cyclists showcase their skill inside the "Globe of Death" at the Riviera Hotel in Las Vegas. Photo by Tom Campbell

Modern Nevada reflects its primordial characteristics of contrasts, contradictions, and extremes in many ways. But nowhere do they manifest themselves in more striking fashion than in the individuality of the state's communities.

The rugged land has always demanded self-reliance. The hamlets and mining camps that mushroomed after a rich discovery were generally so remote that their success depended solely on the boom itself. Those that survived the inevitable busts did so mostly by luck: they happened to spring up at spots where prospectors struck it rich near one of the roads or railroads.

Some flourish even today. They are likely to be either off-highway tourist attractions, or on-highway towns—communities where travelers pause and ranchers, miners, and nearby homesteaders come in from the range to shop and play.

These are the exceptions. Hundreds of less fortunate camps, their mines long since depleted and abandoned, have returned to the age-old solitude and silence of the vast Great Basin deserts.

Only a few of the settlements have grown into cities, and none of these qualifies as a metropolis by any standard measure. Nevada's permanent population in 1988 of about 1.2 million people (10 per square mile) would altogether make up only a fraction of the teeming throngs of a major U.S. city.

Yet, remarkably, although Americans tend to measure the importance of almost everything by its size, the state's two largest communities, Reno and Las Vegas, are as well-known by name throughout the civilized world as London or New York, as Paris or San Francisco. But each city, although operating under exactly the same state laws and regulations, became prominent in the beginning in its own fashion, and for different reasons. Divorce made Reno famous; gambling made Las Vegas "the entertainment capital of the world." Gambling has long since become the main attraction for both cities, yet each remains totally independent of the other in personality, philosophy—and especially growth.

Las Vegas contrasts with Reno in everything from age to influence. Reno functioned as a full-fledged city for about 50 years before the oasis called Las Vegas (Spanish for "The Meadows") became more than a railroad tank town.

It had taken many years to reach even that status. Spanish Franciscan missionaries had approached the general region as early as 1776, but fear of the "Northern Mystery" led most of them to pass the oasis well to the south.

By 1829 the Old Spanish Trail, which carried trade between Santa Fe, New Mexico, and Los Angeles, had started to run through the area. It soon grew from a route limited to commerce into one for the emigrant wagon trains from the East. (Even the great John C. Frémont had gone by Las Vegas Springs in 1844, when he was on his way home from his trailblazing trip through the northern part of the Great Basin.)

But as a place to settle it had even less to offer than some other parts of the Great Basin. Las Vegas lay 2,200 feet above sea level in the Mojave Desert, and it had a climate that baked in 100-degree heat on a daily basis in the summer. That might be a bearable condition for hardy prospectors, but they looked in vain for a big enough mining strike to make Las Vegas the kind of boomtown that had created other Nevada communities.

In short, almost everyone who happened upon it found Las Vegas to be just another oasis in the desert wilderness. Records indicate that the only reason travelers paused even briefly was to drink from its springs, which offered blessed relief to any wayfarer foolish enough to have been caught in the parched expanse around it.

When it finally did become a city in 1905, Las Vegas still didn't catch on. It looked as if it might in the 1930s, when the building of nearby Hoover Dam swelled the population to about 8,000. But that turned out to be as temporary a situation as experienced by so many of the state's early mining boomtowns—Las Vegas served mainly as just a transient home for the laborers who had poured in to work on the dam. Most left when that great structure was finished, and the town returned to its state of somnolence, not even to begin to awaken until the 1940s, when the first resort hotels were built on the Strip.

In other words, almost all of the history of Las Vegas as a true city goes back no further than World War II; it is said that only one of its buildings still standing predates 1905. And more than half the casinos that were to put Las Vegas on the entertainment map were built in just the 11 years between 1963 and 1974.

Today a score of high rises towers over the desert, proclaiming Las Vegas to be Nevada's biggest city. Some 600,000 people live in the metropolitan area—Las Vegas itself and nearby communities.

Both economically and by reputation, Las Vegas dominates Nevada's legalized gaming industry so overwhelmingly that nearly all potential visitors, whether from New York or New Delhi—from Cairo, Egypt, or Cairo, Illinois—will not say to their friends, "We're going to Nevada." Instead they will say, "We're going to Las Vegas." Most of them don't know—and probably don't care—that the same laws that allow them to gamble in the plush palaces of Las Vegas also allow the owner of a convenience store at any remote crossroads in the Silver State to apply for a gambling license. (He probably only wants a slot machine or two, but still must pass and pay for a background investigation by the Gaming Control Board although the investigation is less intense than it would be if he wanted table games.)

Revenue figures confirm that more visitors from out-of-state go to Las Vegas than anywhere else in Nevada. In 1987, for example, the $2.1 billion in gross gaming revenues taken in by Las Vegas alone amounted to about two-thirds of the statewide total. The rest of Clark County, of which Las Vegas is the seat, reflected the strong influence of Vegas by adding another half-billion dollars. The biggest contributor from that source was Nevada's latest gaming boomtown—Laughlin, on the Colorado River at the southern tip of the state. It raked in just under $210 million in gross gaming revenues.

Despite recessions that have affected the national economy adversely, Las Vegas continues to lead the way in cushioning the state against disastrous slumps. With that city leading, gambling has outlasted the spectacular mining bonanzas in the past. Today it competes only with the state's production of gold, which is the highest in the nation.

◄ Both economically and by reputation, Las Vegas dominates Nevada's legalized gambling industry. Photo by Tom Campbell

◄ Las Vegas has become famous throughout the world for its stage shows. Photo by Tom Campbell

The way Las Vegas achieved its fame and economic superiority was through a combination of highly professional promotion and advertising. It ignored the criticisms leveled at the very idea of legalized gambling, opting to make the most of it. By emphasizing excitement, glamour, and a sophisticated carnival atmosphere, it drew crowds like a magnet. People continue to come in droves—about 25 times Nevada's permanent population visit the state every year. It is they, not the residents, who keep the economy going.

And among them, surprisingly, are large numbers of people who wouldn't dream of approving legalized gambling in their own states, but who shed their qualms and indignation as soon as they arrive in Nevada and start playing the slots and table games themselves.

However, the promoters, being sharp businessmen, know that many who come to Nevada either don't want to gamble or genuinely disapprove of it on moral grounds. So almost right from the start they offered a broad variety of attractions to overcome or bypass both objections, concentrating on entertainment, sports—and culture.

They did it so successfully that Las Vegas has long since become famous the world over for stage shows featuring the top stars of the time, the best music, the finest

● What Las Vegas cannot import from Hollywood, it creates on its own. These are before and after views of a troupe of female impersonators from the "An Evening at La Cage" show at the Riviera Hotel. Photos by Tom Campbell

dancing troupes and the biggest and best production numbers. What it couldn't get straight from Broadway or Hollywood, it designed and staged on its own—such as the elaborate "Hello Hollywood" stage shows that included everything from earthquakes to waterfalls, from an onstage airliner to topflight choreography.

As the hotel casinos increased in size and number, their operators and owners added and perfected other non-gambling facilities. A score of championship golf courses sprang up along and near the Strip. Las Vegas alone has 3 private and 15 public courses. The city built its famed convention center and the hotels added their own convention facilities, so today Las Vegas can handle scores of conventions of any size. In 1987 the city hosted 556 conventions with a total of 1,677,716 attendees—delegates and hangers-on. One of the biggest conventions took place in 1988, when the Consumer Electronics Show attracted a total of 100,000 people.

Developments like this, both in and out of gambling itself, have not been limited to the Las Vegas valley. But they have been done there with far more flash, far more glitz, and certainly far more fanfare than in the Reno-Sparks-Carson City area. With the state's second-largest population cluster, those cities lie 450 miles to the north in geographical distance and a quarter of a century behind Las Vegas in flashiness.

Reno leads the area with about 150,000 souls. Its eastern boundary adjoins the western boundary of Sparks, a separate city and township which is home to about 57,000 people. The state capital, Carson City, located just 30 miles to the south, is number five with only 39,420 permanent residents.

That may seem puzzling. After all, Reno had been a city for half a century before Las Vegas even reached that status. But that difference in age is at least part of the reason. Reno started out as what would pass elsewhere as an almost normal community; it settled into a staid, conservative development pattern long before anyone dreamed that the state would legalize anything as daring as gambling, especially since only a few years before Nevada had enacted one of the nation's toughest antigambling laws.

So when it did become legal again in 1931, gambling at first had little impact on Reno. Most of the gaming establishments had the secretive air of a Prohibition speakeasy; almost surreptitiously, the men who frequented the dingy, back-alley clubs helped maintain the low profile.

The city feared that if it drew too much attention to what was going on, the antigambling forces would rise up and outlaw the embryonic industry once again.

That grim aspect didn't last long. Within a few short years the stark contrast of casino flash and glamour took over. Instead of hiding in dark alleyways, people went to the casinos even in broad daylight. They were urged on by the likes of Harolds Club's "Pappy" Smith, whose advertising beckoned the common man to his establishment. Reno itself erected an arch over its main street proclaiming in lights that Reno was "The Biggest Little City in the World"—a slogan that still shines from the third-generation arch that bears it.

In those pre-Las Vegas days all this garish boasting was enough in itself to shock a nation. But in addition to legal gambling, Reno had easy legal divorce and even legal prostitution. Leading the national criticism against this new target of sin were several religious publications and institutions. "Reno—a Wide Open Town," cried the *Christian Century*, a national Protestant magazine. Echoed the International Society of Christian Endeavor: "Reno is a blot on civilization, a menace to the American home and national prestige."

Today comments that disparaging are seldom made even about Las Vegas, and much less Reno. And despite any sense of shock about its inherent sins, "The Biggest Little City in the World" has had far more restrictions than its booming sister to the south. For years Reno prohibited major gambling casinos from being built anywhere but in a small downtown area. That has lately been relaxed considerably, but Reno still has no "Strip" like the one that has become the major area for the spectacular gaming expansion in Las Vegas. And strong resistance against there ever being one still remains among many area residents. As one impatient and progressive-minded native Nevadan put it recently: "The Reno area is the New England of Nevada."

▼ The Reno-Sparks-Carson City area forms the state's second-largest population cluster. This is downtown Sparks. Photo by Tom Campbell

◀ Carson City is home to the state Capitol. Photo by Tom Campbell

The embryo from which Reno emerged was a toll bridge that crossed the Truckee River, the outlet from Lake Tahoe. The bridge, a crude structure built about 1860 by one Charles W. Fuller in the broad valley known as the Truckee Meadows, attracted the attention of a shrewd businessman named Myron C. Lake. He saw it as a promising enterprise because of increasing activity in mining, especially in Virginia City, some 25 miles to the southeast. Noting that it was the only road in the area to the Comstock Lode, Lake bought the bridge and the toll franchise from Fuller in 1861.

Lake knew it was a gamble. There was no telling how long the burgeoning boom in the Comstock would last, or if the transcontinental railroad then being built would ever come through the valley. But he forged ahead with improvements to the area. A new bridge and an inn he called Lake House both did well, and Lake used the profits to buy more land around them. For the rest of the decade the spot was known as Lake's Crossing, and the man who owned it continued to prosper.

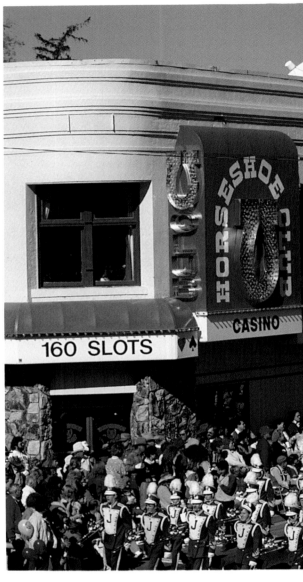

Lake's gamble began to pay off in 1868. The Central Pacific Railroad, building eastward from Sacramento to its eventual meeting with the Union Pacific at Promontory Point in Utah, chose the Truckee River Canyon for its route. But if the trains just passed by his bridge and his inn without stopping, Lake would get no income.

Being a shrewd businessman, it didn't take Myron Lake long to figure out a deal that would convince the railroad that his crossing would be the best place in the Truckee Meadows for their station. He would deed 40 acres of land at the bridge for that purpose to Charles Crocker, a top official of the railroad.

Crocker not only agreed and built the depot, he also agreed to deed back to Lake a number of the lots after he had them surveyed. Within a month after the railroad auctioned off 400 of its town lots, more than 100 homes and businesses had been established.

But the name Lake's Crossing disappeared. In those days the railroad named its own depots, sometimes capriciously. For reasons that remain somewhat obscure, it chose to name the new Truckee Meadows depot for a Civil War general, Jesse L. Reno, who had

◄ A parade swings by the state Capitol on Nevada Day in Carson City. Photo by Tom Campbell

been killed at the Battle of South Mountain in Maryland in 1862. (The general's family name had actually been "Renault" but was anglicized from the French. As a result, many residents of the new Nevada town pronounced it "Raino.")

The railroad gave the newly named Reno a basis for potential economic stability. At the moment it depended, however, on the glamorous but uncertain monetary achievements of the nearby precious-metal mines. So the dazzling events going on at the Comstock Lode left Reno in the shadow of Virginia City during its first decade.

Still, from a population of a little more than 1,000 in 1880, Reno grew to 3,300 by 1890 and to 4,500 in 1900. Slim as that sounds, it was quite remarkable because it showed a steady growth at a time when Nevada as a whole was losing about 35 percent of its residents in a disastrous depression: the state's population fell from 62,226 in 1880 to 42,335 in 1900.

Dr. William D. Rowley, a professor of history at the University of Nevada, Reno, wrote in his 1984 history of the city:

These 20 years of depression froze Nevada and its surviving communities into the social and political mold of the late 19th century. While neighboring states urbanized, vastly increased their population, and moved confidently ahead toward the 20th century with industrial and agricultural development, Nevada and its communities lingered in the shadows of the past. A poverty of human and material resources stood at the root of Nevada's problem. Those who were kind described the state as "quaint." Others, not so kind, spoke of revoking Nevada's statehood.

But the state and its communities, especially Reno, survived and eventually prospered. Since the area didn't enjoy the kinds of resources most other states had, Nevadans had to rely upon their traditional sense of personal independence. Instinctively and fearlessly, they acted boldly on ideas and causes that others shunned or rejected outright. With such freewheeling actions that lay outside the puritanical traditions of the rest of the country, Reno led the way in establishing Nevada as a state which could make the most of a desert environment through its own economic ingenuity and imagination.

▼ World-class airports, excellent roads, and comprehensive rail service make it possible for virtually every city in the contiguous west to be served from Nevada overnight. This is Cannon Airport in Reno. Photo by Tom Campbell

Although Reno managed to get a station stop on the railroad, it didn't get the big switching yard. At first that went to Wadsworth, a spot on a bend of the Truckee River, some 30 miles east of Reno. But in 1904 the railroad, by then renamed the Southern Pacific, moved its yard, shops, turntable, and roundhouse to the eastern edge of Reno and created a community to support it.

Since an anti-railroad rebellion was gaining steam in the state legislature at the time, the Southern Pacific decided it might be politic to change the name of the new settlement. Originally called Harriman, after the famed Eastern railroad tycoon, it was quickly rechristened to honor the governor of Nevada, John D. Sparks. It didn't look like too blatant a political gesture because the governor also happened to own a ranch nearby.

If northern Nevada in general was a Western version of New England in terms of set attitudes, the City of Sparks seemed to reflect it specifically. Its inhabitants—mostly hardworking, family-oriented railroad laborers—spent their days in the yards and their nights at home. Yet things apparently got boisterous enough on occasion to lead the city council to outlaw the growing local custom of driving up to a saloon in a buggy and having drinks at the curb.

Things have changed considerably. The city has a thriving tourist business, thanks mainly to one of the largest hotel-casinos in northern Nevada. John Ascuaga's Nugget, a relatively small operation by Nevada standards when it opened in the late 1950s, now has more than 2,500 employees, 975 rooms (including those in its adjacent inns), 64,000 square feet of gaming space, and 8 restaurants. Its public space would cover three-and-a-half football fields. Such additions as a pool, a spa, and a health club will be completed this year.

The Nugget's success reflects the individuality displayed by each of the next-door neighbor cities. Yet both Reno and Sparks have been able to join forces to promote the area's economic development while retaining their independence. They recognize that their continuing growth has pushed both communities nearly to the natural limits of the Truckee Meadows, demanding increasing cooperation not only between themselves but with Washoe County.

That cooperation is more than lip service. Instead of separate agencies, the two cities share the Reno-Sparks Chamber of Commerce and the Reno-Sparks Convention and Visitors Authority, which oversee everything from convention sales and finances to tourism and the Pioneer Theater Auditorium. In turn, they work closely with the Washoe County Commission in trying to resolve mutual and overlapping problems.

Virtually all those problems have to do, directly or indirectly, with Nevada's economy. A lot of outsiders would automatically assume that means gambling and tourism; for more than 50 years they have indeed been the heart of Nevada's economic livelihood. Although it has had its ups and downs, especially in the early 1980s, tourism has proved to be far more recession-resistant than mining, which experiences booms more spectacular and busts more complete than anything else.

Still, tourism can be fickle. Right from the time legalized gambling sparked the boom in the tourist industry, Nevadans have recognized the inherent economic dangers of putting all their eggs in one basket. The state and its people have long nurtured and fostered tourism as the prime component of their economy. But they also have recognized that it makes sound business sense to back it up by broadening that fun-and-games base with industries that cater to needs and necessities both inside and outside the state.

In short: to diversify.

It's a challenge not easy for any desert state to meet because of inherently limited resources. No one knew that better than Nevadans, but they also knew that by relying on ingenuity, imagination, and inventiveness, they could make economic development a thriving industry in itself.

One of the first Nevadans to accept the challenge head-on was Edwin S. Bender, a successful Reno warehouseman. During the 1920s Bender had done well in his business of storing goods on their way from the East to California. But shippers had to pay taxes to the states where the goods were stored, including Nevada.

Bender figured he might get the tax eliminated if he could persuade the legislature to make Nevada an inland free port. It would operate on the long tradition of the nation's seaports, which offered tax-free storage for goods being shipped out of the country. Nevada would become the major distribution center for the West Coast not only because of its geographical location, but because goods could be stored there and transshipped without excessive taxes or government pressures. It would double or quadruple the warehousing business Nevada already enjoyed.

Bender did convince the 1949 session of the state legislature to pass his idea into law. It would provide tax-free warehousing on goods stored, assembled, disassembled, repacked—or whatever—in transit through the state, with no time limit to disrupt inventory control.

But there was a problem. Many shippers figured it was too good an idea to last, especially in a state that had the dash and flair to take risks like legalizing gambling. The legislature could repeal the law even more easily than it passed it—and would be tempted to do so if the storage business blossomed into too good a revenue source to pass up.

The voters took care of that in the election of 1960 by passing an amendment to the state constitution which guaranteed that Nevada would remain a free port.

As a result, warehousing burgeoned and still flourishes as one of the state's most stable industries. Bender Warehouse Co. leads the way under the management of the founder's son, Frank Bender, who also contributes his business expertise to the State of Nevada as an "ambassador" for the Nevada Commission on Economic Development.

Nevada businessmen saw the free-port law as just a beginning, a sound basis for diversification. Although they welcomed the nice panoply of new service industries created by the spectacular growth of gaming and tourism, these did not qualify as a true diversification. Ranging from dealers and slot-machine mechanics to restaurant workers and hotel personnel, such jobs could not survive a major economic setback suffered by their employers.

The possibility of such problems seemed remote, to be sure. Gaming and tourism had weathered recessions and setbacks with flying colors and clearly would remain the state's major industries. But that was no reason not to use Nevada's other positive assets.

About the time Bender got his free-port law through the legislature in 1949, chamber of commerce officials began sending out the word that the greater Reno area had "an availability of stable and productive labor, and a highly respected air of livability," a combination they felt businessmen elsewhere would do well to consider.

But the Nevadans made the area's limitations clear. Politely but firmly, they pointed out that in a general sense the Silver State was not suited for heavy industry—large, smoke-belching factories would pollute the air. They especially discouraged anything that would require more water than could possibly be found in such an arid state.

That approach has worked well ever since. Small- to medium-sized industries which need little or no water and limited power—electronics, for instance—have found many advantages unique to Nevada. Among them are:

Location. Excellent roads, world-class airports, and good rail service across both the northern and southern parts of the state make it possible for virtually every city in the contiguous West to be served from Nevada overnight. Because of tourism, the state imports all sorts of products by truck, creating a surplus of cheap outbound trucking in all directions.

The most important direction is toward the West. Nevada's next-door neighbor, California, is the largest market in the United States; if California was a nation, it would have the seventh-largest gross national product in the world. The geographical fact that it adjoins Nevada for almost the entire length of its eastern border obviously gives it a special place in the Silver State's whole diversification program.

Tax structure. Businessmen elsewhere find particularly compelling the fact that Nevada is one of four states with the lowest tax rates in the nation at all levels. Both companies and their employees benefit from the light tax burden.

To start with, Nevada is one of only six states without a personal income tax—and if the voters approve a proposed amendment at the general election in November 1990, it will be unconstitutional for the legislature ever to approve one. On top of that, Nevada is one of five states without a corporate income tax.

Property owners pay some of the lowest property taxes in the nation—the highest rate anywhere in the state cannot exceed $3.64 per $100 of assessed valuation. There is no inheritance, estate, or gift tax and no franchise tax.

Nevada does, of course, have taxes and fees similar to those in other states, although most of these are lower. One that affects businesses is workers' compensation. Except for self-insured employers, coverage must be purchased from the State Industrial Insurance System. Rates are generally low, and are especially favorable for plastic and electronic assembly, textile manufacturing, and retail and professional classes. Benefits rank in the top third of all states.

General fund revenues come primarily from a sales tax, entertainment taxes, and a tax on casino gross income at a rate of 6.25 percent. (It surprises many outsiders to learn that of all the states that receive gambling tax revenues, Nevada ranks 11th.)

The 5.75 percent statewide sales and use tax, imposed at the retail level, is about average for the nation. It does not apply on food for home consumption, rentals, prescription

A Need For Doctors

Even today long miles stretch between habitations in much of rural Nevada. Just over 1.2 million residents live in the state's 110,540 square miles, or about 10 inhabitants per square mile.

Among the many difficulties in communication and travel these distances involve has been a chronic lack of easy access to medical services, including local physicians.

For nearly 100 years the state had no means to train doctors itself, and medical schools elsewhere would accept only about five Nevada students a year. Persuading graduates from those institutions to move to these remote reaches to begin their practices was no easy task.

It's still a problem, but it has been helped considerably by a move-

ment that started in the mid-1950s. By that time, the growth of the state population had begun to make the doctor shortage serious.

One obvious step toward a solution was for Nevada to have its own medical school. But even more obviously, a major project of such proportions is not taken on easily or without obstacles and objections. In this case the idea seemed so far-out, so dreamlike, that at first most people laughed it off.

Not much happened until 1965. But the idea was still simmering on the back burner, so some advocates in the University of Nevada system decided to move it to the front burner via a feasibility study. The results indicated that a medical school might not be such a laughing matter after all.

About the same time, champions of the idea got what they figured was a real boost when the federal government showed its concern about the growing national shortage of rural doctors, offering to match funds used to establish medical schools. It would give such schools an annual grant of $2,500 per student.

But the Nevada Legislature took a dim view of the idea. For openers, the potential cost looked enormous to the traditionally conservative lawmakers. Nevertheless, the advocates persisted, and finally the idea of feasibility began to stir some interest. Then internal battles erupted between northern and southern Nevada legislators over which branch of the university should have the school if it came to be a reality. Even after several more grants were pledged by wealthy philanthropists, the two sides remained deadlocked.

Undaunted, the proponents persisted with constant but friendly persuasion, led by some of the state's most distinguished and prominent people. One was Dr. Fred Anderson, a physician and then a university regent, who would come to be known as the father of the school. With him stood another Reno physician, Dr. Wesley Hall, then national president of the American Medical Association.

But the person who finally made it possible was none other than Howard Hughes. Out of the blue and in

the midst of the heated debate, Hughes made a pledge of $6 million, the amount estimated to be the state's share in running the school. (The pledge was cut to $4 million after Hughes' death.) And on March 25, 1969, the bill creating the University of Nevada School of Medicine squeaked through the legislature.

The bill specified that the school would be located on the university's Reno campus, and that it would start with a two-year curriculum. Its first classes were held in 1971, and by 1977 the school was able to take advantage of federal money to convert to a four-year program.

The school started with little or no physical property; at first it borrowed classrooms in existing campus buildings. But by the time it celebrated its 20th anniversary in 1989, it had built four buildings of its own, funded with federal and private money. It had graduated 624 students, 92 percent of them Nevadans, and most of them now practice in communities in the state.

Over the years the school has built a reputation beyond the borders of the state as an institution of superior standing, manifested by the increase in the number of outside grants given to faculty members. Since the school's research program began in the early 1980s, the grants have grown from $250,000 to $3 million. On a per capita basis, that figure puts the institution in the top 10 percent of all 127 medical schools in the country. Dr. Robert Daugherty, dean of the Nevada school, says this is an especially impressive feat because the school is one of the five smallest in the nation.

Not every lawmaker has become ecstatic over all these accomplishments. Yet in 1989, the legislature unanimously passed a resolution which read in part:

"Resolved by the Assembly of the State of Nevada, the Senate concurring. That the members of the 65th session of the Nevada Legislature commend and congratulate the University of Nevada School of Medicine on its 20th anniversary for the outstanding service it provided to the people of the State of Nevada."

drugs, or services. The state general fund gets 2 percent of the sales tax; the school districts, 1.5 percent; and the county relief fund, 2.25 percent. (In seven of the state's 17 counties, voters have approved a quarter-percent sales tax increase to meet local needs.)

The state gives businesses an additional break: they can defer payment of a sales tax on the purchase of capital equipment for up to five years with no interest, thus relieving new and expanding companies of some of the up-front costs.

Nevada's highly favorable tax climate for business and for individuals was recently spotlighted dramatically on a national basis. In a study of the 50 states and the District of Columbia to determine the total state and local tax burden on a hypothetical manufacturing firm, Nevada ranked 51st, the lowest. A similar study of individuals at four income levels, from $17,500 to $100,000, showed Nevada to be 48th or 49th in the nation in terms of the per capita state and local tax burdens its people carry.

Labor. Nevada's right-to-work law has long been an important incentive in attracting out-of-state industries. Recent studies indicate less than 17 percent of the total nonagricultural work force belongs to unions. Most who are union members work in the tourist industry—casino/hotel occupations such as waiters, bartenders, housekeepers, dealers, musicians, and the like.

About 65 percent of Nevada's total labor force lives and works in the Las Vegas area in Clark County. The Reno area has 18 percent, and the remaining 17 percent of the labor force is found in rural Nevada, due mainly to the gold-mining boom.

A problem fully recognized by the state is that its million-person population results in a relatively small labor force, with a limited range of skills. One tool the Nevada Commission on Economic Development has found to be valuable in dealing with this challenge is "Quick Start," a job training program designed to provide initial training for employees of new businesses. It uses the community college system for classroom-type instruction, and produces videotapes and on-the-job training. The program pays for training for up to 30 days, sharing the cost with the employer.

Formal education. State officials and business leaders together constantly strive to improve this important key to an adequate labor pool. The whole system, from kindergarten through higher education, presents a special challenge because of Nevada's small population and limited financial resources, yet it ranks well nationally.

Indeed, there has been especially striking progress at the University of Nevada. Although it is a tax-supported state university system, it has benefited in recent years from millions of dollars in contributions from private business in Nevada. With such cooperation and the normal growth of the population, the system has already attained a stature beyond the predictions of its supporters as recently as a decade ago. Particularly noteworthy are the advances it has made in science and engineering, and in the community colleges' vocational education programs.

The University of Nevada was born in 1874, more than 100 years ago, on a small campus in Elko. The eastern Nevada site was chosen because it had made the best offer to the state legislature. It struggled with a one-man faculty and staff and no more than 30 students a year until 1885, when the tiny land-grant institution moved to more populous Reno.

Today the system has grown into a statewide network encompassing not only under-graduate and graduate programs—including a school of medicine—but unique, special-ized entities such as the Mackay School of Mines and the Desert Research Institute. The basic, publicly supported elements include the University of Nevada, Reno; the University of Nevada, Las Vegas; and community colleges in Elko, Reno, Carson City, and Las Vegas as well as several community college satellite programs in smaller communities.

The University of Nevada, Reno, has 10 schools and colleges and offers a wide vari-ety of academic programs in more than 100 fields of study to over 10,000 students a year. Its library system has 763,000 volumes, 5,700 periodicals, and 2 million microforms, and is the state's regional depository for federal documents.

● The University of Nevada has grown into a statewide network encompassing not only undergraduate and graduate programs, but also features specialized entities like the Mackay School of Mines, a School of Medicine (below), and a museum (facing page). Photos by Tom Campbell

● The University of Nevada, Reno, has
10 schools and colleges and offers a
wide variety of academic programs.
Photos by Tom Campbell

● University of Nevada, Las Vegas, offers 50 graduate and 29 undergraduate degrees to a student population of more than 12,000. Photo by Tom Campbell

◄ The Thomas and Mack Center at the University of Nevada, Las Vegas, has been the scene of many an exciting basketball game. Photo by Tom Campbell

The Reno campus also houses the National Judicial College. Founded in 1963, this nationally recognized institution trains judges from around the country in courtroom management and shares an academic program with the University of Nevada, Reno, leading to a master's degree in judicial studies. The affiliated National Council of Juvenile and Family Court Judges—also at the University of Nevada, Reno—grants a similar degree.

Since its inception, the National Judicial College has trained more than 15,000 judges. The Honorable Warren E. Burger, former chief justice of the United States and one of the school's leading alumni, calls it one of the most significant developments affecting the administration of justice in this country.

The University of Nevada, Las Vegas (UNLV), was founded only 30 years ago but has a faculty of more than 350, 75 percent of whom hold doctorate degrees. The school offers 50 graduate and 29 undergraduate degrees to a student population of more than 12,000. The university has been growing rapidly with the help of private donations—in one year-and-a-half period it received more than $10 million in gifts for programs and facilities.

UNLV's library contains more than a million periodicals, microfilms, records, tapes, and films. It is the depository for more than 200,000 federal, state, and local government documents, and it houses one of the world's most complete collections of gaming-related materials.

The system's graduate programs offer master's degrees in arts, business administration, education, music, public administration, and science, and doctorates in education, psychology, and philosophy.

All these elements have combined in less than 125 years of statehood to create a university system that today works with Nevada's economic development programs. It contributes its academic expertise not only to existing businesses, but to the public-private sector network's continuing success in economic diversification.

● The University of Nevada system includes community colleges like Clark County Community College (above), North Nevada Community College (right), and Western Nevada Community College (facing page). Photos by Tom Campbell

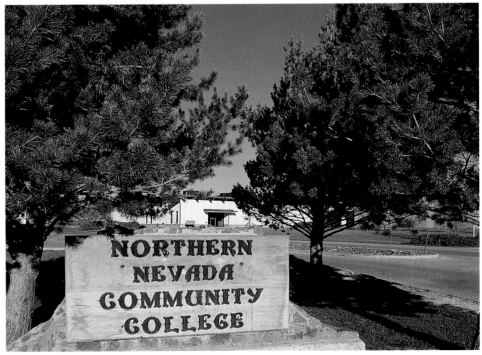

.5.

GOVERNMENT AND THE ECONOMY

◆◆◆◆

State officials are well aware of the role they must play in attracting business to Nevada, and they fill it well. Federal officials favor the site as an ideal military site.

◆◆◆◆

● Maintaining F-15 jets for flight preparedness is a full-time job at Nellis Air Force Base. Photo by Tom Campbell

The hallmark of Nevada's economy during most of the first 100 years of statehood was the ability of its settlers to make do with what was at hand. The awesome demands of the Great Basin's harsh landscape had made self-sufficiency and ingenuity the essential tools for human survival. So the homesteads, the ranches, the booms and busts of mining—and even the early days of legalized gambling—grew and failed and flourished without much outside economic help.

State officials didn't begin to give much thought to broadening Nevada's economic base until the mid-1950s, and even then the thinking was marginal. The legislature established a Department of Economic Development at its 1955 session, but the lawmakers gave it only enough funding to make it little more than a formal symbol, a standby to be activated in case of emergency. They saw no need to do more. Legalized gambling had been a giant of economic strength since 1931. It had not only pulled the state out of the Great Depression almost single-handedly; it had remained untouched by every national economic downturn since.

The fledgling agency was not entirely idle, however; its early efforts did persuade a respectable number of small industries to move to the state. But these seemed of such minor importance that some legislators began to grumble that the department was an unnecessary government expense, not worth even its tiny budget. In the 1971 session, one angry senator made a fiery speech on the floor of the upper house demanding that it be abolished. The effort failed, but a vocal minority of lawmakers continued to regard the department as an unwanted government stepchild.

That view would not change materially for another decade . . .

In 1981 legalized gaming's proud record of carrying Nevada through recessions virtually unscathed ended. This time the national economic downturn had a serious impact on the state's economy. Nevada's unemployment rate climbed above the national average. Not only did a no-growth period affect the usual recession victims like mining, manufacturing, and construction; now, for the first time, the casinos found themselves in the unfamiliar situation of little or no expansion. Fortunately, the stalled economy did no permanent damage to Nevada's major industry, but it was severe enough to shake everybody into the realization that legalized gambling was not recession-proof after all.

That revelation shocked the state government into taking action. In 1983, at the urging of Governor Richard Bryan, bipartisan support in both houses of the legislature created a Commission on Economic Development. Although a new agency, it used as its foundation the 28-year-old Department of Economic Development—revitalizing, refurbishing, and expanding it to give it new dimensions and a stronger impact.

A key part of those changes involved the commission's ability to draw on the expertise of the private business sector by getting the active participation, directly or indirectly, of successful Nevada executives. To that end, the lieutenant governor normally chairs the commission, composed of six private-sector executives, all appointed by the governor. A full-time executive staff of eight state employees handles day-to-day operations.

▲ Nevada has an active Economic Development Division, whose task is to inform the national and international business community of the advantages of Nevada as a place to expand or locate commercial operations. This is the Lear vision plant in Reno. Photo by Tom Campbell

The commission itself has two separate entities—the Division of Economic Development and the Division of Motion Pictures and Television. Principal financial support for both segments comes from the state general fund, but the legislature approved an aviation fuel tax in 1983 specifically to add to that support.

The primary goal of the Economic Development Division is to inform the national and international business community of the advantages Nevada has as a place to expand or locate commercial operations. The division serves as a clearing house for information and technical assistance on the whole spectrum of business activities, from production to marketing. The requests for information, now coming from throughout the world, cover such topics as the state's tax structure, labor market statistics, education and training programs, land availability, and financing alternatives.

The division does not work alone. It relies heavily on six regional development authorities across the state, which not only deliver client services but organize the local resources for development. Funding for each of these groups comes from private donations, state grants, and local governments.

The development authorities are separate, independent entities, established locally with the help of the Commission on Economic Development. Each assumes the responsibility of helping interested clients reach the decision to locate in its area. As an information clearing house, the local authority provides data on the city, county, or region being considered.

The commission backs up the local authorities with strong outreach efforts to out-of-state and foreign prospects. For instance, it has appointed more than 100 "Nevada Ambassadors" to "carry the message" of Nevada's advantages into their industry associations and in their travels.

In its letter telling a candidate it would like to nominate him or her as an Ambassador, the commission warns that while "this is intended as a very real honor . . . acceptance would also imply a responsibility to the economic diversification program of the state . . ." The letter continues:

An Ambassador is a volunteer who, without compensation, assists the Commission on Economic Development and our local development authorities.

Those nominated by the Commission, with the assistance of the development fall

◄ This bustling printing plant is one of the thriving businesses found in the Reno industrial core. Photo by Tom Campbell

▼ A technician at Southwest Color Graphics, another thriving high-tech industry enjoying the advantages of a home base in Nevada, uses the latest in state-of-the-art color scanning equipment, a Hell color scanner. Photo by Tom Campbell

● Companies that have relocated to the state include West Germany's Porsche Cars North America, with headquarters in Reno employing 447 workers. Photos by Tom Campbell

into two basic categories. The first is a person who is the head of a business that has moved to Nevada, or expanded here, in the past several years. People in this category can speak from their own experience about how they have been treated and the advantages of doing business in Nevada.

The second category are those Nevadans in business or government who have played a leadership role in our development efforts at the state or local level . . . We also want to be able to bring someone who "speaks their language" in terms of employees, wages, suppliers, transportation, markets and the like. Our government Ambassadors may be called upon to assist a client in arranging for services and complying with requirements.

Early in its career the commission recognized the strong economic interests in Asia and made a major effort to sell them on the advantages of Nevada. In August 1985 Governor Bryan began an international trade initiative to organize a trade/investment mission to the Pacific Rim area. That resulted in a 1986 state mission to Japan, Korea, and Hong Kong. Follow-up missions returned in October 1986 and June 1987.

By that time it had become evident that even more concrete steps should be taken. On the basis of Governor Bryan's recommendation, the 1987 legislature appropriated funds for a representative office for economic development in Tokyo. On August 10 of that year, the Board of Examiners approved a contract between the commission and

EPISTAT, a U.S. company with a Tokyo office. The new office was formally opened on October 16, 1987, with Governor Bryan and Lieutenant Governor Bob Miller both attending. (Bryan was elected U.S. Senator in 1988. Miller is acting governor through 1990, and remains chairman of the Commission on Economic Development.)

The success of this Asian venture, rather bold for a desert state, has been borne out by the advent of some 25 Asian companies now operating in Nevada. These include not only such common industries as electronics, plastics manufacturing, and printing, but partial or full ownership by Japanese interests of four Las Vegas casinos.

But at the same time it was concentrating its major efforts to get Asians to invest in Nevada, the commission by no means neglected other foreign countries. About a dozen companies from such European countries as West Germany, Hungary, and Italy, as well as one each from Israel and Canada, have established themselves in Nevada. All of these foreign investments have meant the employment of several thousands of Nevadans in operations that 10 years ago did not exist even in dreams.

The influx into Nevada of American corporations from other states has been proportionately larger. In 1985 and 1986, for example, over 130 businesses relocated or expanded in Nevada—more than double what had been recorded in the previous two years. That activity resulted in more than 5,000 new jobs, and used more than 3 million square feet of office and warehouse space.

Relocated companies range from West Germany's Porsche Cars North America, with

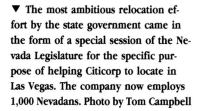

▼ The most ambitious relocation effort by the state government came in the form of a special session of the Nevada Legislature for the specific purpose of helping Citicorp to locate in Las Vegas. The company now employs 1,000 Nevadans. Photo by Tom Campbell

▲ The film industry had made intermittent use of Nevada locations for many years, but without much official help from the state. The Commission of Economic Development has since established a Motion Picture Division to promote Nevada's location advantages, and the change in commercial film activity has been dramatic. Photo by Tom Campbell

ESCAPE
FROM
HOLLYWOOD

One of the most famous American entertainers, who loved the desert enough to buy seven ranches in the state, never performed for money in a Nevada casino. Bing Crosby, a devoted hunter and fisherman, discovered the fascination of the broad reaches of the Great Basin in the 1940s. It came about when his equally outdoor-loving Hollywood friends, Gary Cooper and Roy Rogers, introduced him to the rugged beauty of Elko County.

The most popular male baritone singer in the world at the time, Crosby fell in love with the area as a perfect retreat from the clamor that surrounded him on the entertainment circuit. Despite his fame as a singer, Nevadans treated him as one of their own; he could go into the town of Elko in blue jeans, a plaid shirt, and a cowboy hat and be accepted as a rancher rather than as the national celebrity that everyone who saw him knew he was.

"Elko is . . . one of the last bastions of the Old West," Crosby wrote in his 1953 autobiography, *Call Me Lucky.* "I've been going there for more than 10 years now, and I haven't been asked for an autograph or to do a benefit show, or contribute to charity, or to do anything but mind my own business, by any resident of the county. As nearly as I can figure it, if I'm known at all, it is simply as that fellow from California with a pretty nice cattle—cow and calf—outfit up near Wild Horse." And best of all, they let him pursue his love of the outdoors as an avid golfer, hunter, and fisherman uninterrupted.

Crosby was so grateful for this understanding of his strong desire for normalcy, for being treated as "that fellow from California," that he contributed both time and money to the community. This included his taking part in a few local celebrations and, despite his fierce desire for privacy, even accepting his appointment by the townsfolk as honorary mayor of Elko. Crosby regarded it enough of an honor to hold the post until his death in 1977.

His appointment as honorary mayor was a major event in Elko, and to celebrate it the town declared February 7, 1948, "Bing Crosby Day." At ceremonies at the Ranchinn, Crosby accepted the key to the city from Mayor Dave Dotta, saying, "I pledge my support to help you any way I can." He immediately began to carry out that pledge by donating $5,000 toward a new swimming pool for the city. The second thing he pledged was to close down all the saloons in town—after everyone in town was inside.

"The Groaner" closed out the day by attending a banquet in his honor with his wife, Dixie—herself a former Fox starlet—then picking up the tab for the whole affair. He capped the evening by singing several songs for the audience.

But Crosby couldn't prevent word of his new post from spreading far and wide. Not long after that celebration, the honorary mayor fulfilled his civic duty by pushing a broom down the gutter of Elko's main street. A photograph of the gag showed up in newspapers all across the country.

headquarters in Reno employing 447 workers, to Chicago's big printing company, R.R. Donnelley & Sons, which expanded to Reno and employs 250. The most ambitious effort by the state government came in the form of a special session of the Nevada Legislature, called by Governor Richard Bryan in 1984 for the specific purpose of helping Citicorp to locate in Las Vegas. The company now employs 1,000 Nevadans.

The commission's Motion Picture Division was created in July 1983, to promote Hollywood's already present interest in Nevada as an area with a wide variety of sites for filming on location. The film industry had made intermittent use of Nevada locations for many years, but without much official help from the state. These included such well-known classics as *The Misfits* (the last major movie starring Clark Gable, Marilyn Monroe, and Thelma Ritter) and the long-running television series, "Bonanza." Hollywood was clearly a potential cinematic gold mine for its next-door neighbor, but until the division's formation, no official agency had taken a full-time, active part in promoting Nevada's location advantages.

The change has been dramatic. The year before the division came into being, Nevada generated a total of $5.6 million in commercial film activity. After one full year of the division's operation, that total reached $13.1 million. In 1985 and 1986 it generated nearly $60 million in location production, and the number of motion pictures; TV movies, specials, and episodes; and other productions went over the $100-million mark. And in 1987 alone, motion picture and TV companies spent $44.5 million in Nevada.

Examples of the major motion pictures completely or partially produced in Nevada during the 1987-88 fiscal year include the Oscar-winning *Rain Man*, starring Dustin Hoffman and Tom Cruise; *Midnight Run*, featuring Robert DeNiro and Charles Grodin; *Things Change*, with Don Ameche; *Steal the Sky*, costarring Mariel Hemmingway and Ben Cross; *Homer & Eddie*, with Whoopi Goldberg; and *Rambo III*, starring Sylvester Stallone.

Television productions included 20 episodes of "Crime Story," 13 episodes of "High Mountain Rangers," two episodes of "Brothers," and one episode apiece of "Matlock" and "Rags to Riches." Made-for-television movies included *Bonanza: The Next Generation*, *Once Upon a Texas Train*, and *Elvis & Me*.

Production of commercials was as hardy and healthy. Clients included Chrysler, Pontiac, Peugeot, Jeep, Goodrich Tires, Mercedes Benz, Buick, Whirlpool, and Amtrak. Producers from Japan, Mexico, Italy, England, Australia, and France used Nevada as their location filming choice. The Silver State now ranks eighth in the nation in spending by all these industries.

The division has accomplished this by actively recruiting production companies. It maintains a vigorous advertising and marketing campaign in a variety of industry publications, including *Variety* and the *Hollywood Reporter*. Ads focus on the location advantages of Nevada, highlighting the 24-hour availability of help, rural attractions, and a blend of scenery with urban centers not typically found in most states.

The division takes pride in its sound record of providing reliable service. The most obvious and most crucial thing is to get the production into the state by meeting the

needs of the script. The division uses photographs, videotapes, and site tours to present a wide variety of choices.

When necessary, the division gets special use permits to provide one-stop service for a production company, or troubleshoots by taking care of unanticipated problems for production companies unfamiliar with Nevada. It publishes a directory of services which is distributed to more than 5,000 companies worldwide, and which enables production companies to make direct contacts with local services. The 96-page, four-color manual provides information on services, locations, talent, and support facilities available to production companies. And since the division came into being, two production companies have located in Nevada.

It is not only the state government that plays a strong part in the economy through its cooperation with private industry—so does the federal government, despite the state's love-hate relationship with the owner and operator of 87 percent of Nevada's land.

The federal economic impact manifests itself most sharply in the number and importance of military reservations the Department of Defense and the Department of Energy oversee and operate in Nevada. Today more land than in any other state—4.069 million acres—is dedicated to military activity, and nearly 40 percent of Nevada airspace is

▲ TA-4 jets line the airfield at Fallon Naval Air Station. Photo by Tom Campbell

◀ Aerial activity is common throughout the Nevada region. The U.S. Air Force Aerial Demonstration Squadron, more commonly known as the Thunderbirds, practice their intricate maneuvers over Indian Springs. Photo by Tom Campbell

restricted to military use. Units of the army, navy, air force, and Department of Energy (the Nevada Test Site) now make use of this land and airspace for everything from weapons development, storage, and testing to troop and pilot training.

All this came about as a direct result of World War II. Most of the bases and testing grounds functioned through Korea and Vietnam. They also have survived the presidential commission's 1988 recommendation that some 86 military installations across the nation be closed. They avoided the cuts not because of some special political influence, but because, as Senator Harry Reid of Nevada said, "all are unique and an integral part of the national defense." And what made them so was, again, the contradictions and contrasts of the landscape itself.

It all started for that reason when, in 1926, lightning struck a huge naval arsenal in northern New Jersey, blowing it sky-high. Near the Atlantic Ocean and in a heavily populated region, the thousands of tons of highly explosive ammunition killed and wounded many navy men and neighborhood civilians, and fire damaged or destroyed many homes.

It didn't take long for military leaders to decide that the ammunition depot had best be rebuilt in a region not only less populated but well inland from either ocean, yet convenient enough to ports for ammunition to be transported with relative ease to naval vessels. That meant the Far West, preferably in a desert area. The site they chose lay just outside Hawthorne, a town in central Nevada some 300 miles from the Pacific Ocean, well back behind the protective wall of the Sierra Nevada mountain range.

Established by the builders of the Carson and Colorado Railroad in 1881, Hawthorne had been a freight center for the area's mining towns, but faded when the mines played out. It avoided completely fading into a ghost town largely because it became the seat of local government when Mineral County was created.

But that was not enough to make it prosper until the U.S. Navy decided it was the ideal spot for its highly explosive caches—to be spread over a wide-enough area not to blow up all at once—where they would be a lot safer from attack.

Despite the odd fact that it would serve the U.S. Navy from one of the driest deserts on the continent, Nevada's first important defense installation mushroomed from its opening in 1930 to one of the largest ammunition depots in the world 10 years later. During World War II it carried the responsibility of supplying ammunition to American naval vessels all over the world.

Performing such an awesome mission required a tremendous amount of acreage. To meet that requirement, the navy built its ammunition depot completely around the small community of Hawthorne. Today the area is once more an active military installation (it has been transferred from the navy to the army). Motorists driving through Hawthorne and along the highway that runs from Reno to Las Vegas still see the scores upon scores of concrete mounds or earthen dumps where the ammunition is stored in the desert countryside.

When the arsenal was built, Hawthorne itself was too small to serve the several thousand people who came to work at the site, so the navy built a new community just outside of town. Called Babbitt, it contained several hundred family units and was the headquarters for the naval officers.

The depot itself contains more than 200 miles of railroad track (no longer used) and 550 miles of paved roads, a complex transportation system needed to haul the highly explosive cargo. The installation had to have all the other requirements of a fair-sized city, including an intricate system of power and water lines and hundreds of vehicles of all kinds. During the height of World War II, all these and more were needed to service not only the sprawling base but its massive collection of bombs, naval depth charges, rifle bullets, missiles, and other devices.

With the nation not at war, the depot naturally operates much more quietly these days. But it still plays a key role in the defense program. Although local officials felt it would be the most likely Nevada target on the "hit list" for closure of military installations, Hawthorne has not only survived but may get 34 more civilian jobs.

It became clear in 1940 that the need to prepare for the possible involvement of the United States in World War II would require much more than ammunition depots. It would take many new military bases to train men for possible combat and to cope with any emergencies.

No place appeared more ideal to the military brass in Washington than the harsh deserts and tough terrain in the wide-open spaces of interior Nevada. Although they continued to defy man's best efforts for development, these very attributes of Nevada would become highly desirable assets in the training of thousands of American and Allied airmen. The state's clear and cloudless skies provided perfect flying weather year-round; the natural topography of mountains and canyons in vast areas of unused and sparsely occupied public domain provided ideal backdrops for cannon and machine-gun practice.

▼ Nellis Air Force Base recognizes the human needs of its inhabitants. Its grounds include a golf course, mobile home park, and child-care facilities. Photo by Tom Campbell

● Nellis Air Force Base offers full-fledged child-care facilities. Photo by Tom Campbell

▲ A golf course on an air base? You'll find it at Nellis! Photo by Tom Campbell

Military development started in earnest in January 1941. The U.S. Army Quartermaster Corps acquired the Western Air Express runway and field eight miles north of Las Vegas. The purpose was to establish a flexible gunnery school to train men to use the weapons on World War II planes in what was then the Army Air Corps. The school later became the Las Vegas Army Air Field, and, finally, Nellis Air Force Base.

Named in honor of Lieutenant William Nellis, a Nevadan who was killed in combat over Europe in 1944, Nellis became the largest tactical air base, in area, in the free world. As such, it played a key role in training most of the American pilots and other airmen who fought in all theaters during World War II.

Following that war, the base became relatively inactive for about four years. But when training environments were sought elsewhere, none matched the advantages of climate and terrain of Nevada. Nellis was reactivated in 1949 and became a world-renowned training institution.

Today the 2.9-million-acre Nellis Air Force Range comprises the largest air and ground space available for military operations in the Western world. Its activities have expanded from instruction in all phases of air combat to a laboratory and test range for developing concepts and methods for perfecting and updating tactics and techniques. By the mid-1980s it had developed into a virtual independent community, with more than 1,400 sets of family quarters and a large mobile-home park for privately owned units.

The base has recreational facilities ranging from a golf course and hobby shops to swimming pools and a rod and gun club. In addition to the usual commissary and exchange facilities, it also boasts a child-care and preschool program as well as undergraduate college courses through Clark County Community College.

Nellis also oversees the nearby Indian Springs Air Force Auxiliary Field, which lies on the southern edge of the bombing and gunnery range. Located about 45 miles northwest of the main base and operated by the 554th Combat Support Squadron, the field has a population of about 2,000 including active duty personnel, 300 dependents, and some 1,250 civilians.

About the same time Nellis got started and 300 miles to the north of it, the U.S. Navy established its own training base for air personnel. In 1942 army engineers had laid out the runways for a small airport near Fallon, some 60 miles east of Carson City. It got little use until the navy took over in 1944 and commissioned it as an auxiliary naval air station. Under the control of the naval base in Alameda, California, it trained thousands of pilots and aviation technicians during World War II, then was deactivated in 1946.

For a while it appeared that this would be the end of the base's career. But three years later it suddenly bounded into headlines around the world because of an unusual and dramatic local emergency. It had nothing to do with training fighter pilots, but it was the kind of emergency that only an air base like Fallon could resolve. It was the historic "Hay Lift" of 1949.

The winter had been so severe across the northern part of the state that deep snows had isolated thousands of head of livestock on the desert ranges. Unable to dig down deep enough to get at the sparse forage, the animals faced certain starvation without help.

The help came in the form of military planes. In an almost steady stream, scores of them took off from the temporarily reactivated Fallon base, each of them loaded with feed. By the time the lift was over, they had dropped hundreds of tons of hay, and had saved most of the snowbound cows, sheep, and horses in central and eastern Nevada.

In 1972 the base became the Fallon Naval Air Station in its own right, designed to train naval air personnel to fly and support the most modern fighting aircraft. Ever since, graduates of those programs have been carrying out assignments at naval stations and on aircraft carriers throughout the world as key elements of the national defense.

The air station obviously contributes heavily to the economic health of Fallon. A city of about 12,000 permanent civilian residents, it also enjoys the additional influx of money from another 1,500 naval personnel who live on the base and rely on the town for everything from groceries to entertainment.

Yet the training activities have lately caused increasing tension between the station and local citizens throughout the area. The reason is the sonic booms that daily shatter the once-quiet atmosphere. The jets fly low-level training routes across a large area of desert country. When they break the sound barrier so close to the ground—from 400 to 3,000 feet high—the sonic booms they create are so earth-shaking the residents complain they cause health problems not only for the human population of ranchers and miners, but even for livestock.

▲ High-tech industries can be found throughout Nevada. This is a lithium battery plant in Henderson. Photo by Tom Campbell

Although the navy laid out the routes over sparsely populated areas, even its own Environmental Impact Statement acknowledges its training course still does not lie far enough away from cows, sheep, and people to prevent problems. The statement reports: "Sonic booms could have adverse effects on the autonomic nervous systems, including short and long-term changes in the vascular, respiratory, endocrine and/or gastrointestinal system."

A partial solution has been the purchasing by the navy of private property from longtime settlers in the regions directly affected. This can amount to a lot of land, since the airspace controlled by the military specifically as the navy's Supersonic Operations Area in northcentral Nevada currently stands at more than 7,675 square miles. In addition, a current total of 25,541 square miles of Nevada airspace is designated Military Operations Areas, where non-supersonic aircraft operate.

What worries many Nevadans about all this is that the use of Nevada land and airspace by military and other defense activities may be expanded even further. Citizen Alert, a nonprofit organization based in Nevada, is in the vanguard of efforts to keep such expansion to a minimum. While recognizing the value of the presence of such federal government installations—and with a kind of grudging gratitude for the money they bring to the state—Nevadans feel they have done enough for national defense and scientific advancement. In a 1986 report Bob Fulkerson, executive director of Citizen Alert, pointed out the dichotomy of thinking among Nevadans on this subject:

Federal control of all but 13 percent of land in Nevada, combined with low population density and a desert wasteland image, make this state a prime testing ground for the latest military hardware. No doubt there are economic benefits from Nevada's close ties with the military: The total projected economic impact of the Department of Energy in 1985 approaches $1 billion in payroll and expenditures, and exceeds 20,000 persons employed . . .

But recently Nevada has been deluged with additional proposals for military use of

*public land and airspace, and many citizens and public officials are becoming
extremely sensitive to the impacts these projects may have on the health, economic
livelihoods and recreational interests of Nevadans and the people who visit here.*

And then we have the famous (or infamous) Nevada Test Site. Located on 864,000
acres in southern Nye County, this fearsome piece of land has experienced the explosions of more than 675 nuclear weapons since 1951.

Since the official recognition of the insidious and inherent hazard of radioactivity,
the tests have taken place underground instead of in the open air. But many residents in
the rural areas of southern Nevada and in western Utah have filed suit against the federal government, claiming that there has been a higher than normal incidence of cancer among
the area's population since testing first started and implying that there may well be unde-
tected leakage from the deep underground explosions.

Nonetheless, nuclear experts in and out of government not only regard the area as
ideal for such testing because of its remote and still-primitive natural qualities, but have
in recent years indicated it might be one of the few locations ideal for the storage of high-
level nuclear waste.

Most Nevadans saw this possibility as an even more ominous health threat than nuclear bomb tests—so potentially dangerous that it could be a hazard to future generations for as long as 10,000 years.

The project proposes a $30-billion repository for the burial of high-level nuclear
waste from commercial and military projects. Against strong objections by Nevada officials and—according to professional surveys—from 70 to 80 percent of the population of
Nevada, Congress has favored the test site's Yucca Mountain as the best location.

Lying only about 110 miles northwest of Las Vegas and tentatively scheduled to
open in 2003, the nuclear waste dump would hold an estimated 75,000 tons of used fuel
rods from commercial and military reactors.

In theory, there would be little or no danger of radioactivity escaping into the atmosphere because the waste would be buried thousands of feet deep. But serious questions
have yet to be answered about the geological suitability of the proposed repository. Located near Death Valley close to the Nevada-California border, Yucca Mountain lies between an area of recent volcanic activity and that part of the test range where hundreds
of nuclear bombs have disturbed the earth with their mighty blasts for the past 40 years.

Nevada claims these technical considerations had not been researched before the
site was selected as the probable location. This lack has left unresolved doubts about the
ability of Yucca Mountain to contain leaks, and ignores some indications that water in
the soil could corrode the containers and dissolve the waste itself.

In any case, because of the engineering, geological, and practical complications involved, it may be a long time before the issue will be resolved. Meanwhile, it has not
become enough of a factor even to slow down the influx of more and more people who
have learned of the attractions of this unspoiled land.

.6.

THE DREAM BECOMES REALITY

◆◆◆◆

*Although they may not
immediately come to mind when
one thinks of Nevada, the arts
flourish throughout the state.
And of course, sports and
recreation have always been
big draws.*

◆◆◆◆

● Nevada offers an extremely wide range of diversions, from the ultimate urban microcosm, to the quiet solitude and exciting possibilities of the wilderness. These snowmobilers are watching the curtain close on yet another beautiful day on the shore of Lake Tahoe. Photo by Tom Campbell

The primordial upheavals have quieted. The restless noise of creation has become a stillness, and the jagged scars formed in a trembling land have softened into a rugged beauty.

But the passing centuries did not erase the deep geological impact of the violence that molded the Great Basin. Today, eons later in the register of time, the stark contrasts and contradictions the violence caused still give the Nevada landscape its strange dual quality.

On the one hand, it reflects an unrelenting harshness, a clarity so bright and brilliant as to be almost blinding; on the other, subtle, unseen pulses and silent harmonies impart to it a tranquility that seems to come from another part of the cosmos.

Disparate tones and textures, to be sure. But by some mysterious alchemy they have combined into a compelling mystique, beckoning dreamers and daredevils alike to take on its unique challenge.

Some could not meet that challenge. Those early adventurers who tried to force their civilized ways on the raw, demanding desert not only failed, but became its victims. The bones of uncounted hundreds of them lie in nameless graves, scattered across nameless hills, the crude wooden markers long ago lost to the restless winds.

Their mistake had been to fight the land, to try to subdue it. Those who followed saw the futility and elected instead to work with the land, to use what it had to give as a tool. There lay the road not only to survival, but to the means for building a new society and creating a successful, working economy.

Today the dreamers and the adventurers live and work in harmony with the natural gifts Nevada offers—a vast array of minerals beneath the land, an endless variety of topography on its surface, an infinite clarity of sky and air above it. They have learned how to apply these values not only to shape their own lives and fortunes, but to help improve the lives and fortunes of those beyond the state's borders with their economic, scientific, literary, and cultural contributions.

Sometimes the dreamers and the adventurers join forces and use the tools at hand to turn bold new ideas into reality.

A case in point in Nevada was the establishment of the Desert Research Institute (DRI) in 1959, by a special act of the state legislature. A division of the University of Nevada System, the fledgling organization announced its primary purpose would be to learn how Nevada could most effectively manage the unusual natural resources of this desert state, and to use that knowledge in the development and diversification of Nevada's economy. As it turned out, that would be just the start of efforts that would be felt across the world.

DRI says its basic tool has been "a unique combination of an academic tradition of high quality, basic research, and the productive application of new technology . . . This novel approach has developed an effective, flexible research organization in Nevada capable of rapidly transferring new knowledge into technology in a cost-effective and fiscally viable manner."

During the past quarter-century, that approach has involved DRI's scientific specialists in locations reaching from both polar regions to every major continent—and to all but five of the 50 United States. Some efforts have even extended well beyond the institute's home planet to examine "such diverse topics as the atmospheric physics of Venus, the possibility of life forms on Mars, and the potential for growing exotic, advanced crystalline materials in the zero-gravity of space."

To reach out to all these areas, the 30-year-old Desert Research Institute now has 280 scientists, technicians, and support personnel conducting about 100 research projects every year. They work out of the DRI offices and laboratory facilities at Stead, a few miles north of Reno; at the Dandini Research Park in Reno; and at Las Vegas and Laughlin in southern Nevada.

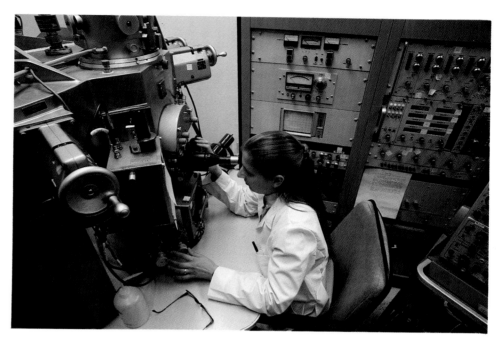

▲ The Desert Research Institute studies the effective management of Nevada's diverse range of unusual natural resources. Photos by Tom Campbell

To much of the outside world, Nevada has only two claims to fame or, in the eyes of some, notoriety. One is its widely touted reputation as the "entertainment capital of the world." The other is the current and greatest of the state's long list of mining booms—the state's becoming the largest producer of gold in the nation.

Less known but of more lasting and wider significance is the important part Nevada plays in the worldwide efforts to solve a problem that threatens not only the quality of life, but life itself on this planet—the rapidly increasing deterioration of the environment. The Desert Research Institute has become a national leader in those efforts. Because the overall problem is so complex, DRI has assigned parts of it to several of its research centers, each organized around a "selection of scientific disciplines" that relate to that center's particular environmental expertise.

The Water Resources Center, the oldest and largest of DRI's divisions, concentrates on Nevada's most precious natural element: water. It has developed special computer simulation models for high-tech research on all aspects of water quality and quantity, historically this arid state's toughest environmental problems. The center's research includes everything from planning and evaluating groundwater flow to geothermal resources and hydroelectric applications. It examines present management systems and studies the feasibility of new techniques for conserving or increasing water supplies.

Water quality, tricky at best, became more critical with the advent of the Nevada Test Site and the storage of certain hazardous wastes. To deal with this, the center monitors groundwater for evidence of pollution and researches means of improving its quality. This work has made it possible for the state to advise potential new businesses of locations that have safe and ample water for their projects.

The Energy and Environmental Engineering Center does for air quality what the

Water Resources Center does for water quality. This DRI division's research has developed new techniques and instruments for identifying the relative amounts of pollutants that come from different kinds of emissions.

First applied to characterize air quality conditions in Las Vegas and Reno, these advanced scientific methods have since been used in Phoenix, Arizona, and in Santa Barbara and the San Joaquin Valley in California. Now these methods have become so effective that the center has been called upon to lead the state of California's battle against acid rain, and to take a major part in national studies currently being conducted on acid deposits.

Finally, what the center calls a "major ground-breaking effort" is its current investigation of the impact of pollutants moving from metropolitan areas into the relatively pristine air of the vast, open desert and mountain regions of the Southwest. Scientists use a complicated, highly technical development developed by the center to track and measure, with remarkable accuracy, even infinitesimal amounts of particulates affecting the scenic resources in national parks and recreational areas, such as the Grand Canyon.

During his long residence in the Nevada Territory, Mark Twain often took note of the weather, a subject that fascinated him so much that some claim (perhaps erroneously) that he was the source of the famous line, "Everybody talks about the weather, but nobody does anything about it."

The thing that most intrigued Twain about Nevada's weather was the high wind that often sweeps down from the peaks of the Sierra Nevada Mountains to race across the valleys on summer afternoons. Since it can reach gale force, Mark Twain labeled it "The Washoe Zephyr," a nickname Nevadans still tend to apply to any breeze over 20 miles an hour.

The Atmospheric Sciences Center of the Desert Research Institute has taken the famous complaint to heart—it is actively doing something about the weather.

In fact, the Atmospheric Sciences Center has developed an international reputation in the areas of cloud physics, air motions, and weather modification research and become one of the largest and most comprehensive such groups in the world. For instance, its scientists participate in such research projects as how Gulf and Atlantic hurricanes are formed, how to suppress hail in the high plains, and weather modification techniques to increase the winter snow pack (the chief water source in many parts of the world) in the Sierra Nevada Range, in Utah, and in several foreign nations.

DRI gives this rundown of some of the Atmospheric Sciences Center's accomplishments:

[It was a pioneer in research] in atmospheric ice crystal formation, in the fundamental atmospheric phenomena involved in cloud system formation and the dynamics of air turbulence, and in the self-cleansing processes of the atmosphere.

ASC operates the federally-funded Western Regional Climate Center, coordinating climatic research, data analysis and climate information distribution for 11 western states. Prototypes of the research tools ASC has developed are now in use by scientists throughout the world.

Because ASC scientists operate in an area where adequate research technology is often non-existent, the center has developed exceptional instrumentation capabilities to support its own investigations. Prototype DRI research tools are now being used by other scientists on related research efforts worldwide.

Anthropology figures heavily in the Quarternary Sciences Center's research into the record of climatic changes in the western United States during the last 1.8 million years (the Quaternary Epoch). It extends the information supplied by that history into the more recent development of human cultures in arid lands, especially how they relate to the anthropology and archaeology of the western and southwestern United States.

Lately the alarming spread of industrial and housing relocation has created an increasing demand for practical applications of this research. The center is being called upon more and more to conduct surveys and analyses of ancient cultural resources so often found on undeveloped land. Says DRI: "The center's scientists are heavily involved in cultural resource surveys for government and industrial sponsors to interpret anthropological sites prior to land-disturbing activities throughout the Southwest." QSC also conducts similar studies in the Middle East, especially on important recent discoveries of ancient cultures in Jordan and on Cyprus.

The Biological Sciences Center, DRI's smallest and fastest-growing research group, is in the vanguard of research in an extremely important field which has only recently begun to get widespread attention. It focuses on changes in global climate and the implications those changes have for the environment of the intermountain West.

The Desert Research Institute takes the view that it must constantly direct its efforts toward keeping a delicate balance between the two goals of its mission—preserving the state's natural resources and enhancing economic diversification. In his speech marking the 30th anniversary of DRI in March 1989, President James V. Taranik made a point of these potentially contradictory positions:

Many of us came to Nevada because of the quality of the environment, and we are alarmed when we see poor air quality in Nevada's urban areas, congestion on highways, and hear concerns of water shortages.

Yet we know that we would like to see Nevada's economy expand and diversify. The attraction of high-technology industry with highly skilled labor will bring permanent citizens to our state that will enhance our quality of life. Therefore, it seems because we live in a delicate environment, Nevada must be careful to balance its agenda for development with its agenda for effective management of its natural resources.

It comes as a surprise to many outsiders that Nevada would think of balance of any kind. Even in these days of enlightened and technically proficient communication, they find it hard to believe that such barren, high desert country could be the home of so much advanced scientific research as that at DRI. It seems totally out of character with the common perception that Nevada is the last stronghold of the Old West, the one remain-

▲ Hundreds of entertainers who have made Nevada their permanent home supply the area with a rich base of talent. Photo by Tom Campbell

ing bastion of freewheeling, rugged individualism.

Even harder for many outlanders to visualize is that anything resembling the arts could exist in a place they regard as a cultural as well as a geographical desert. They question whether the glitz of opulent show-biz stage and cabaret productions in the casinos—however professional and polished—can be described as artistic. Certainly, say the purists, they are far too garish and gauche to qualify as true art. The result is that many people planning to move to the state—especially from the East—fear they will never again experience anything resembling culture as they have known it in their less raucous environments.

They may be pleasantly surprised. Nevada certainly has nothing to approach the great orchestras and art galleries of the nation's metropolitan areas, but newcomers used to them don't have to suffer from cultural anemia. More than 200 organizations support the dance, budding and advanced literary efforts, music (classical, operatic, jazz, rock, bop, and chorale), theater, painting, and visual arts throughout the state.

Visitors and critics alike from those metropolitan areas who have discovered these activities have generally been impressed that the quality of these artistic and cultural endeavors is higher than would be expected.

One reason is the unusually rich supply of talent available in Nevada. Hundreds of entertainers who have come to the state to perform at the casinos have become permanent residents—more professional musicians and dancers live in Nevada than any other state in the Union. When they are not working for pay, many provide free entertainment at hospitals, parties for children's organizations, and at local cultural events in both urban areas and small towns throughout the state.

But the state can also boast considerable amateur artistic talent in the general population, thanks to locally organized groups in even the smallest, most remote communities. Writing classes crop up in private homes in tiny towns, or in isolated ranch houses. Choral groups meet weekly in local Elks clubs and Eagles halls. Artists of varying capabilities take over schoolrooms in the evenings for classes in oil painting and watercolors, or to work on the pottery wheel. Gymnasiums become rehearsal halls for local orchestras or ballet troupes.

In Las Vegas the Nevada Dance Theater, a professional ballet company, makes periodic tours throughout the nation . . . the city's Rainbow Company Children's Theater has performed at Washington, D.C.'s Kennedy Center on national television . . . the Nevada School of the Arts has a continuous curriculum for children of all ages, including a summer arts camp at nearby Mount Charleston . . . the Las Vegas Symphonic and Chamber Music Society, the New World Brass Quintet, and a host of community theaters offer regular programs . . . and the UNLV Master Series concerts feature such visiting artists as Itzhak Perlman and Aaron Copeland.

In Reno the chief offerings, most of which have a long history, are the Nevada Opera Association, the Reno Philharmonic, the Reno Chamber Orchestra, the Sierra Nevada Museum of Art, the Reno Little Theater, and the Nevada Festival Ballet.

The University of Nevada, Reno, hosts the Nevada Repertory Company, which has on two occasions been one of the 10 companies invited to the American College Theater Festival at the Kennedy Center. A new $5-million wing to the university's Fine Arts building will be the center for a greatly expanded series of cultural programs and events.

Rural Nevada shares in this wealth of arts offerings. The Nevada State Council on the Arts serves more than 65 communities throughout the state, and the University of Nevada campuses in both Las Vegas and Reno offer professional instruction in the arts, regularly bringing professionals to schools and towns.

Even small local communities offer cultural events that attract visitors from throughout the West. Virginia City's historic Piper's Opera House has summer concerts. The world-renowned Utah Symphony gives annual performances in Ely. The little community of Panaca (population 300) has a folklore ballet, and the annual Cowboy Poetry Gathering

▼ The Rainbow Company Children's Theater has performed at Kennedy Center on national television. Photo by Tom Campbell

► The Reno Philharmonic is always a large draw. Photo by Tom Campbell

in Elko gets national attention in news outlets and on television.

Carson City offers a community concert series, and its Brewery Arts Center has extensive and ongoing cultural activities, including many art classes and theater productions.

More than 40 public and private museums dot the state. Their galleries feature exhibits devoted to history, anthropology, and biology. Chief among them is the Nevada State Museum, housed in what was once the Carson City branch of the United States Mint. It was here that the famed (and now priceless) Carson City silver dollars were produced from 1870 through 1893. Today the historic building is recognized as one of the most outstanding museums of its size in the country. Its displays feature Western and Nevada history, the most famous being a unique walk-in replica of a gold mine, built in the basement of the old mint building.

Other displays unique to Nevada include the world-famous Harrah automobile collection in Reno, now housed in an elaborate museum building opened in November 1989, and the Liberace Museum in Las Vegas, which displays memorabilia of that late entertainer's flamboyant life-style. And a favorite of television fans is the Ponderosa Ranch at Lake Tahoe, locale of the long-running "Bonanza" TV series.

▲ The Las Vegas Dance Theater makes periodic tours throughout the nation. Photo by Tom Campbell

On the research, information, and literary front, Nevada has developed a substantial and expanding structure. At its heart stands the Nevada State Library and Archives, headquartered in Carson City but connected by an elaborate electronic, computerized network linking it with about 100 other libraries across the state.

These include 68 public libraries and their branches, 2 university libraries, 4 community college libraries, and about 27 other special libraries. So no matter where they live, virtually all Nevada residents have quick access not only to specialized collections, but to extensive research materials needed by students, teachers, writers, and public relations and media people.

Extension and improvement of the library system is an ongoing project. For example, a $10-million bond issue is currently going toward the construction and expansion of public libraries, and the Nevada Legislature in 1989 appropriated $20,283,000 for the construction of a new main building for the Nevada State Library in Carson City.

Recent improvements in sophisticated electronic communications have extended Nevada's overall information and educational capabilities tremendously. Translators and cable systems now carry Public Broadcasting System programming, in both radio and television, across virtually all 110,540 square miles of the state. Almost every remote ranch house now has the capability of receiving this programming directly, without the expense of a personal satellite dish.

Out of this broad background have come a proportionately large number of talented and widely recognized Nevadans. A major example is the late J. Craig Sheppard. A native Nevadan and professor of art and head of the art department at the University of Nevada, Reno, he lived to see his paintings hung in major exhibitions throughout the United States and Europe.

In 1962 the exclusive Coard Gallery in Paris held a one-man show of 24 of Sheppard's oil paintings and 8 of his watercolors. Said one French critic: "The paintings of Craig Sheppard distinguish themselves by their originality, their explosive force and their striking colors. They are done with refinement and rare distinction."

Sheppard also had shows at the Museum of Beaux Arts and the French Museum of Modern Art, both also in Paris. During the latter exhibition, the Museum of Modern Art took the unusual step of buying

▼ The Lost City Museum, in Overton, examines the more basic technologies and cultural practices that formed the original character of the region. Photo by Tom Campbell

one of the paintings in the show. Reported the *Nevada State Journal*: "The purchase by that highly critical and nationalistic gallery was the first acquisition of a work of art done by an American artist in more than nine years, and established Sheppard as one of the outstanding internationally-known artists in America today."

There has been similar recognition of both native and transplanted Nevada writers. Best known of the early group, of course, was Samuel Clemens, who took the pen name Mark Twain while visiting his brother and working on Virginia City's lusty newspaper, the *Territorial Enterprise*.

Nearly as famous was a cowboy/artist/writer named Will James, who drifted in and

▲ The University of Nevada, Las Vegas, is home to the Performing Arts Center, offering a wide range of theatrical productions. Photo by Tom Campbell

◄ The Sierra Nevada Museum of Art, in Reno, is one of the many galleries throughout the state. Photo by Tom Campbell

out of Nevada between 1910 and 1917. A skinny, 22-year-old rider and bronc-buster from Canada, James had wandered through Montana, Wyoming, and Idaho during the same period, traveling from ranch to ranch, hiring out to break broncos at three dollars a head. After World War I he finally settled in Nevada, where he would live more than half his life (he died in 1942). It was in this period that James became famous across the country for his portrayals of the West in paintings, songs, and books.

His biographer, the late Anthony Amaral, wrote that the publication of one of his books, *Lone Cowboy,* "gave Will James a tremendous popularity, even outside the United States." Amaral indicated the reason was that it and most of the other 14 James books "were written without excessive Wild West frills. They are deep-rooted in western lore and written in a language that has the gloss of the cowboy speech. They ring true to the mood and tempo of the cow country of the early 20th century, and significantly help fill the literature of that period."

International fame came to the late Walter Van Tilberg Clark for his classic Western novel, *The Ox-Bow Incident.* Critics and Western experts alike acclaimed it for its definitive portrayal of what the early West was really like. Wrote one reviewer, L.B. Salomon, "In Mr. Clark's account of the Ox-Bow lynching, there were no villains nor special heroes, and the book was one of the first in Western fiction that did not glamorize the West of the rancher and the cowboy." Another, G.G. Stevens, said the book "stands by itself for its high grade of psychological insight and expert crafts-manship."

Clark's equally popular *The Track of the Cat,* published nine years later, was highly praised for capturing the same mystical quality. Said reviewer Edmund Fuller: "The actions have implications that go far beyond their limited context. It is masterful, consistently sustained story telling, and it purges with pity and terror."

These and other Clark works were translated into 20 languages including Arabic, Urdu, Korean, and Japanese. In 1943, 20th Century Fox filmed *The Ox-Bow Incident*; Warner Brothers filmed *The Track of the Cat* in 1954. Both movies became box-office and critical successes.

Although born in Maine, Clark considered himself a full-blown Westerner. He moved to Reno at the age of eight when his father was named president of the University of Nevada, from which the young Clark was graduated. He earned a master's degree from the University of Vermont and taught creative writing courses at universities in Iowa and Montana and at San Francisco State before returning to teach the same courses at his alma mater, the University of Nevada, before his death in 1971.

Although Clark remains Nevada's most famous writer, he is not the state's only literary giant who has more than made his mark across the land. The most outstanding today is Robert Laxalt, one of four children (the eldest is Paul Laxalt, former Nevada governor and U.S. senator) who were born to Basque immigrants. Laxalt grew up in Carson City, was graduated from the University of Nevada, and worked for the United Press before concentrating his writing efforts on articles and books.

His first book, *Sweet Promised Land,* about his father's sheepherding years in the hills

● Other displays unique to Nevada include the world-famous Harrah's Automobile Collection in Reno and the Liberace Museum in Las Vegas. Photos by Tom Campbell

▲ A display of discarded license plates makes a ghostly exhibit in Berlin, Nevada. Photo by Kerrick James

▶ Much of Nevada offers a whirlwind of sights and sounds, 24 hours per day. Photo by Tom Campbell

and valleys of Nevada, received wide acclaim for its insight into a little-known but vital Western industry. Laxalt's knowledge of his heritage led to a Fulbright Research Fellow- ship in France, and an assignment as a consultant in Basque culture to the Library of Congress. Later, in recognition of his knowledge of Nevada, Laxalt was hired to write a book on Nevada as part of the 1977 series on the States and the Nation, published for the national Bicentennial of the American Revolution.

Of equal importance to the quality of life in Nevada has been Robert Laxalt's oversight of the University of Nevada Press. He became its first editor in 1961, when he was director of news and publications for the university.

"Laxalt intentionally charted a modest course for the new press," said a university report on the operation. "Nevada obviously did not have the resources to compete with larger organizations. From the beginning, the press received guidance from experienced staff members of the University of California Press in Berkeley."

Since those early days, however, the University of Nevada Press has published between 150 and 200 titles, 90 of which are currently in print. They cover a wide spectrum of subjects, from its unique Basque Book series and specialized publications on Nevada and the West to general titles, monographs, and even a number of art portfolios.

These penetrating and broad-based forays into culture contrast sharply with Nevada's Wild West reputation, and with good reason. The sheer physical and emotional forces that made it the Wild West in the first place demanded special, flinty tools to tame it. That meant bold, brash muscle and brawn, directed by a mentality that had to concentrate on ingenuity, not on art. The tranquility of culture had to come second to the difficult job of making a hostile environment livable.

Yet the yearning for "the good things in life" persisted. Nevadans took advantage of every break in the sweat and toil to sing or dance or play an instrument, to gather in community festivals in distant, tiny towns.

Today Nevadans can and do enjoy the luxury of a wide variety of cultural activities, but it is still the more earthy aspects of the state's development that remain the most visible to outsiders.

They have been from time immemorial. Legalized gambling was not the first venture to shock the nation with what many saw as excessive flash and boldness. Long before that the state became a target for abuse when it legalized prizefighting in 1897.

Virtually every part of the country had outlawed boxing, so when the state legislature passed a bill authorizing it under state auspices, newspapers around the nation came unglued with indignation. Cried the San Francisco *Post*: "If the brutal sport is to be tolerated, we know of no better place adapted to it than Nevada."

Nevada adapted immediately. Within a matter of days, the state began a long career of aiming to become the boxing capital of the nation. During the first 17 years after the law was passed, it hosted three of the most famous prizefights in history.

The first took place on March 17, 1897, after the ink had barely dried on the new law—and in no less a location than the state capital of Carson City. In what is still regarded as an epic title bout, James J. "Gentleman Jim" Corbett, the reigning heavyweight champion, and Bob Fitzsimmons fought before some 8,000 people who "were treated to a thriller," according to one reporter. Although Corbett decked his opponent for a nine count in Round Six, Fitzsimmons came back to take the title by a knockout in the 14th round.

The next major fight was the first to be promoted by the famed Tex Rickard, and it turned out to be grueling, long, and dirty. The world lightweight championship battle between Joe Gans, the titleholder, and Oscar Mathew "Battling" Nelson, took place in 1906 in the mining town of Goldfield. It lasted 42 rounds—nearly three hours—and drew a gate of $69,715 from 8,000 fans.

In the 12th round, Nelson butted Gans. That happened to be illegal even in those raucous days. But the referee didn't stop the fight, so in Round 27 Gans got back at Nelson, in a way. Gans hit Nelson so hard he broke a bone in his hand, but kept fighting. In the 42nd round, Nelson knocked Gans down with such a powerful blow to the groin that it left Gans "quivering." It was so obviously against the rules that this time the referee had no choice but to declare Gans the winner on a foul. One writer called the whole performance "undoubtedly the foulest bout on record."

The third major set-to of the time, billed as "The Battle of the Century," took place in Reno on July 4, 1910. It had strong racial overtones because it was a showdown between Jack Johnson, the first black heavyweight champion, and Jim Jeffries, who had retired unbeaten in 1905. Promoter Tex Rickard, who had talked Jeffries out of retirement to recover the title for the white race, had wanted to stage it in either Salt Lake City or somewhere in California. When both Utah and California refused to allow a prizefight in their states, Rickard moved it to Reno.

Tickets went for as high as $50 apiece, at that time the highest ever paid for a prizefight. Such famous writers as Jack London and Rex Beach joined 19 wire services to flash a blow-by-blow around the world.

▲ Nevada has hosted some of the
most famous prizefights in history.
Photo by Tom Campbell

THE OLDEST LIVING THINGS ON EARTH

High on the slopes of 13,063-foot Wheeler Peak, in the Snake Mountain Range of eastern Nevada, grow the oldest living things on earth. Gnarled and twisted by the gales and cold of high-altitude winters, the rare bristlecone pine trees grow only in this general region. And although those found in Nevada are more than 3,000 years old, they still have many years of life ahead of them.

The oldest bristlecone ever discovered had been growing in one of the groves here for nearly 4,900 years when someone cut it down, while still alive, in 1964.

Bristlecone seeds come from dark purple cones, and are scattered by autumn winds each year. The trees grow so slowly that they are still saplings at the age of 50, still in their youth at 500. Even when a tree dies it can remain standing for hundreds of years, and when it falls it does not rot because the air at that high altitude is too dry.

Now the Nevada bristlecones have become a unique feature of the Great Basin National Park. Established in 1986, America's newest national park encompasses 76,800 acres of rugged wide valleys and the high mountain ranges where the bristlecones grow. Its unusual biologic, scenic, and geologic attractions range from Sonoran sagebrush animal communities to the Arctic Alpine tundra life zone. The park also includes Lehman Caves, one of the largest limestone caverns in the western United States. It contains stalactites and stalagmites—huge, fluted columns of various colors—and a number of cave rooms, all different and all joined by a two-thirds-mile-long paved trail with stairways.

Some bristlecones also grow in the nearby White Mountains of eastern California.

▶ The rare bristlecone pines of the Snake Mountain Range in eastern Nevada are some of the oldest living things on earth. Many are more than 1,000 years old. Photo by Tom Campbell

But the biggest blow came to the audience, when Johnson kept the title by knocking out "the great white hope" in the 15th round. Jack London summed up the crowd's disappointment: "Once again has Johnson sent down to defeat the chosen representative of the white race, and this time the greatest of them all."

Ever since those days big fights have been bringing fans to Nevada from all over the world. Virtually all of the most famous boxers of the century, including world champions in all divisions, have won and lost major and minor bouts in the state, mostly in Reno and Las Vegas. They range from Jack Dempsey (who also refereed and managed fights in Nevada, where he lived for some time) to Sugar Ray Leonard, from Max Baer to Muhammad Ali, from Sonny Liston to Mike Tyson.

An example of the growing importance of boxing to the state's economy and entertainment base is Caesars Palace in Las Vegas. It has hosted at least 35 title fights, plus scores of lesser bouts, just in the last 10 years.

But despite its widespread activity, boxing, like gambling, relies mainly on fans from out of state for its commercial success. So do such annual events as the Reno Championship Air Races and Virginia City's camel races. They attract local fans, of course, but Nevadans as a whole get more involved in their area's high school and university basketball, baseball, football, and Little League games. (Nevada has 293 baseball and softball fields.)

Yet the greatest appeal lies in the lure of outdoor recreation, thanks to Nevada's generally favorable climate that makes possible a rich variety of activities of one kind or another year-round. The 1986 Rand McNally *Places Rated Almanac* guidebook, for instance, ranked the Reno-Tahoe area first in America for vacationers seeking fun outdoors. Almost immediately behind came Las Vegas, with its 18 golf courses; fishing and boating on nearby, spectacular Lake Mead; and hiking, picnicking, and camping in the Mount Charleston area, only 30 miles away.

Winter offers world-class skiing. More than a dozen resorts in the Sierra Nevada Range around Reno and Lake Tahoe have upwards of 150 surface lifts, chairs, and aerial tramways serving nearly 240 miles of groomed downhill runs. They offer an additional 300 miles of groomed trails at 13 Nordic centers for cross-country skiers. Snow-making equipment at the major resorts virtually assures ideal conditions regardless of the weather. And despite being in a more semitropical clime, Las Vegas has excellent alpine and Nordic ski areas at Mount Charleston and Lee Canyon.

Desert state or not, Nevada has enough lakes and streams to rank 20th in the nation, with a total water surface of 775 square miles. This breaks down into 6,577 miles of rivers and streams (684 of them for water-sport use), and 55 lakes and reservoirs with a total of 352,928 acres of surface area to support fishing, water-skiing, and boating.

Among these is southern Nevada's Lake Mead National Recreation Area. This 3,000-square-mile parkland, nurtured by the Colorado River, contains Lake Mead itself. Formed by Hoover Dam, Lake Mead covers 230 square miles, the largest man-made lake

► Rockhounds can have a field day almost anywhere in Nevada. This intrepid scrambler is trying his luck in the terrain of Red Rock Recreation Area. Photo by Tom Campbell

● Winter in Nevada brings world-class skiing. Photo by Tom Campbell

LONESOME ROADS

Although Nevada's population grew by a staggering 31.7 percent between 1980 and 1988, John C. Frémont would feel pretty much at home were he to show up today by some magic reincarnation.

True, he would probably avoid Las Vegas and Reno; the glitter and traffic gridlocks would terrorize a horse-and-buggy man even of Frémont's renowned courage. But the old explorer would feel comfortable just a few miles from the heart of either city and its immediate environs because about 90 percent of Nevada today looks pretty much as it did when Frémont's party first braved the unknown wilderness.

By far, the majority of Nevada's 1.2 million residents are clustered in the state's few urban areas. If they were all spread out evenly, the Nevada population comes down to only about 10 people per square mile. The main intrusions upon the landscape as Frémont would remember it are the relatively few paved roads in the rural areas.

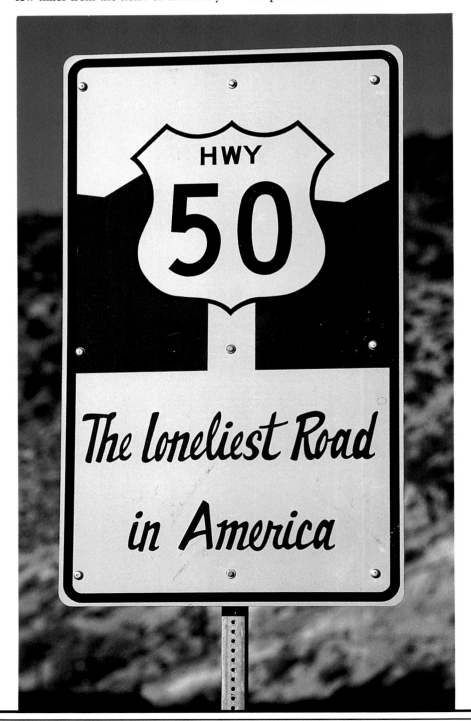

● U.S. Highway 50, the first transcontinental route in the country, received national attention in 1986 when *Life* magazine called it "The Loneliest Road In America." Photos by Tom Campbell

The two vital transcontinental arteries crossing the state take up only a small part of the land. The northern route, Interstate 80, runs from the California border through Reno to the Utah border on its way to Salt Lake City. About 450 miles to the south, Interstate 15 skirts Las Vegas on its route between Southern California and Arizona. Except for some four-lane highways in and around the major communities, most of the paved roads are two-lane ribbons of asphalt.

One of those paved two-lane roads received national attention in 1986 when *Life* magazine called it "The Loneliest Road in America." It is U.S. Highway 50, which was part of the Lincoln Highway, the first transcontinental route in the country.

Like the two interstates, Highway 50 transverses Nevada from east to west, running some 300 miles from Lake Tahoe to the Utah border east of Ely. About half the route parallels the original Pony Express Trail, and remains of some of the stations are still visible.

The magazine found that the road indeed seems to stretch out forever across the sagebrush-covered desert valleys and mountains, across open range where cattle wander onto the road at will. Watching for them is one of two diversions. The other is passing an oncoming car. Sometimes there is no traffic as far as the driver can see; the road may run straight across a 20-mile-wide valley.

Yet Highway 50 does pass through settlements containing people. They include Carson City, the state capital; Dayton, one of Nevada's oldest communities; and, some 30 miles farther east, Silver Springs. Later comes tiny Hazen, site of the state's last lynching, then Fallon and the old mining towns of Austin and Eureka, and finally Ely.

Most of these places could be passed in the blink of an eye, an appalling idea to the Eastern magazine writers and photographers. By the time they got to Ely, they must have felt as if they were in the big city. After all, it has a population of nearly 6,000 people. And, as Richard Moreno of the Nevada Commission on Tourism reported recently, "There's a white bandstand in the city park, a corner drugstore that serves shakes, and a JC Penney's with wooden floors." It even has a sizable, modern convention center.

As for the *Life* story, most Nevadans thought it was great. Reported Moreno: "The folks on Highway 50 were so proud they developed Highway 50 Survival Kits for travelers and successfully petitioned the 1987 State Legislature to erect signs along the route carrying that designation."

But if the magazine people had done a bit more research, they would have found that Highway 50 is pretty crowded compared with some other Nevada roads. The Nevada Department of Transportation says the least-traveled primary in the state is the 109-mile stretch of U.S. Highway 93 from Ely to Pioche—it averages a total of 550 to 700 cars a day.

Some paved secondary roads are even lonelier. For instance, one 63-mile stretch from Major's Place to Pioche averages 205 cars on a big day.

But the loneliest paved road of all is closer to the teeming city of Las Vegas than is Highway 50. It is the 98-mile span of state Route 375 from Hiko to Warm Springs. Running just north of the Nevada Test Site, it averages only 80 cars each day.

in the United States. In the north, Lake Tahoe, split between California and Nevada, covers an area about 15 by 22 miles at an altitude of 6,226 feet above sea level. Rock-hounds can have far more than one field day. The seemingly barren desert offers a wide variety of petrified woods, and gems and minerals including agate, jasper, beryl, garnet, opal, and turquoise.

Especially the last two. Nevada produces most of the world's turquoise—and a nugget found near Battle Mountain in 1954 weighed 152 pounds. The world's largest black opal, now displayed at the Smithsonian Institution in Washington, D.C., was found in the Black Rock Desert near the Nevada town of Gerlach.

The effects of rapid population growth on Nevada's wide open spaces have been infinitesimal: it's possible to camp or picnic undisturbed within a few miles of every urban area. To assist those who want some semblance of civilization, the state or local entities together have laid out 9,732 campsites, 1,860 tent campsites, and 8,193 vehicle/trailer campsites. There are also 138 group picnic areas.

● The Lake Mead recreation area offers everything the avid sports enthusiast could want in a vacation setting. Photos by Tom Campbell

● Windsurfers catch the breeze on Lake Mohave in Laughlin. Photo by Tom Campbell

Even all that doesn't make enough of a dent in this vast landscape to preclude anyone from finding a spot to be entirely alone. Nor does one have to stay in one place: 1,509 miles of trails for hiking, backpacking, or horseback riding and 102 miles of nature trails can provide more than enough exercise. So do the 155 miles of bicycle trails.

Yet despite the wide reach of the public domain, the growing population has made it necessary for the Department of Wildlife to impose increasingly tight restrictions on two of Nevada's favorite pastimes: hunting and fishing. During a five-year span some 30 years ago, hunters from Nevada and California killed as many as 30,000 deer annually, almost at will. Today, with the total number of deer in the state estimated at around 120,000, deer tags are rationed.

Hunting antelope and bighorn sheep has become an even greater luxury. Herds of antelope numbered in the hundreds of thousands a century ago, but only about 3,000 antelope remain in northern and western Nevada today, and some 4,500 bighorn sheep reside in a 1.5-million-acre refuge in southern Nevada. Both antelope and bighorns attract so many would-be hunters that getting one of the few available licenses may take years.

But hunters have plenty of other targets. Bobcats, gray foxes, raccoons, muskrats, beavers, and otters abound. Even the former predators, mountain lions and coyotes, have become sport animals, but are protected to some extent by licensing requirements. Equally plentiful are game birds such as ducks, geese, chukar partridge (introduced into the western United States from India), quail, and pheasant.

Anglers can try their luck among the 30 different species of game fish swimming in Nevada's rivers and lakes. At least one of those species reaches back into Nevada's prehistory: the cui-ui (pronounced "kwee-wee"), a species of sucker, lives only in Pyramid Lake.

The restrictions on hunting and fishing in Nevada have generally been lenient compared to those of other states, and have been imposed fairly recently. But they provide the Department of Wildlife with the authority and the tools to prevent the extinction of any species of fish and game at the hands of sportsmen. That virtually guarantees that future generations of Nevada hunters and fishermen will know the quick exhilaration of bringing down a buck or landing a trout.

Clearly, a full spectrum of colorful elements makes up the intriguing tapestry that is Nevada—elements ranging from entertainment to mining, from science to art, from manufacturing to hunting. But the predominant theme of the tapestry, the one that has made this spectrum possible, is freedom. More than any other element, it has lured the adventurers and dreamers to meet the challenge of an awesome land ever since the white man dared to venture into the "Northern Mystery" 150 years ago. The great ideal of freedom has inspired them to use their ingenuity, their strength, and their inner spirit to build an enviable life-style and a workable economy.

The process goes on. The people have made it work by combining the contradictions, extremes, and contrasts that have always been the soul and sinew of Nevada into a tapestry of harmony.

◀ These sunbathers have found their mecca right here in Las Vegas, at the Sahara Hotel. Photo by Tom Campbell

● State Highway 163 leads into Laughlin, Nevada, and a whole range of possibilities. Photo by Tom Campbell

PART

.2.

NEVADA'S
ENTERPRISES

◆◆◆◆

174

·7·

BUILDING THE FUTURE

◇◆◇◆

Economic development agencies are attracting new businesses and creating jobs in this land of enterprise by building a partnership between government and business, promoting business opportunities; and bringing economic diversity.

◆◆◆◆

EXIT

The Commission on Economic Development: 178

Nevada Development Authority: 179

Economic Development Authority of Western Nevada: 180

Photo by
Tom Campbell

THE COMMISSION ON ECONOMIC DEVELOPMENT

The Commission on Economic Development (CED) is the agency that turns the state government into an active partner of private business, working to build Nevada's economy and her future. CED carries the message around America and around the world that Nevada is "America's premier location for new and expanding businesses."

The state legislature in 1983 established CED as a streamlined agency with new, dynamic programs to leverage Nevada's position as a freeport state astride important transportation routes—and a state with favorable tax and business climates. CED's job was to create a more diversified and prosperous economy.

Since then Nevada has attracted new businesses from 17 foreign countries and 25 states—companies with names such as Citicorp, Porsche Cars of North America, R.R. Donnelley, Salomon Ski, T.J. Maxx, and Ocean Spray. The new firms created 150,000 new jobs, which represents the highest per capita rate of new-job growth in the United States.

CED's trade missions and other efforts to promote Nevada around the Pacific Rim have paid off as well. In 1983 there were no Japanese businesses in Nevada. Today there are 17, including four hotel-casinos and a variety of manufacturing, warehousing, and distri-

▼ **Pacific Western Systems located in Winnemucca specializes in semiconductor diagnostic equipment and has added to the vitality of northwestern Nevada's economy.**

▲ **The exciting slopes of Lake Tahoe challenge and entice discriminating skiers from all over the world. This winter feeds a vital tourism economy in western Nevada.**

bution businesses. In 1988 the first Korean-owned business arrived in Nevada. CED has also helped Nevada firms increase their exports.

Chaired by the lieutenant governor, there are six CED commissioners appointed by the governor. A professional staff, headed by James L. Spoo, works out of offices in Carson City and Las Vegas.

With direct financial grants, information, and technical help, CED supports the work of regional agencies such as the Nevada Development Authority (NDA) in Clark County and Economic Development Authority of Western Nevada in the Reno area.

CED sponsors major programs such as Quick Start to help new businesses train workers quickly, Silver Star Communities Program to help rural Nevada communities realize their full economic-development potential, and Industry Appreciation Days to honor new and expanded Nevada businesses. CED also helps new businesses obtain financing.

CED's Motion Picture and Television Division promotes the state as a filming location for movies, television programs, and commercials. Nevada has been a setting for such recent productions as *Rain Man, The Wizard, Midnight Run, Pink Cadillac,* and *Top Gun.*

In 1989 the state legislature established an Export Office in Las Vegas, charging CED with conducting the Procurement Outreach Program to help Nevada's small businesses win their fair share of government contracts. POP has the potential of aiding more than 80 percent of the companies in Nevada that qualify for special help as small businesses.

Nevada's accelerated rate of growth is projected to lead the nation into the next century. And the Commission on Economic Development will be there to help Nevada secure the economic benefits that accompany that growth.

NEVADA DEVELOPMENT AUTHORITY

While tourism will always be Las Vegas' high-profile industry, a diversity of other business is what keeps Clark County's economy balanced and protected against extreme business swings.

Encouraging that diversity is the job of the Nevada Development Authority (NDA), the state's oldest and largest regional development agency. Supported by more than 500 members, NDA works with the Nevada Commission on Economic Development to persuade new businesses to come to southern Nevada and to encourage existing businesses to expand.

Major companies have relocated to Nevada with NDA's help. Bally Manufacturing Corp., which makes slot machines, video games, and other recreation devices, is located in a new 150,000-square-foot plant in Las Vegas' Hughes Airport Center. Ocean Spray will be bringing its big bottling and distribution facility to the Gibson Business Park in Henderson.

T.J. Maxx, a chain of factory-outlet centers for name-brand merchandise, is building a 400,000-square-foot warehouse in North Las Vegas.

Financial services companies such as Montgomery Ward Credit Corp., which

processes receivables at its new financial center in Las Vegas, and Citicorp, with its huge credit-card processing center at The Lakes, are located in Las Vegas as well.

In a typical year NDA is responsible for 50 to 100 new or expanded businesses in Clark County, handles almost 3,000 inquiries, and helps create more than 2,000 new jobs. Though creating new business is among NDA's chief goals, improving the quality of business life in southern Nevada is also important to the organization, according to Dennis H. Stein, NDA's president and chief executive officer.

NDA helps to develop working relationships between businesses and local government, to strengthen the region's financial stability, to achieve a balance between the environment and economic growth, and to support educational efforts that will improve the quality of southern Nevada's labor pool.

Located amid major highway and rail links between Los Angeles, Salt Lake

▼ Citibank Nevada's regional credit card-processing center began operations in 1984 and has already doubled in size. NDA assisted and encouraged Citicorp in opening the facility.

City, and the rest of the nation, and with a world-class airport, Las Vegas has powerful lures for new business, Stein believes. In addition, the city's Foreign Trade Zone No. 89, easing the burden of high U.S. tariffs on imported goods, is expected to make Las Vegas an international business center.

The current emphasis for NDA's marketing program targets businesses in California, where taxes are relatively high, and on overseas companies, particularly those around the Pacific Rim, which can use Nevada's tax advantages to help open the U.S. market.

NDA uses successful newcomers to southern Nevada as leverage to lure more newcomers. Stein says, "When more businesses see the success of businesses that have come here, that is something that continues to feed on itself."

And he credits the state's supportive business climate as the Nevada Development Authority's most powerful selling tool. "The attitude of the people here is pro-business," Stein says. "There is a pro-growth outlook in both the public and private sectors in southern Nevada—and that makes my job a lot easier."

ECONOMIC DEVELOPMENT AUTHORITY OF WESTERN NEVADA

A seatmate on an international flight ticks off the advantages of doing business in Washoe County.

An advertisement in a trade journal explains that Reno is in the geographic heart of the rich West Coast marketplace.

A visiting trade delegate shows the tax advantages of operating in Nevada, rather than one of its neighboring states.

These things do not happen by accident. They are part of the program orchestrated by the Economic Development Authority of Western Nevada (EDAWN) to diversify the economic landscape of the Reno-Sparks area.

With its staff of six and a $.5-million budget, EDAWN has lured 200-plus new businesses to the Reno-Sparks area that have pumped almost one billion dollars into the economy.

EDAWN, a nonprofit organization supported by both business and government, has more than 200 corporate members—companies and individuals

interested in making sure the area's economic future is bright. "Our interest is the diversification of the economy in western Nevada," says Kenneth G. Lynn, EDAWN's executive director.

EDAWN's job is to spread the story—particularly in California and around the nation and the world—of Reno's proximity to West Coast markets, its low taxes, its quality of life, and its friendly business climate. *Inc.* magazine has rated Nevada as the number-one state for business. The accounting firm of Grant Thornton has rated Nevada's business climate fourth best among emerging manufacturing states, and Rand McNally rates Reno among the top 20 transportation hubs in North America.

EDAWN's goal, says Lynn, is to bring "wealth, not just jobs, to the Truckee Meadows." He cites R.R. Donnelley's catalog-printing plant, which opened in the Stead industrial district in 1987. "There was the impact of a major payroll, of course," says Lynn. "These are high-skill employees. In addition, Donnelley has a major investment in roto presses here." The Donnelley plant employs almost 400 people now, with plans to expand to 1,000.

Lynn proudly ticks off the firms that EDAWN has helped bring to the area: America West Airlines (reservation center), Hi-Shear Technologies (aero-

▲ EDAWN helped bring to Reno the national headquarters of Porsche Cars North America, as well as the company's regional distribution center.

space), Salomon (ski equipment), Daimler-Benz Freightliner (truck parts), Home Shopping Network (distribution), and many others.

He is especially proud of the growth of Porsche Cars North America, whose national headquarters and big regional distribution center came to Reno in 1984. Porsche prepares and ships cars and parts from its plant at Reno Cannon International Airport to dealers in the western half of the United States. Its newly built headquarters office building is one of the largest in downtown Reno.

In addition to its outreach programs, EDAWN has a place within the community, Lynn says. "We want to be a catalyst to make sure the infrastructure is in place for future business growth. We're concerned with improving water, air quality, transportation, and so on. We want to make sure there's a cohesive regional plan.

"Nobody will ever buy an EDAWN. But they'll buy a Reno-Sparks. We want to make sure the product continues to be a good one."

▼ Bringing strength and diversity to the Reno-Sparks area, EDAWN has been successful in attracting new businesses into the area.

.8.

NETWORKS

◆◆◆◆

*Nevada's communication and
energy providers keep information
and power circulating throughout
the Silver State.*

◆◆◆◆

**Photo by
Ken Davies/Masterfile**

SIERRA PACIFIC RESOURCES

Sierra Pacific Resources is using innovative solutions—and the talents of 1,900 skilled employees—to meet the challenge of a 24-percent increase in Nevada's population; the state is projected to be one of the top five fastest growing states through the remainder of this century. This rapid growth will be answered with the corporation's pledge to provide quality service and products for its customers at the lowest-possible prices.

Sierra Pacific Resources evolved from the many small gas, water, and electric utilities that were formed to serve Nevada's early gold and silver mines in the late 1800s and the turn of the century.

Sierra Pacific Resources is an investor-owned diversified energy and resource company. Its operating units include Sierra Pacific Power Company, which supplies electric power to more than 216,000 customers in northern Nevada and northeastern California; Westpac Utilities, a division of Sierra Pacific Power Company, which supplies natural gas and water to the Reno-

▲ **Sierra Pacific Resources' new administration building is occupied by the parent company and three of its operating subsidiaries. The 320,000-square-foot facility is part of a 160-acre office park complex to be developed by Lands of Sierra.**

Sparks area of Nevada; Lands of Sierra, Inc., which buys, develops, leases, and manages real estate in Nevada and California; Sierra Energy Company, which explores for natural gas and oil in a half-dozen western states; Great Basin Energy Company, which will build and operate a series of nonutility coal-fired electric-generating plants at Thousand Springs in northeastern Nevada; and Clean Air Fuel Systems, which provides compressed natural gas motor vehicle systems.

The Thousand Springs Energy Park, located some 35 miles north of Wells, is an opportunity for Sierra Pacific Resources to showcase its management skills and technical expertise, along with several nonutility partners, to provide for the electricity needs of the western

United States. This innovative private enterprise project will generate electricity for sale to western utilities at competitive wholesale prices.

The Thousand Springs power project includes the construction of up to eight 250-megawatt, coal-fired generating plants over a 15- to 20-year period at a cost of $4 billion. The first plant is expected to come on line in the mid-1990s. Later units will be constructed on a schedule to match the need for new electric capacity in the West.

Another aspect of Sierra Pacific Resources' involvement in energy development is Sierra Energy Company, which explores and develops through joint venture oil- and gas-producing properties in Canada and in states such as North Dakota, Wyoming, Colorado, Utah, and California.

Lands of Sierra, Inc., owns, develops, and manages more than one million acres of diversified properties with interests ranging from 750,000 acres of ranching property under lease to the 160-acre Sierra Plaza in southwest Reno, which will be the site of a regional of-

▲ The Truckee River, which flows from Lake Tahoe through Reno to its terminus at Pyramid Lake, is western Nevada's major water supply.

Both utilities work in partnership with the communities they serve. Sierra Pacific Power continually works with business to develop energy management plans, while Westpac Utilities Yard Fitness Plan educates residents on water conservation.

The partnerships of Sierra Pacific include working with the state of Nevada to create and maintain a healthy and invigorating business climate. Nevada has been the nation's leader in the per-capita creation of new jobs in the past five years and will see 54,000 new jobs created in northern Nevada by 1995.

Working with state and local agencies, Sierra Pacific Resources offers an economic development program that assists businesses moving to northern Nevada and helps existing businesses expand. In just three years more than 100 new mining, manufacturing, and distribution firms have located in Reno-Sparks, a testament to the success of regional economic diversification efforts and Sierra Pacific Resources.

BELOW LEFT: Sierra Energy Company now has several producing wells in five western states, including this one located northeast of Bakersfield, California.

▼ Two 250-megawatt, coal-fired generating units make up Valmy Power Station, jointly owned by Idaho Power Company and Sierra Pacific Power Company. These units have received national recognition for engineering efficiency.

fice park. This company develops the best uses of properties to enhance their value.

Sierra Pacific Resources' utility operations—Sierra Pacific Power Company and its Westpac Utilities division—are pledged to supply reliable and inexpensive energy and water while responding to growing customer needs.

For example, Sierra Pacific Power supplies electricity to Nevada's rapidly expanding gold-mining industry. In the near future 14 new Nevada gold-mine projects are scheduled to begin production, and each will require from two to 10 megawatts of energy capacity, accounting for almost a 10-percent increase in total electric demand from Sierra Pacific by the end of 1989.

Westpac Utilities currently serves more than 70,000 natural gas customers and 50,000 water customers in the growing Reno-Sparks area. The number of gas customers has increased by more than 52 percent in the past 10 years.

NEVADA BELL

"The telephone was put into operation in the Consolidated Virginia mine yesterday afternoon," wrote the *Virginia City Chronicle*. "It worked to perfection and gave entire satisfaction!" It was November 15, 1877.

Today, of course, the telephone is such an integral part of our lives that its use is habitual, and taken for granted. But the amazing invention of Alexander Graham Bell, a teacher of the deaf, revolutionized the lives of almost every person on the globe. Its social impact is almost immeasurable. As mankind struggles through its labors, the telephone has become so unobtrusive that it blends quietly into the background of our lives.

But the impact of Nevada's first telephone system, installed up at the mine just a year after its invention, could not have come at a better time. The state was in the midst of a spectacular mining boom. It was rumored that Virginia City, a metropolis that boasted nearly 10,000 residents, sat atop an entire mountain of silver. The rush to Nevada was on.

But the vein of precious quartz-bearing ore was maddeningly elusive.

▼ **Laser pulses are used to demonstrate the feasibility of ultrafast photonic switching.**

Unlike the gold fields of California, which yielded their treasures with relative ease, Nevada's silver lay deep underground where temperatures reach as much as 120 degrees. Constant cave-ins, fires, and explosions made working conditions hazardous at best. The telephone became the vital link with the surface and freedom.

Nevada Bell has come a long way since the days when the fabulous Comstock Lode turned the eyes of the world on Nevada. Today the simple transmission of voice, which seemed so miraculous more than a century ago, is now only a small part of Nevada Bell's stable of communications services. The movement of data digitally and the use of fiber optics, video teleconferencing, facsimile, and other services are all components in today's telecommunications network.

Voice Mail, in reality an electronic mail box, is now possible. The introduction of fiber optics to northern Nevada has enabled the new Washoe County detention facility to arraign prisoners via a video screen. Soon one will be able to monitor many customers' household chores, such as cooking, home security, and movie viewing, with the help of a telephone. The list of new products and services is nearly endless.

▲ **R.C. "Bob" Blanz, president and chief executive officer of Nevada Bell.**

The vast majority of Nevada Bell's customers now have access to software-controlled computerized switching equipment. And implementation of state-of-the-art digital switching brings the advantages of higher quality, speed, and accuracy in both voice and data communications.

Nevada Bell has changed dramatically, but its commitment to customers remains the same. It's a total telecommunications company, dedicated to meeting the needs of an ever-growing, ever-changing community.

What does the future hold for Nevada Bell and the state it has served for more than 75 years? Says Bob Blanz, president and chief executive officer, "It will be exciting beyond your wildest dreams. Our people will be doing some pretty bold things in the next few years and introducing new products that will have a tremendous impact on our daily lives. We will be the leading edge of communications technology in northern Nevada."

KRLR-CHANNEL 21

▲ KRLR TV-21—the Las Vegas Valley's unique community TV station.

Television station KRLR-Channel 21 plans its programming especially for the unique community that is Las Vegas as only Las Vegans know it.

Spotlighting family entertainment, TV-21 is the Las Vegas Valley's family-owned station. The family, the Scotts, has a commitment to the community that goes back more than 50 years, so "TV-21, the Home Team," is more than just the station's slogan.

The family's patriarch, Frank E. Scott, first came to Las Vegas as a child with his parents in 1934. His father was employed by the Union Pacific Railroad, and Las Vegas was a small town of 5,000. Recognizing the opportunities in this rapidly growing desert oasis, Scott remained in Las Vegas where he has been instrumental in building it into the modern city of 700,000 it is today. He has owned and operated several companies providing roofing, ready-mix concrete, and general construction services during the booming growth of Las Vegas. Scott built and operated the Union Plaza Hotel before his retirement from the Scott Corporation, which also bought and restored the historic Mizpah Hotel in Tonopah, Nevada.

TV-21, which went on the air in 1984 on the UHF band, was the city's first

new television station in 16 years— "Evidence of the growth of this community," according to Scott's son Rick, the station's executive vice-president. "It was just another way our family found to take part in the city's growth," he says.

Frank Scott's wife, Charlene, serves as the company president, and his other children, Richard and Elizabeth, are included in the station's name. The station's call letters are: K (which signifies all stations in the West), R (for Rick), L (for Liz), and R (for Richard). Station manager Wayne Gartley also takes an active role in all station business.

TV-21 has increased its market share at a rate of one percent per year since it started, according to Rick Scott. He laughs now about the station's early days as the city's first UHF station. "People asked, 'Where is it on my dial?' We had to educate them on how to receive UHF," Scott recalls. "To get them interested, we started out as a 24-hour music-video station. We sold UHF antennas for 99 cents in all Las Vegas area 7-eleven stores. We used press promotions and had TV sets tuned to TV-21 in all

Las Vegas area Burger Kings. We built the audience, and after six months, we weaned them into regular programming"

And that regular programming is aimed at the heart of the town. TV-21 produces and airs Runnin' Rebel basketball games. In a town crazy about sports, TV-21 airs the Los Angeles Lakers, the San Diego Padres, and the Oakland A's, in addition to UNLV football. It also telecasts Brigham Young University football, a reflection of the Las Vegas Valley's Mormon heritage. TV-21 is the only Las Vegas channel to telecast the twice-yearly Latter-day Saints Conference from Salt Lake City live.

More than 30 movies each week, cartoons for kids, and shows including "Highway to Heaven," "The Best of National Geographic Specials," "Hunter," and "Kate & Allie" make up the rest of KRLR Channel 21's family programming. "We like action movies," says Scott, "but we pay attention to the words that are used and scenes that are shown when we select them."

Scott and his family believe in "the importance of a local station identifying itself as a local station and keeping abreast of what the community seeks in the way of entertainment and information."

CENTEL

Las Vegas and its telephone company are not what they used to be. Indeed, Central Telephone Company, better known as Centel, and the Las Vegas Valley came of age together.

For years Las Vegas was considered the vacation spot only for fun seekers, jet-setters, and high rollers. But barely a decade ago, like a slow-boiling kettle, Las Vegas' mystique and appeal spilled over to vacationing middle-class American families and business—and the rush was on.

Visitor volumes shattered records, more hotels and expansions sprang up, the economic base diversified, and people by the thousands abandoned other cities to make southern Nevada their home.

When Las Vegas was a dusty little resort town, dial tone, that magic sound Alexander Graham Bell created a century ago, was basically the only service a caller needed.

Today voice transmission is just one ingredient in Centel's communications recipe. Video, data, and facsimile— transmitted at incredible speeds—have joined voice on global electronic highways that will have a profound impact on the economic fortunes of southern Nevada.

"In the mid-1960s we provided direct-distance dialing from here to the rest of the United States and called it a breakthrough for our customers," says James J. Kropid, Centel-Nevada vice-president. "Now you can direct-dial much of the world and send them a fax, data, or video pictures and talk to them, too."

As a unit of Chicago-based Centel Corporation, which became an integral part of the Las Vegas community in 1961, Centel has become a major competitive player in a telecommunications world driven by change and innovation.

Competition means the phone company not only must be a dependable service provider, but a creative one. "Competition is good for us, and it results in multiplied benefits for our customers," says Kropid.

Digital technology, which transmits via a code, came along for Centel about the time southern Nevada was straining with new growth.

In the late 1970s the company committed to making the area's telephone network the most modern for a metropolitan area of its size. That meant eight years and a $250-million investment to replace old mechanical machines with digital call-processing equipment linked by fiber-optic cable. Digital equipment boosts voice-transmission speed and clarity, opening the door to features that forever changed the concept of basic phone service.

Customers were urged to make their phones work harder for them with call waiting, call forwarding, speed calling, and three-way calling. These features were just a flurry before the technology blizzard hit. A whole new class of features is waiting in the wings.

Digitized information speeds along hair-thin glass fibers on pulsating laser beams. Fiber optics, another Alexander Graham Bell invention, is the clearest known medium on which to transmit high-speed voice, data, and video signals.

Field trials of another link in the revolution, ISDN (Integrated Services Digital Network), promises to revolutionize the way businesses function in southern Nevada.

▼ Centel's advanced digital network allows customer service representative Jill Valenti to serve customers from her electronic home office. The program is designed to employ the handicapped.

ISDN is a customer-controlled system of integrated voice, data, facsimile, video, and other messages that can be carried simultaneously over a single set of telephone wires. It is the global network of the future and a tremendous bargaining

▼ The Centel Singers make more than music with southern Nevada's senior citizens. They bring joy and friendship to those who are making the area a retirement mecca. Photo by Bruce Davidson

chip when the area's economic developers go courting new industry.

At home, Centel has taken seriously its responsibility to be a company giving back to the community—from helping to meet basic needs of residents to supporting youth sports, the arts, and cultural activities.

The firm's nonprofit community service organization, Silver State Telephone Pioneers, is a national award winner. The Pioneers' programs of helping the less fortunate continue to inspire others.

▲ Centel's Nevada and Texas regional head-quarters in northwest Las Vegas is a community landmark just off the U.S. 95 Oran Gragson Expressway.

Centel employees ring up thousands of hours of community service each year and raise like amounts of money for Pioneer projects.

Centel also is the recipient of the Governor's Service to the Arts Award for ongoing assistance and underwriting of worthwhile programs and events. Among them is the annual directory cover competition, which showcases local artists and gives Centel another way to help nonprofit community service organizations through the competition entry fees.

About 50 years ago the telephone industry adopted a philosophy of universal service and set out to provide reliable, reasonably priced, and widely available telephone service for Americans.

At Central Telephone Company, technology and a changing world marketplace are giving new definition to the term "universal service." In addition to contributing time, energy, and money to furthering the quality of southern Nevadans' living, Centel is their voice, data, facsimile, and video link to the world.

SOUTHWEST GAS CORP.

Since 1931 Southwest Gas Corp. has been providing energy to residents of the American Southwest—a sizable land almost uninhabitable in some places but for modern technology. Southwest Gas' commitment is to use technology to provide a dependable source of efficient, reasonably priced energy for its customers. Southwest Gas, today a diversified, natural-gas utility and financial-services organization with corporate headquarters in Las Vegas, serves 2.5 million people throughout Nevada, Southern California, and Arizona. It is a service area that stretches south to the Mexican border, north to the Idaho-Nevada line, east to the New Mexico border, and west almost to the Los Angeles city limits.

While Southwest Gas recognizes that electricity is also a vital form of energy, the company provides incentives to

▼ A liquefied natural gas storage facility near Lovelock helps Southwest Gas meet its customers' heating demands on the coldest winter days.

builders to install appliances that use natural gas for those things gas does best: space and water heating, cooking, and clothes drying. A home fitted with gas appliances for those tasks costs up to $200 per year less to operate than an all-electric home.

New uses for natural gas are making the nation's energy supplies go even further, lowering costs and helping to reduce air pollution. Compressed natural gas (CNG), for example, is being used by many fleet operators to fuel cars and trucks. The company's fleet of 450 vehicles runs on CNG. Because there are few pollutants, engines run more efficiently and at a lower cost than by using gasoline. And there is less wear on engines, reducing maintenance costs.

Commercial and industrial firms are using natural gas for cogeneration to produce multiple energy forms. Cogeneration systems capture energy that is normally wasted with conventional systems and puts it to work performing other functions, such as providing steam and generating electricity.

The technology and new, more efficient equipment is making feasible the use of natural gas for home cooling. Southwest Gas is a leader in testing that technology.

The firm began as a bottled-gas company with 160 customers in dusty Barstow, California, during the Depression. When Pacific Gas & Electric Co. built a high-pressure natural-gas line from Arizona to San Francisco in 1951, Southwest tapped into the line and converted from propane to natural gas. Because of rapid growth in Arizona and Nevada, Southwest Gas relocated its corporate

headquarters to Las Vegas in 1958.

The firm built its own transmission line from Idaho into northern Nevada in the 1960s to bring natural gas for the first time to Carson City and Lake Tahoe and nearby farming communities. Acquisitions of gas properties from Tucson Gas & Electric and the Arizona Public Service Company, each one doubling Southwest Gas' customer base, have made the company one of the na-

▲ Headquartered in Las Vegas, Southwest Gas provides natural gas service to most of Nevada and Arizona, as well as small portions of eastern California.

tion's largest gas utilities.

In 1987 Southwest Gas entered the financial services field by acquiring Nevada Savings and Loan Association, now PriMerit Bank, to give the company the added financial safety of diversification.

Today the firm's Nevada employees number 400 at its Las Vegas headquarters, almost 300 operations people in southern Nevada, and more than 130 in northern Nevada, not including those employed by PriMerit Bank. Northern Nevadans are served by a division headquarters in Carson City and district offices at Tahoe, Fallon, Elko, and Winnemucca. Southwest Gas also provides natural gas for resale in the Reno/Sparks area, selling natural gas to Westpac Utilities.

To make sure there is always enough energy available for its customers—25 percent of whom are located in Nevada— Southwest Gas buys natural gas from three suppliers whose reserves are among the best in the country—El

deliverability by 25 percent.

To ensure a steady natural-gas supply in the South, the company plans to tap into a major new pipeline being constructed by another firm between the gas fields of Wyoming and Southern California.

As well as being economical energy, Southwest Gas makes sure natural gas also is safe energy. The firm conducts regular safety education programs for customers, the public, contractors, and municipal fire and safety departments. And the company has an ongoing program of inspection and maintenance throughout its distribution system.

Because of its size and commitment, the corporation maintains a high level of customer service. Whenever there is a massive disruption, as in the Truckee River flood that knocked out gas service to several thousand northern Nevada customers in 1986, Southwest Gas can bring in work crews from as far away as Tucson and Phoenix to repair pipeline and relight pilot lights.

In Nevada, Southwest Gas service technicians make scheduled house calls free of charge to check furnaces and repair gas appliances. The com-

▲ Helping to ensure a steady supply of gas to customers, a Southwest Gas welder works on a natural gas line.

Paso Natural Gas in the south, Northwest Pipeline Corp. in the north, and PG&E in California—as well as on the spot market.

Even so, the company is developing its own facilities for the future. At the firm's Harold G. Laub liquefied natural gas (LNG) plant near Lovelock, natural gas is taken out of the pipeline in summers and stored in liquid form. In the winter the gas is reconverted into vapor and put back in the pipeline to meet in-

creased customer demand. Natural gas processed at the LNG plant can heat 12,000 homes for a year.

At a liquid petroleum gas peak-shaving plant in Reno, the company mixes propane, air, and natural gas, increasing

pany has a toll-free 800 number for customers to use to ask questions about natural gas and its use in the home.

"Each community has its own needs," says Kenny C. Guinn, Southwest Gas Corp.'s chairman and chief executive officer. "It is our goal to balance those needs and to answer them to the best of our ability. At Southwest Gas, we are the energy specialists."

.9.

MANUFACTURING AND MINING

◆◆◆◆

With rich natural resources, a qualified labor force, and a favorable economic climate, Nevada is becoming the West's new mecca for manufacturing and mining operations.

◆◆◆◆

Hunt-Spiller Manufacturing
Corporation: 194

Echo Bay Mines: 196

Reno Iron Works Co., Inc.:
198

Dura-Bond Bearing Co.: 199

American Pacific Corpora-
tion: 200

Timet: 202

Nishika Corporation
American 3-D Corporation:
204

Pioneer Chlor Alkali Com-
pany, Inc.: 206

Ford Aerospace: 208

Newmont Gold Company:
210

Kerr-McGee Chemical
Corp.: 212

Photo by
Mike Dobel/Masterfile

HUNT-SPILLER MANUFACTURING CORPORATION

▲ Turbochargers are computer tested to ensure maximum efficiency and structural integrity.

Sometimes a simple phrase not only sums up the products a company makes, but also says a lot about the people who own it and run it. For Hunt-Spiller Manufacturing Corporation and its sister company, Globe Turbocharger Specialties, Inc., that simple phrase is "the best in the business."

The business they're best at is the manufacturing and remanufacturing of diesel engine turbochargers and other diesel engine components. With a single-minded dedication to making the products they sell both the highest quality and most reliable on the market, the people behind Hunt-Spiller and Globe have not only made Reno the center of turbocharger manufacturing, they've also set—and continue to raise—the standard for the industry to follow.

Hunt-Spiller was founded in Boston in 1810. One of the firm's first products was cannonballs used in the War of 1812. The company's founder, metallurgist Cyrus Alge, also developed a new form of iron to be used in the manufacture of cannons. Given the name "gun iron," this product was three times stronger than iron produced by ordinary means.

In the years following the Civil War, Hunt-Spiller diversified, manufacturing castings for hydraulic presses, beds for

marine and stationary engines, mining machinery, and railroad locomotive parts.

In the early 1960s Hunt-Spiller was purchased by Paul W. Chartrand, who moved it from Boston to San Francisco. By that time the company's major product focus had become diesel engine parts: cylinder heads, cylinder liners, pistons, and rings.

Chartrand had an extensive background in diesels as a technician, salesman, and consultant. He developed the computer technology and operating methods that Hunt-Spiller uses today. He also expanded the company's markets and extended its product line with innovative designs and creative manufacturing and product-testing techniques.

One of the new products Hunt-Spiller developed under Chartrand is a new Super Cylinder Head for diesel engines. Analyzing why ordinary cast-iron cylinder heads tended to crack, Hunt-Spiller engineers isolated the problem and the cause as steam. They designed new head cast from a type of iron that is stronger and harder than cast iron. Quality control was ensured through the use of sonic measuring instruments. Hunt-Spiller now markets this successful

new product with a pledge "guaranteed not to crack."

Seeing a problem, designing a new product that will eliminate or minimize the problem, constructing the product from the best materials available, and then rigorously testing the design and the materials to guarantee quality and reliability is a process Hunt-Spiller calls its "policy of perfection."

The same commitment to quality that Hunt-Spiller was founded on continues under Chartrand's visionary leadership. The expertise gained by Hunt-Spiller in manufacturing diesel replacement parts proved invaluable when the company diversified in 1975. As Globe Turbocharger Specialties, Inc., the firm took on the challenge of manufacturing and remanufacturing turbochargers and turbocharger parts.

▲ The expansive headquarters of Hunt-Spiller and Globe Turbocharger is geared to a future of opportunity for expansion.

Turbochargers are components of diesel engines that help them burn fuel more cleanly to meet EPA standards and operate more efficiently with greater power. Integral to the operation of the diesel engines that power railroad locomotives, oceangoing vessels of every type, and stationary engines such as those used by utility companies, turbochargers run constantly at speeds exceeding 16,000 revolutions per minute. The job of keeping them running at top efficiency is Globe's specialty.

Entering the field of turbocharger manufacturing in 1975, Globe soon established a reputation that matched that of its parent company. The joint success of Hunt-Spiller and Globe caused the businesses some growing pains in the early 1980s. Skyrocketing rents in the

▲ Globe turbocharger components are manufactured to perfection, using aircraft-quality materials.

Bay Area combined with a lack of room to grow to make relocation a necessity.

In 1984 Chartrand brought his companies to Reno. There, they found a favorable business climate, a plant facility available at a reasonable cost, and a 10-acre site that could accommodate future expansion.

Today, in its 80,000-square-foot Reno plant, Hunt-Spiller and Globe employees (who number about 40) utilize increasingly sophisticated techniques in manufacturing their own products and remanufacturing those of international firms such as Alco, General Electric, and Electromotive Division/ General Motors. There, the advanced metallurgy, the state-of-the-art tooling, and the high-tech testing that Hunt-Spiller and Globe are known for are applied in the development of the new products that the companies market worldwide.

From this plant came a product such as the Black Cat, a monitoring and control system for both turbochargers and diesel engines. The Black Cat's sensors monitor, analyze, and evaluate the critical functions a turbocharger is expected to perform and keep it working within operational specifications.

From this plant came other innovations such as the Super Clutch that

▲ Commitment to the advancement and perfection of turbocharger technology is reflected in Hunt-Spiller products.

Chartrand and his team developed specifically for application to diesel turbochargers. The device, designed and built by Hunt-Spiller, practically eliminates the breakdowns experienced by original equipment clutches and outlives them by three to four times.

With the volume of his business constantly growing, Chartrand is looking at plans to double the size of his plant. The success of Hunt-Spiller and Globe has always been based on their ability to respond to the needs of the industries they serve with creative solutions through quality products. With growth come more opportunities and more challenges to be met, or, in the words of Chartrand, "new mountains to be scaled." Finding innovative ways to scale those mountains is the characteristic that keeps these two Reno-based companies ahead of the competition. In their field, nobody does it better.

ECHO BAY MINES

Round Mountain and McCoy/Cove blend into Nevada's basin-and-range country until they are almost invisible, except from the air. No wonder these places are almost unknown, even to longtime Nevadans.

Yet below these sites are more than $5 billion worth of mineral reserves. And with its "Gold+Growth" formula for operations, Echo Bay Mines is sure to find more.

Round Mountain and McCoy/Cove are just two of Echo Bay's four open-pit operations in Nevada. Exploration continues, and by the time present reserves of gold and silver are extracted, Echo Bay expects to find more in mineral reserves to replace them, according to Donald L. Simpson, Echo Bay's vice-president. "We're really here for the long haul," he says.

Echo Bay, a successful Canadian mining company, came to Nevada in 1985 when it acquired part interest in the Round Mountain mine. It acquired other Nevada mines from Tenneco, Inc., in 1986 and discovered enormous new reserves at McCoy/Cove, where exploration continues, in 1987.

Echo Bay also operates mines in western Canada. Echo Bay has joint ventures with operating mines in Nevada, eastern Canada, and Colorado. The company's Nevada operations include:

Round Mountain-Manhattan—Sixty

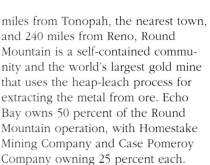

miles from Tonopah, the nearest town, and 240 miles from Reno, Round Mountain is a self-contained community and the world's largest gold mine that uses the heap-leach process for extracting the metal from ore. Echo Bay owns 50 percent of the Round Mountain operation, with Homestake Mining Company and Case Pomeroy Company owning 25 percent each.

● A rich supply of gold and silver are processed at the giant McCoy/Cove mine site, located just south of Battle Mountain in north-central Nevada.

Gold was discovered there, on the western slope of the Toquima Mountains in Nye County, in 1906. Miners who rushed to the Tonopah District found gold showing on the mountainsides and lying in the creek beds. Underground and placer mining continued intermittently in the district until the 1950s, when the rich vein and available placer seemed to be exhausted. But there was still lots of mineralized gold in the ground, at Round Mountain.

The Manhattan mine, 10 miles south, is operated as part of Round Mountain. Together, the two mines have at least 8 million ounces of mineral reserves—more than half of Echo Bay's total in Nevada.

Because of the mine's isolation, Echo Bay has literally built a town for the 600 workers and their families at Round Mountain, complete with streets, water and sewage systems, schools, and recre-

◀ The world's largest heap-leach operation, Round Mountain Gold Corporation processes low-grade ores, utilizing environmentally safe technology.

ounces of silver have been discovered in the ground at Cove, and more will be discovered as exploration goes to deeper levels, Simpson says. A new $155-million mill processes ore from both McCoy and Cove pits into bullion. Together, the two mines have at least 5 million ounces of mineral reserves.

Even though Battle Mountain is an established community, Echo Bay has spent $13 million there, developing subdivisions and making mortgage loan guarantees available for its workers.

Borealis—In operation since 1981, the Borealis mine, near Hawthorne,has been a major producer, but will close in 1990 when known reserves have been mined.

Echo Bay Mines employs more than 1,100 workers at its Nevada mines and has an annual payroll of almost $40 million. Its workers earn about twice the state's average wage, Simpson says.

"All this contributes to Nevada," he adds. "They don't spend all that money just in Round Mountain and Battle Mountain."

ation facilities. Echo Bay spent $1.3 million to build a new junior high school, and it provides housing for all the town's teachers. There's a clinic with a full-time physician's assistant. And Simpson adds proudly: "We operate probably the best child-care facility in the state of Nevada at Round Mountain. It cares for more than 100 kids a day." In all, he says, the company has spent more than $22 million on the community.

McCoy/Cove—The McCoy mine, Echo Bay's third-largest producer, is just a few miles south of Battle Mountain in north-central Nevada.

Echo Bay acquired the McCoy operating mine and heap-leach operation in 1986 from Tenneco.

The real bonanza came at Cove, just over a ridge from the McCoy pit—the result of Echo Bay's commitment to exploration. The Cove orebody is still being explored and developed. So far, 4 million ounces of gold reserves and 250 million

What Is Heap-Leaching?

Gold is taken from some of the ores from Echo Bay Mines' Nevada mines by the heap-leach process, particularly suitable for lower-grade ores.

In the typical process, ore is hauled from the open pit by truck to the mill, where crushing reduces it to gravel about a half-inch in size. Then it's stacked 20 to 40 feet high into a leach pad, where it is sprinkled with a weak cyanide solution for up to 100 days. The weak cyanide solution dissolves the gold and silver from the ore.

The mineral-bearing cyanide solution (pregnant solution) is pumped through a series of tanks containing actuated carbon, which removes the gold and silver from the solution. The barren solution is then recycled back to the leach pads. The carbon, stripped of its precious metals through electrolysis, is used again. The metals are formed into "doré bars," containing gold, silver, and a few impurities, which are shipped to precious metal refineries for processing into pure gold and silver.

"We think we do a good job of protecting the environment," says Echo Bay's Don Simpson. "We recycle and reuse almost everything. Our environmental permits require a zero-discharge policy, and we take great pains not to contaminate the ground water.

"When mining is completed, we will ensure that the disturbed areas can return to rangeland for cattle and the desert wild animals and that the entire area is safe."

RENO IRON WORKS CO., INC.

Since 1909 Reno Iron Works Co., Inc., has been helping to build Nevada—and a good part of California and other western states as well.

Almost every building erected in Reno before the mid-1970s contains structural steel beams fabricated at Reno Iron Works. That also applies to structures ranging from Harrah's Hotel towers to Citicorp's sprawling credit card center in Las Vegas, the new Washoe Hospital Tower and Porsche Building in Reno, and the R.R. Donnelley & Sons printing plant in Sparks.

The third-largest steel fabricator on the West Coast, Reno Iron Works is the only Nevada building contractor to hold a Category I, II, and III AISC unlimited license (No. 95) worldwide and a Los Angeles city license (No. 1269). Reno Iron's president, Andrea Pelter, notes that is because her company produces structural steel to meet today's stringent earthquake standards.

Reno Iron has been under the same family direction from the beginning; Pelter's father, the late Andrew

Ginocchio, began the company. By trade a forger of steel, Ginocchio made everything from mining tools to railroad cars, and truck bodies to hoisting equipment. Ginocchio was a consultant on San Francisco's Golden Gate Bridge and Bay Bridge construction.

His daughter, Andrea, grew up in the business. "My dad had me in the drafting room by the time I was 12." She assumed leadership of the firm in 1967.

Now Reno Iron Works Co., Inc., is primarily a fabricator and erector of structural steel for buildings and bridges. The firm buys steel in the form of beams, tubes, and other structural shapes from the likes of Bethlehem Steel and USX, and fabricates it into structural, seismic-approved components.

Reno Iron Works can manufacture 2,000 tons or more of structural steel each month at its 92,000-square-foot facility in Sparks. The robotics that permitted a sevenfold increase in steel beam production also permitted Reno Iron to expand its markets beyond Nevada, Pelter says. Having recently expanded its site to more than 26 acres, the firm can now bid on major bridge work as well.

Pelter believes that diversification is the key to profits in the troubled U.S. steel industry. Reno Iron Works' new products include pollution-control

▲ Andrea G. Pelter, president and chief executive officer of Reno Iron Works, is the only female structural steel contractor in the United States to hold an AISC category III license (No. 95).

equipment, earth-moving machinery, and processing equipment for the mining industry. The company is building library and office towers in Los Angeles, the Civic Center in Seattle, and military facilities throughout the West. Another recent project was building a mockup of an aircraft carrier deck, where fighter pilots train, at Fallon Naval Air Station.

Pelter is as proud of her employees and her company's safety record as she is of its buildings. During erection of the Porsche Building, crews logged 100,000 man-hours without an accident. As a member of the board of directors of the State Industrial Insurance System, Pelter appreciates the importance of safety.

She is most proud of Reno Iron's contributions to the community—and her own role in community activities. "We believe that to make our community strong, we must give back to it, and we feel an enormous gratitude to this area—to the pioneering spirit of Nevadans," she explains "I feel it's important for people to get involved and be a part of their community—our strength comes from within."

▼ Reno Iron Works fabricated and erected the structural steel for the seismic-approved Porsche Building in Reno. At the tree-topping ceremony, company officers and community dignitaries signed their names on the last support beam and displayed a pine tree that was later planted at the UNR Arboretum.

DURA-BOND BEARING CO.

Dura-Bond Bearing Co. is typical of the kind of clean industrial neighbor northern Nevada development officials seek for the state's future growth.

At its 87,000-square-foot plant in Carson City, the firm makes more than 400 kinds of camshaft bearings for auto engines. In 1988 Dura-Bond moved its factory to a spectacular six-acre site overlooking Eagle Valley and the Sierra Nevadas, from Palo Alto, California, where it had been in business for 40 years.

Dura-Bond, a division of Landover Corp., dominates its market. "If you're driving a car with a rebuilt engine in the United States," says Robert Gilkey, Dura-Bond's president, "chances are 95 percent that it has Dura-Bond camshaft bearings." Two percent of all American automobiles and light-truck engines are rebuilt each year.

Camshaft bearings, basically, are metal rings that hold in place the rotating shaft that carries power from the engine to the axle of an auto.

Dura-Bond supplies the bearings to the automotive aftermarket through national and international distributors and major engine rebuilders, who resell the engines to parts distributors worldwide.

What makes Dura-Bond bearings special is the exclusive process for producing them from steel tubing to which a lining of babbitt metal, an alloy, is

▲ Dura-Bond's six-acre plant in Carson City is responsible for producing about 95 percent of the camshaft bearings used in rebuilt car engines in the United States.

bonded. Other manufacturers roll bearings from sheet steel. The tube method, which eliminates a split or interlock, allows Dura-Bond to mass-produce higher-quality camshaft bearings at less cost to the engine rebuilder. The bearings are easier to install and fit more precisely, and they don't break under pressure.

Though water is used in the bearing production process, Dura-Bond's on-site disposal system cleans the wastewater before it is recycled into the system, used for irrigation, or discharged into the Carson City sewer system. The process produces no smoke, noise, or smells outside the plant.

Dura-Bond brought 18 employees to Carson City when it moved from Palo Alto, then hired and trained almost 100 new workers. The firm employs machinists, bore and screw machine operators, inspectors, and computer operators, in addition to unskilled workers. Gilkey credits the state's Quick Start Program, which provides accelerated training for workers, and other state-sponsored financial aids for giving the firm a running start at its new Nevada plant.

Other sites in California and Arizona were considered, but the welcoming attitude of Carson City residents was a strong selling point in bringing Dura-Bond to Nevada. "We talked to a lot of people around town, some natives and folks who recently had come over from California," says Gilkey. "We didn't find one person who regretted the move . . . They all told us, 'You'll just love it over here.'

"I think every citizen of Carson City is an unofficial member of the chamber of commerce."

▼ The 87,000-square-foot plant is a model for productivity and environmental safety.

AMERICAN PACIFIC CORPORATION

◀ Western Electrochemical Company, a principal subsidiary of AMPAC, is located in Iron County, Utah. The plant is one of only two U.S. producers of AP, a vital oxidizing agent essential to the nation's space and military programs.

▲ Steam pipes at the WECCO facility.

American Pacific Corporation (AMPAC), long an important southern Nevada manufacturer, has evolved into a holding company on the leading edge of space-age technology.

AMPAC's diversified activities ensure its continued growth. Under the leadership of the Gibson family for almost 45 years, AMPAC is a key supplier to America's space and military rocket programs, an important player in the war against pollution, and a developer of one of the Las Vegas Valley's top business parks.

AMPAC has three principal subsidiaries. PEPCON Systems, Inc. (PSI), designs, builds, and installs odor abatement equipment and water-treatment systems for large industrial and municipal applications. Western Electrochemical Company (WECCO) is one of only two U.S. manufacturers of ammonium perchlorate (AP), the oxidizing agent used in solid-fuel rocket motors. AMPAC Development Company (AMDECO) is the developer of the 500-acre Gibson Business Park in Clark County, southeast of Las Vegas.

AMPAC's operations have their beginnings with Fred D. Gibson, Sr., a mining engineer who came to Nevada in 1929 as an employee of Kennecott Copper Corporation in McGill. During World War II Gibson helped build the government's giant magnesium plant in

Henderson. After the war Gibson was the principal operating officer of Western Electrochemical Company, a manufacturer of various chlorates, perchlorates, and manganese dioxide. In 1955 Gibson and his associates, John Mueller and Edgar Marston, founded Pacific Engineering & Production Co. of Nevada, which later developed a new process for the production of AP. AMPAC and Pacific Engineering merged in 1982.

The manufacturing process developed by Pacific Engineering was based in major part on the use of a special electrode invented and patented by Fred D. Gibson, Jr., a graduate of the University of Nevada's Mackay School of Mines. This invention replaced the costly platinum electrodes formerly used in producing perchlorates, and is also the heart of today's pollution control equipment built by PSI. Pacific Engineering designed and built a pilot plant for the production of AP using its new process and the younger Gibson's electrodes in 1959, and expanded that plant several times over the next three decades. Today Fred D. Gibson, Jr., is chairman, president, and chief executive officer of AMPAC.

The late James I. "Jim" Gibson, another Gibson son, was also instrumental in the development and growth of AMPAC. Jim Gibson served as president

of Pacific Engineering from 1985 until his death in 1988. Jim served the people of Nevada as an assemblyman for eight years and as a state senator for 21 years, earning the respect and confidence of all who knew him for his integrity and able leadership.

In addition to Fred D. Gibson, Jr., the principal officers of AMPAC and its subsidiaries are C. Keith Rooker, executive vice-president and general counsel of AMPAC; David N. Keys, vice-president and chief financial officer of AMPAC; and James J. Peveler, president and chief operating officer of WECCO.

WECCO's plant near Cedar City, Utah, is one of only two American producers of AP, a vital oxidizing agent essential to the nation's space and military programs.

The Titan IV space launch vehicle requires almost one million pounds of AP to reach space; the Delta rocket takes 150,000 pounds. A single launch of the space shuttle uses 1.7 million pounds of AP. In all, AP is used in more than 80 rocket programs.

Built at a cost of approximately $92 million, WECCO's new 122,000-square-foot facility is housed in a 22-building complex on a 217-acre site 15 miles northwest of Cedar City, near the Nevada-Utah border. Active 24 hours per day, seven days per week, it can produce 30 million pounds of AP each year. This capacity is readily expandable to meet growing national needs.

AP, a stable chemical, is shipped by truck or rail from WECCO in 4,000- to 5,000-pound metal containers to customers such as NASA, the military services, Thiokol, Aerojet, United Technologies, Atlantic Research, and Hercules. Though AP manufacture is not especially hazardous, WECCO personnel neverthe-

▲ The 500-acre Gibson Business Park was developed by AmPac Development Company, a subsidiary of AMPAC. Kidd Marshmallow Co. is one of the occupants in the business park.

▶ PEPCON Systems, Inc. (PSI) designs, builds, and installs pollution abatement systems for large industrial and municipal applications.

less receive at least 400 hours of training in plant safety, first aid, and fire fighting.

America's renewed quest of outer space ensures that WECCO will be producing AP at near or full capacity for many years, and, according to Peveler, that WECCO will almost certainly expand its operations.

The equipment designed and produced by PSI is found in more than 250 installations around the globe from San Diego to Yanbu City, Saudi Arabia. These systems have proven effective in the control of noxious odors, the chlorination of sewage effluents, and the treatment of seawater to control the growth of marine organisms.

Many coastal power plants, offshore

platforms, and desalination plants use seawater as a coolant. PSI equipment rids the seawater of impurities that could clog pipes and shut down an installation. Its OdorMaster systems remove contaminants in air. The heart of all these systems is the electrode and associated electrolytic cell developed by Fred D. Gibson, Jr.

PSI systems require little maintenance and regenerate much of the chemicals needed to operate them, eliminating costly transporting and storing of chlorine. Only the proprietary electrodes need periodic replacement.

The units are individually engineered and are assembled at PSI's plant in Las Vegas. The electrodes are manufactured at the WECCO plant in Utah.

Buildings at AMDECO's multiple-use Gibson Business Park, with easy access to rail

and freeway transportation, will have an estimated 10 million square feet of industrial, commercial, and office space when completed.

Current occupants of Gibson Business Park include Ocean Spray Cranberries, Inc., and Kidd Marshmallow Co., both nationally known food-processing firms.

American Pacific Corporation continues to serve the Las Vegas community and the state of Nevada as its operations grow. The company supports many public service activities, and its officers are prominent in civic organizations.

The many activities of Fred D. Gibson, Jr., are illustrative. He is a past president of Nevada Development Authority, a member of The Commission on Economic Development, and chairman of the State Commission on Mineral Resources. He also is a director of the Nevada Taxpayers' Association, a trustee of the Desert Research Institute Foundation, and a member of the advisory boards of the Mackay School of Mines and Clark County Community College.

TIMET

Titanium metal produced in Nevada helps America send rockets into space, helps make U.S. fighter planes the world's fastest and strongest, helps golfers lengthen their drives, and helps archaeologists hold together the Parthenon.

The amazingly versatile metal is the product of Henderson-based Titanium Metals Corp. of America (Timet), the world's leading producer of titanium. At Timet, what was once part of the World War II government-owned magnesium plant in Henderson has become one of the largest integrated titanium-sponge plants in the world. What was once a fledgling company with four employees has become the largest industrial employer in Nevada. And what was once just a tiny research laboratory has become the nation's largest dedicated titanium technical center.

Timet was established in 1950 as a joint venture of Allegheny Ludlum Steel Corp., a specialty steel producer, and National Lead Co. Allegheny Ludlum recognized increasing needs for titanium metal. National Lead's interest was in the production of brilliant white titanium dioxide pigments for use in paints. Both products require the use of natu-

rally occurring ores of titanium as a starting point.

This start-up operation produced titanium tetrachloride and housed a titanium "sponge" plant and a melt shop for casting ingots of commercially pure titanium. However, the pure titanium lacked the strength required for many applications, particularly those involved in aerospace, so it was necessary for Timet to set up the Henderson Technical Laboratory to assume leadership in developing titanium alloys that would meet the variety of demanding requirements.

▲ Titanium mill products produced by Timet include slab, plate, billet, and coil.

The laboratory's three jobs are developing new products and processes, helping customers to find new uses for titanium mill products, and, as a corrosion laboratory, demonstrating titanium's resistance to attack in aggressive environments. Since then the Henderson Technical Laboratory has become the nation's largest dedicated titanium technical facility, and visitors from all over the world come to Henderson to confer with Timet's technical staff.

Titanium is not quite as light as aluminum, nor as strong as some other metals. Yet its combination of strength and light weight, coupled with its resistance to corrosion and high temperatures, are virtually unsurpassed. Such a metal is produced through a complex manufacturing process.

Rutile, a component of many beach sands, is the principal ore of titanium. At Timet's Henderson plant, the rutile is converted to titanium tetrachloride, a clear, colorless liquid. Impurities are distilled out, then the purified titanium tetrachloride is exposed to molten magnesium in a closed, inert-gas-filled steel vessel to produce elemental titanium sponge—so called because of its appearance—and magnesium chloride.

The titanium sponge is combined

▼ Aerial view of Timet's Henderson, Nevada, plant.

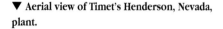

▲ A 14,000-pound ingot produced by Timet.

with the appropriate alloying elements and high-quality scrap metal, then formed into a cylindrical electrode. This operation and the recycling of magnesium chloride into magnesium and chlorine requires huge amounts of electricity. Thus, Timet is one of the largest consumers of electricity in Nevada—a good reason to have Hoover Dam as a close neighbor.

The ingots are remelted and shipped to Timet's Toronto, Ohio, plant where they are formed into a variety of mill products such as plate, sheet, bar, billet, tube, and the like.

The largest single market for titanium and titanium alloys is the aerospace industry. As long ago as the birth of the DC-8 airliner, titanium was used to replace a number of steel structural components, thus lightening the airframe sufficiently to allow for additional passengers and luggage.

In the early 1960s titanium was used extensively in the Century Series fighter planes and the Pratt & Whitney J-57 jet engine, which powers the B-52.

One of the truly significant achievements of Timet's technical laboratory was the development of fabrication techniques for a special alloy used extensively in the SR-71, an all-titanium aircraft designed to operate at Mach 3 and fly at altitudes exceeding 100,000 feet.

Designers of today's military aircraft continue to use significant amounts of titanium. All of our leading fighters rely on the high-performance strength-to-weight ratio offered by titanium alloys.

In the commercial aircraft market, titanium also plays a leading role. The largest single consumer in this area is the Boeing 747. The airframe and engines require more than 85,000 pounds of titanium for each of the giant commercial jetliners. As for titanium's value to America's space program, every time a space shuttle flight roars off the pad, more than 7,000 pounds of titanium moves into Earth orbit.

While vast amounts of titanium and titanium alloys are consumed in the aerospace industry, this unique product has found other niches in which its combination of properties makes a major contribution. Notable among these is the use of titanium in heat exchangers for power plants and in oil refineries. Titanium's corrosion resistance makes it ideal under conditions where the metal is exposed to a variety of corrosive elements, from seawater to hydrogen sulfide in gas wells.

Recreation-equipment producers use titanium for water skis, boating propellers, hardware for sailboats, tennis racquets, golf-club shafts, bicycle frames, and mountain-climbing pitons. The medical prosthesis industry has successfully used titanium for hip-replacement components and for valve assemblies in the Jarvik artificial heart.

Titanium has been used in appliances, cookware, watches, jewelry, writing instruments, electric razors, lightweight wheelchairs and crutches, ultrasonic baths, dental crowns, and even for replacement pins in archaeological restorations, such as the Parthenon.

In the four decades since Timet began operations in Nevada, it has grown to employ more than 600 workers and contributes more than $25 million in payroll and purchases to the state's economy.

The firm has been honored as a Distinguished Nevada Business of the Year at the annual Governor's Industry Appreciation Luncheon.

Timet's goal in Henderson is to continue to capitalize on the growing demand for the remarkable metal, to produce the best-quality titanium available to the ever-growing marketplace, and to constantly improve its quality.

NISHIKA CORPORATION
AMERICAN 3-D CORPORATION

Nishika Corp. of Henderson has a special niche in the world of photography. This new company is the only producer of a three-dimensional camera system that does not require special glasses or viewers.

The centerpiece of Nishika's product line, marketed exclusively by American 3-D Corp., also headquartered in Henderson, is the unique N8000 35-millimeter 3-D camera. This futuristic-looking four-lens device allows ordinary people using standard 35-millimeter film to take their own striking three-dimensional photos. Due to patented breakthroughs in technology, the dramatic feeling of depth can be appreciated with the naked eye.

The easy-to-use camera works on a principle similar to ordinary vision. To perceive depth, our two eyes see a scene from slightly different angles, with our brain combining both views into a single three-dimensional image. The Nishika process is comparable, except that to enhance the 3-D effect, the scene is recorded from four different angles. Computerized printers optically slice the four negatives into strips less than 1,000th of an inch wide and align them under the hundreds of microlenses that form the surface of the Nishika photograph. These tiny lenses direct the proper image to each eye, creating the three-dimensional effect.

James Bainbridge is the founder and chief executive officer of both Nishika and American 3-D. A brilliant young entrepreneur with a remarkable background, Bainbridge graduated first in his class in mathematics at Iowa State University, Ames. After receiving his master's and Ph.D. candidacy degrees in mathematics from the University of California at Berkeley while on a full four-year National Science Foundation scholarship, Bainbridge switched gears, obtained a law degree from Harvard, and joined a major Los Angeles law firm. In the late 1970s he set aside his legal career and established a successful consumer electronics company with manufacturing facilities in Hong Kong and South Korea.

In 1985 Bainbridge was looking for an exciting new product to manufacture.

Coming across the no-longer-produced Nimslo 3-D Camera, precursor of the Nishika, he recognized a basically good idea that needed better implementation. Bainbridge acquired the rights to the technology the following year, and set up a research and development team to improve what Nimslo had begun.

The results have been gratifying. The new 3-D printers are many times more efficient than before, the color of the prints is richer and more accurate, the cost of processing is dramatically lower, and the turnaround time for developing and processing 3-D photos has been reduced to three working days. With a completely redesigned camera, lavish packaging, and a new line of accessories, the Nishika 3-D system made its debut in March 1989.

As a result of its favorable commercial and tax environment, southern Nevada won out as the location of Nishika's headquarters. Corporate offices and the state-of-the-art 3-D film-processing laboratory are in the master-planned community of Green Valley,

▲ **A diverse background of mathematics, law, and manufacturing has given founder and chief executive officer James Bainbridge the experience to guide Nishika Corp. and American 3-D Corp. to the success they have known recently.**

on a street that the Henderson City Council officially renamed Nishika Drive. Nishika and American 3-D together employ a staff of more than 150 people in a 58,000-square-foot facility comprising office, laboratory, studio, and warehouse space.

As unusual as the Nishika camera is the marketing strategy behind it. After exploring the more traditional avenues, the management of American 3-D Corp. decided not to sell the camera in stores. Instead it is only available through American 3-D Corp. independent distributors, who sell Nishika products directly to their customers in the manner made familiar by Amway, Mary Kay Cosmetics, and Shaklee. Given the unfamiliarity of the concept of three-dimensional photography among the public and the ex-

citement generated by the 3-D prints themselves, the Nishika system is especially well suited to the kind of one-on-one show-and-tell sales presentation that is the specialty of these direct marketers.

An important factor contributing to the explosive growth of Nishika and American 3-D is the uniqueness of their products. Nothing comparable to the Nishika 3-D system is on the consumer market today. With more than 100 patents on the system worldwide—and with potential competitors mindful of the costly judgment against Kodak for patent infringements on Polaroid's instant photography—this situation is unlikely to change soon. Customers will not find the N8000 or anything like it in camera shops or department stores; direct marketers now have a genuine exclusive on a whole new area of customer interest—not just a brand name.

The Nishika and American 3-D teams realized early that a product as outstanding as its 3-D camera system—the result of more than 15 years of research by hundreds of engineers and technicians at a cost of more than $50 million—requires equally outstanding marketing and customer service. Accordingly, every piece of supporting material for the camera is top notch, including the video

▲ **Nishika Corp. headquarters in Henderson, where photographs take on new dimensions in a state-of-the-art film-processing laboratory.**

Step Into the Third Dimension starring Vincent Price.

A comparable commitment to customer service is indicated by the unconditional one-year warranty on all parts and labor that is standard with every N8000 camera, and by the expert staff and high-tech equipment in the order-taking and sales support departments to deal with both distributors and retail customers as efficiently as possible.

Exciting new developments on the horizon for Nishika include expansion of the direct marketing system internationally and the introduction of new products, such as 3-D greeting cards and 3-D poster-size prints.

If current trends continue, Nishika Corp. and American 3-D Corp. will succeed in making 3-D photography a viable alternative to standard picture taking. For a growing number of photographers and direct-sales marketers, the four-eyed camera is living up to Nishika's slogan and changing the way people picture the world.

▼ **American 3-D Corp. functions as the North American marketing agent for Nishika products and services.**

PIONEER CHLOR ALKALI COMPANY, INC.

Pioneer Chlor Alkali Company, Inc., is located in the BMI industrial complex adjacent to the community of Henderson, Nevada. Although the Pioneer name is new to this chemical manufacturing plant, this facility has, for more than 40 years, provided a major contribution to the development of southern Nevada. It continues to make a substantial economic impact, providing jobs and utilizing local business services.

The town of Henderson, located 10 miles south of Las Vegas, was established because of the BMI complex. The BMI complex was built in 1941 as a federal defense project, producing magnesium for the war effort. As the complex was being built, what is now the city of Henderson sprang up around the complex. Then known as Basic, Nevada, the

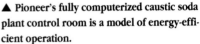

▲ Pioneer's fully computerized caustic soda plant control room is a model of energy-efficient operation.

◀ An operating engineer checks a control panel for Pioneer's steam generation plant.

town was renamed Henderson in honor of a local state senator, Charles B. Henderson. When the war was over, the plant, having served its usefulness, was shut down and was scheduled to be scrapped.

Fearing that the area would become economically depressed, local businessmen successfully lobbied the State of Nevada to purchase the plant. After the state bought the complex, it was then resold to private industry. The Pioneer plant was originally purchased by Stauffer Chemical Co. in 1945. In October 1988 Pioneer, whose corporate headquarters is located in Houston,

Texas, purchased the facility.

While many take for granted the products used in everyday life, few realize that most consumer goods would not be possible without basic industrial chemicals. Pioneer produces three basic industrial chemicals that are crucial in mining, oil refining, and electronics manufacturing as well as in the production of many items such as gasoline, pharmaceuticals, processed food, cosmetics, detergents, paper, steel, and precious metals. They are also utilized by numerous industries as the fundamental building blocks that keep industry operating.

Pioneer products are chlorine, caus-

tic soda, and muriatic acid, all of which are made from common rock salt. These chemicals are extracted from the rock salt by using a simple and safe process. This substance is available in abundance and transported to Pioneer from the Great Salt Lake in Utah. Once on site, the salt is used to make a brine solution that is fed into electrolytic cells. The cells decompose the salt brine to produce both chlorine and a weak solution of caustic soda. An evaporation process further concentrates the caustic soda to an industrial-grade product. Muriatic acid is manufactured by burning pure chlorine in the presence of pure hydrogen.

A new chlorine plant was installed in 1976 and a new caustic soda plant completed two years later. Both of these plants are current state-of-the-art designs, providing for energy-efficient operation, worker safety, and environmental safety.

The economic impact the facility has in the community and the state is significant. Pioneer has a payroll of more

▲ Pioneer's state-of-the-art quadruple effect caustic soda plant operates 24 hours per day.

◀ Shown here is one of four rows of electrolytic cells, which produce chlorine at Pioneer's Henderson facility.

than $6 million annually and yearly purchases from local vendors in excess of $10 million. Pioneer plans to look to the future and have its business presence grow at the Henderson facility.

Safety is a crucial factor at Pioneer. Ongoing seminars, job training, and communication programs are implemented at all levels of management throughout the year. Safety is a daily routine for all employees and visitors of the environmentally conscious Pioneer. As a result of effective training and appropriate supervision, Pioneer holds one of the best safety records in the state.

Pioneer also prides itself on community services. Its memberships and participation in many community emergency programs are extensive. The firm's employees have trained emergency response teams for fire departments, conducted training programs for all local fire departments, and served as members of Clark County Emergency Advisory Committee, the CHEMTREC emergency response team. These activities are considered to be an important part of doing business. Pioneer also supports many other civic activities as well as charitable causes.

In 1990 the Pioneer plant will observe 45 years of exceptional service in the state of Nevada. It has outstanding work and safety records and is committed to the growth of the community. Employees are the backbone of the organization, and their concerns are for the people of Nevada. The firm has become the leader of this fundamental and essential industry in the southwest region of the United States, and it will continue to be a forerunner in the future. Pioneer Chlor Alkali Company, Inc., is a business partner of Nevada.

FORD AEROSPACE

War rages in the Nevada skies several times a year and is fought over the 7.7-million-acre Nellis Air Force Base ranges north of Las Vegas and at Fallon Naval Air Station, southeast of Reno.

Using "weapons" ranging from wooden tanks and electronic bullets to enemy missiles created on computers, Las Vegas-based Ford Aerospace is helping to train America's combat pilots and those of its allies to be the best in the world.

Ford Aerospace runs the highly complex air-to-air and air-to-ground combat arenas that stretch from northern Nevada to the state's southern border. Systems installed, managed, operated, and maintained by Ford Aerospace simulate hostile and antiaircraft artillery and surface-to-air missile systems, record the results of aerial dogfights and ground attack missions so crews can learn from their mistakes, and help test new weapons and tactics to keep America's armed forces fit and modern.

A subsidiary of Ford Motor Company, Ford Aerospace manages similar combat ranges in Florida, North Carolina, New Mexico, Arizona, California, the Philippines, and Sardinia, Italy. The threat systems operated by Ford Aerospace can be configured to simulate the "bad guy," regardless of where he is in the world, and are employed using the most current aggressor nation tactics expected to be encoun-

tered by U.S. forces, whether they be Navy, Marine, or Air Force.

The largest range used for aircrew training is at Nellis AFB, "The Home of the Fighter Pilot." Nellis has been headquarters for the Tactical Fighter Weapons Center since the 1960s and is the free world's leader in developing, training, testing, and evaluating the aircrews' skills—skills that are honed to perfection by U.S. pilots and those of other NATO countries in war games such as Red Flag, which pits Blue Forces against Red Force aggressor experts based at Nellis. In order to avoid an electronic "kill," pilots must dodge simulated missiles and ground fire from multiple cockpit-detectable electronic-threat emitters operated by Ford Aerospace. These enemy-threat systems are designed to simulate hostile antiaircraft weapons employed worldwide.

Other Ford systems continuously monitor the results of aerial dogfights at Nellis and Fallon. Pods full of computers and data communications equipment on each aircraft sense in three dimensions each aircrews' maneuvers and "kills," then transmit the data to Ford Aerospace's ground-based Air Combat Maneuvering Instrumentation system (ACMI), or to a similar system called the Tactical Aircrew Combat Training System (TACTS) at Fallon—which records and relays this data back to the aircraft's base for analysis and pilot debriefings.

To make training effective aircrews must be able to review their performances by actually observing the results of aerial actions and reactions while the experience is still fresh in their minds.

Thus, ACMI and TACTS permit these aircrews to view their actions soon after landing. They review their actions from many angles and perspectives, even from the cockpit of the opposing aircraft, to, in effect, critique their aerial combat techniques.

The solar-powered instrument stations supporting these ACMI and

TACTS systems are housed in weatherproof boxes that have to resist snowstorms and windstorms in remote desert and mountain locations, while providing clear and reliable communications between aircraft, those desert stations, and the home base at Nellis or Fallon. To support these systems and the myriad of communications, data, and video circuits linking the diverse activities within the 12,000 square miles of combat ranges, Ford Aerospace maintains 750 miles of digital microwave relays containing 432 voice and data channels, approximately 150 miles of fiber-optic cable, 150 air-to-ground receivers, and more than 200 radio transceivers.

Not everything in Ford Aerospace's bag of simulated weapons is high tech. Wooden targets that look like tanks, trucks, and missile systems are fabricated at a Ford installation at Indian Springs, then taken out to the ranges to provide realistic targets for the pilots. From an aircrew's aspect, traveling at 400 knots across the desert, they look

▼ Fallon Naval Air Station. Ford Aerospace operates and maintains ground electronic equipment and EW/TACTS Ranges.

very real. Also adding to the battlefield chaos are pyrotechnic devices that simulate smoke-trailing rockets and antiaircraft gunfire. To reach their assigned targets, aircrews must fight their way through this gauntlet of electronic weapons and simulated fire.

Ford Aerospace closes parts of the Nellis bombing and gunnery ranges for cleaning and maintenance each year. Ford range-maintenance crews, in association with Air Force's explosive ordnance disposal teams, replace old targets and clean up munitions residue. Also, complicated electronic instruments and complete radar units are periodically dismantled and brought to Ford Aerospace's new depot in Las Vegas, where they are rebuilt or replaced—and often, through Ford's engineering expertise, upgraded to maintain pace with the state-of-the-art in electronic-combat equipment.

Many of these systems and their components are no longer commercially available, so Ford Aerospace has to design and build them. Its Las Vegas warehouse stocks many few-of-a-kind and rebuilt instruments and their subsystems for these systems, as well as parts for Department of Defense customers worldwide, thus saving the government extensive reprocurement costs.

Thirty-five miles north of Las Vegas on the Weapons Center ranges, Ford Aerospace also operates and maintains a network of precision optical tracking devices—cinesextants and cinetheodolites—that track and record the flights of weapon systems being tested, their impact performance, and even the effect their release may have had on the delivering aircraft.

Since it took over operation of the Nellis ranges from the Air Force in 1981, Fallon NAS range in 1984, and Indian Springs Air Force Auxiliary Field in 1987, Ford Aerospace has been able to reduce by half the number of people needed to run the systems and to reduce system down-time on the ranges, adding sigificantly to the number of test and training missions supported.

Ford Aerospace estimates the savings

▲ Combat simulation devices are operated and maintained by Ford Aerospace, which manages combat ranges in Nevada at Nellis Air Force Base, Fallon National Air Station, and Indian Springs Air Force Auxiliary Field.

to taxpayers on the conversion at Nellis, Fallon, and Indian Springs is in excess of $20 million per year.

Ford Aerospace has been a good Nevada community partner as well. Employees assisted in the installation of a TV satellite system for the community at Beatty and helped upgrade the water system in Tonopah, where many of its range maintenance personnel reside. Ford Aerospace is also a strong financial supporter of the engineering school at University of Nevada, Las Vegas, the Clark County School District, and other nonprofit charitable organizations.

Ford Aerospace employees are not technocrats imported from somewhere else. They work in Nevada and they are proud to live there.

NEWMONT GOLD COMPANY

Prospectors began searching for silver and gold in the foothills of the Tuscarora Mountains in Nevada more than a century ago. However, it wasn't until 1965, when Newmont Gold Company produced significant quantities of gold from its first mine near the town of Carlin, that Nevada was launched on the road to becoming North America's biggest gold producer.

Newmont's Carlin mine, the first modern open-pit gold mine in North America, produced 128,000 ounces of gold in 1965, its first year of operation. Its gold appears as microscopic-sized particles that are disseminated thinly and broadly through rock formations. Today it requires, on average, the mining of 100 tons of material and the treatment of more than 30 tons of ore to recover a single ounce of gold. Since it began operating in 1965, Newmont Gold Company has invested more than $750 million in gold production facilities, and in 1989 its 2,300 employees produced some 1.5 million ounces of gold at its mines located along a 38-mile alignment of gold deposits that has become known as the Carlin Trend.

In 1989 the company operated five

▲ Proper regard for the environment guides Newmont's approach to mining. Here, sunflowers grow alongside its largest mill near Carlin. Hundreds of acres of land have been reclaimed and reseeded by Newmont in 1988 and 1989; eventually, the reseeding effort will lead to a totally natural landscape, blending fully with the surrounding undisturbed lands.

mills and three leach facilities servicing five active open-pit mines near Carlin in the northeastern corner of the state. A major expansion program, begun in 1987 and completed in mid-1989, added three mills, three leach plants, and various support facilities. Milling capacity is 40,000 tons per day compared with 12,000 tons in 1987, while annual leaching capacity has increased to 32 million tons, up from 9.2 million tons just two years ago.

Due to an aggressive long-term exploration program, Newmont Gold Company has been able to increase its reserves even as it has produced and sold record amounts of gold in recent years. As of the end of 1989 the companys gold reserves stood at 20.7 million ounces, the largest reserve position of

any company in North America.

In mid-1989 the company's exploration drilling encountered very encouraging new mineralization about 500 yards from an existing Newmont Gold Company mine named Genesis. The initial hole drilled in this new area, called Deep Star, encountered three-quarters of an ounce of gold per ton over a 350-foot interval. This result is comparable to all but the best high-grade holes drilled on the Carlin Trend, and it was followed by additional drilling that encountered further high-grade mineralization at Deep Star. A record hole on the Carlin Trend was drilled on Newmont Gold Company property in 1988 and averaged .9 ounces of gold per ton over

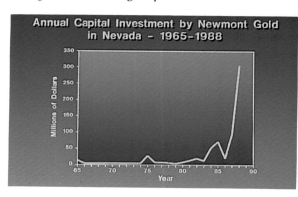

▶ Test tubes, scanners, and computers surround Carl Ray, chemist and project manager at Newmont Gold's new $11-million analytical laboratory in Carlin. The laboratory uses robotics to perform more than 2.3 million assays of gold ore each year. It is the world's largest, most advanced such laboratory known to be operated by any gold-mining company.

an interval of 470 feet. In comparison, the average grade of ore treated by Newmont Gold in 1988 contained less than .05 ounces of gold per ton.

Future exploration opportunities for Newmont Gold Company in Nevada are substantial. Its 20 square miles of property, which are situated along 38 miles of the Carlin Trend, are encompassed by additional land owned by Newmont Mining Corporation. Newmont Mining holds 90.1 percent of Newmont Gold's common stock, and in 1989 Newmont Gold, together with Newmont Mining, invested more than $22 million on exploration and development in Nevada.

Conducting mining activities in Nevada involves more than production of gold. Regard for the natural environment and the communities in which it operates is a major concern at Newmont Gold. Parallel to its gold mining operations, Newmont has one of the state's largest ranches on its Carlin Trend property, with up to 14,000 head of cattle. In addition to paying the highest taxes per employee of any major industry in the state, Newmont Gold has invested more than $20 million on local housing and has made significant grants to schools, hospitals, and other social services, as well as to conservation organizations in Nevada.

Furthermore, in areas where gold ex-

ploration activities have ceased, roads constructed for access by drilling equipment have been and continually are being restored to their natural contours and vegetation. In 1988 some 13 miles of such drill roads were reclaimed. By mid-1989 an additional 19 miles of roads had been recontoured and restored to a natural state. Most of this reclamation was on private land, where reclamation previously had not been mandated by law. During the 1989 legislative session in Nevada, Newmont supported landmark legislation requiring reclamation even on its own and other private land.

"Newmont is committed to excellence in its mining operations. But it is equally committed to preserving and maintaining the quality of the natural environment in which we operate and the quality of the communities in which we live," said Gordon R. Parker, chairman

▲ Newmont Gold has invested more than $20 million to build new homes in the area surrounding Elko, Nevada, where many of its employees live. The company also has contributed nearly $2 million in the past two years to local communities to improve and expand schools and hospitals, as well as police, water, and sanitation facilities.

and chief executive officer of Newmont Gold Company and Newmont Mining Corporation.

"Nevada has always provided a healthy climate for business," said Parker. "And today the gold business is receiving encouragement to invest in the state, to explore for gold, and to operate mines and plants in a responsible manner. Nevada is *the* gold state today—and likely will be for generations to come."

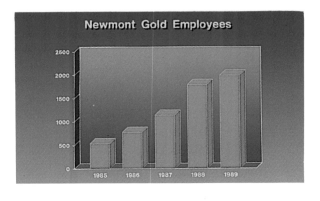

Exploration and Development Spending by Newmont in Nevada

Millions of Dollars

1985 1986 1987 1988 1989

Newmont Gold Employees

1985 1986 1987 1988 1989

KERR-MCGEE CHEMICAL CORP.

Operations at Kerr-McGee Chemical Corp.'s Henderson facility near Las Vegas are part science and part engineering. But at the heart of the world-class chemical manufacturing plant are human skills and commitment of more than 250 employees.

Kerr-McGee employees have been operating the Henderson facility since 1967, when the plant was purchased through an acquisition. The manufacturing site, however, predates even the community of Henderson, which today numbers about 45,000 residents.

During World War II a shortage of

▼ A chlorate plant operator traverses a cat-walk between the salt silo, containing dry salt, and the salt saturator, containing salt slurry. Salt is an integral component of sodium chlorate.

magnesium metal prompted emergency construction of a manufacturing facility at the site that would later become Henderson. Following the war the U.S. government sold the facility to private companies. In some of those buildings designed and built during the war, Kerr-McGee manufactures four basic products: chlorates, perchlorates, manganese dioxide, and boron specialty chemicals. These industrial chemicals have down-to-earth uses such as manufacturing paper products and ceramics, as well as space-age uses in jet fighters and the space shuttle program.

Kerr-McGee's sodium chlorate, for example, serves as a bleach for wood pulp in paper-making processes. Manganese dioxide is used in dry-cell batteries. Boron trichloride is a raw material for manufacturing boron fibers that reinforce critical aircraft components and sporting equipment, such as tennis rackets and golf-club shafts.

Another Kerr-McGee product, ammonium perchlorate, plays a critical role in launching the space shuttle. The shuttle's solid-fuel boosters carry 1.7 million pounds of ammonium perchlorate, which provides a source of oxygen for rocket fuel to burn and helps booster rockets generate 2.6 million pounds of thrust.

Most of the Henderson facility's products are electro-chemicals—made by processes in which electricity, water, and other raw materials are used to recover end products. Two of the most important materials—water and electric-

▲ Ammonium perchlorate is dried in a rotary drier before being made into marketable form. Ammonium perchlorate is of major importance in launching the space shuttle.

ity—come from Lake Mead and Boulder Dam, about 15 miles from the plant. Another natural resource, the weather, helps ensure efficient operations. Low humidity, infrequent rain, and abundant sunshine enable Kerr-McGee to more efficiently produce a line of moisture-sensitive products.

Kerr-McGee's Henderson facility produces 33,000 tons of chemicals per year valued in excess of $60 million. The facility competes with other manufacturers worldwide, and several of its products are recognized as providing the greatest purity and consistency available from any source. Credit for this can be attributed to outstanding professional and technical employees and support staffs that include high-quality plant operators, safety specialists, and marketing experts.

In addition to processing chemicals in Henderson, Oklahoma-based Kerr-McGee Corp. produces other natural resources in locations worldwide. Its products include oil and natural gas, refined-oil products, coal, and forest products. The firm's annual sales of more than $3.1 billion place it among the largest companies in the nation.

.10.

HIGH
FINANCE

◇◇◇◇

*Banks and thrift institutions fuel
Nevada's booming progress,
providing capital needed for
development and growth.*

◆◆◆◆

First Interstate Bank of Nevada: 216

First Western Savings Association: 218

Valley Bank of Nevada: 220

American Bank of Commerce: 224

PriMerit Bank: 226

Citibank (Nevada), National Association: 228

Photo by
Andrew McKim/Masterfile

FIRST INTERSTATE BANK OF NEVADA

First Interstate Bank of Nevada, the state's largest financial institution, started as a single office in Reno in 1902. Currently the institution has more than 70 banking offices statewide and is part of the nation's largest retail banking organization.

Nevada is among the fastest growing states in the country, and First Interstate Bank of Nevada has been a primary factor in the financing of this growth as well as a supporter of the civic needs of individual communities statewide. The bank makes more loans to more Nevadans than any other financial institution. It is consistently the largest lender to the state's number-one industry—gaming—and has been a driving force in the successful efforts for economic diversification in the state.

First Interstate Bank of Nevada does business with more than 50 percent of all the households in the state. The bank has more than 130 automated Day & Night Tellers statewide and banking offices in all corners of the state—from Elko and Wells in the northeastern part of Nevada, to Henderson, located at the state's southern tip. The convenience offered by First Interstate Bank is second to none.

With an 85-year history, locally managed First Interstate Bank of Nevada is part of First Interstate Bancorp, which has a 22-state banking territory with more than 1,000 offices. On the corner of Second and Virginia

▲ The First Interstate Tower in Las Vegas serves as southern Nevada headquarters for First Interstate Bank of Nevada.

of existence from 1984 to 1990. The University of Nevada system will receive $2 million, with half going to each university in Reno and Las Vegas. In addition, the bank supports many of the state's community colleges.

From its early days as a one-office operation to today's sophisticated statewide institution, First Interstate has been an integral part of Nevada's history. It has grown and prospered consistently with that of the communities it serves.

Nevada is an exciting state with a panoply of business and citizenry. As it has for nearly a century, First Interstate Bank of Nevada is playing a leadership role in the state's dynamic future.

◀ The Nevada Museum of Art is one of the many nonprofit organizations throughout Nevada that benefits from the generosity of the First Interstate Bank of Nevada Foundation.

▼ Chairman and chief executive officer Donald D. Snyder.

streets in the heart of downtown Reno, a small group of local businessmen opened the doors of Farmers & Merchants Bank in 1902, the name under which First Interstate Bank of Nevada was originally incorporated.

The state's former state treasurer, William Westerfield, was the bank's first president. One year later, in 1903, the bank received its national charter and became The Farmers & Merchants National Bank. In 1929 the name was changed again to First National Bank in Reno. The bank has grown with the state. With the merger of First National Bank and Las Vegas' Bank of Nevada in 1979, First National had the foundation for a very strong statewide banking system. In 1981 Western Bancorporation, the multistate banking corporation that owned First National, changed its name to First Interstate Bancorp.

Today First Interstate Bank of Nevada, with headquarters in Reno and Las Vegas, is rapidly growing with assets of more than $3.8 billion. The bank

prides itself on the theme, "Nobody makes banking easier," and is working more aggressively than ever to offer innovative services, products, and convenience. The institution is also a leader on the technological end of banking and continues to be among the top performing banks its size in the nation. First Interstate Bank of Nevada has its own International Banking Division, as well as more trust and investment services than any other Nevada financial institution.

The First Interstate Bank of Nevada Foundation pledged close to $4 million to Nevada during its first six years

FIRST WESTERN SAVINGS ASSOCIATION

With a strategy of carefully planned expansion into other western states, prudent loan management, and tight cost control, Las Vegas-based First Western Savings Association is one of the nation's strongest thrift institutions.

"We've achieved this position," says R.G. Taylor, chairman of First Western Financial Corporation, the association's holding company, "by sticking to our purpose—which is encouraging thrift and home ownership."

The association is also one of America's leading savings and loans in operating efficiency, as measured by its operating costs, and is fourth in profitability among 25 thrift institutions of its size. First Western Financial Corporation is listed on the NASDAQ Over-the-Counter Exchange.

Founded in the 1950s, the state-chartered First Western was Las Vegas' first savings and loan association. Taylor, a retired U.S. Air Force major general and World War II ace fighter pilot, began steering the association in 1971, when it listed only a quarter-billion dollars in assets. With a solid management team since that time, he has seen tiny Las Vegas grow into a major metropolitan area and First Western become one of the leading financial institutions fostering the growth of home ownership. In 1982 First Western expanded its northern Nevada operations with the acquisition of American Savings of Reno. Today First Western's assets have increased to more than $1.3 billion.

Taylor points out that 88 percent of First Western's loan portfolio is in home

▲ Major General R.G Taylor, USAF (retired), chairman of the board of First Western Financial Corporation.

▲ Raymond J. Gregor, chairman of the board, president, and chief executive officer of First Western Savings Association.

loans—a high percentage for the industry. And, reflecting the association's prudent loan philosophy, about 25 percent of its home loans are secured by adjustable-rate mortgages, which protect the association from runaway interest rates and give mortgagees the benefits of any interest-rate declines.

"We chose long ago not to compete in a high interest-rate environment," Taylor says of First Western's current financial strength. "After deregulation in

▼ Customers of First Western's headquarters branch have come to expect excellent customer service at the teller line.

1981, we remained a traditional savings and loan and have not engaged in the type of investments that have caused the industry problems."

With more than 300 employees, First Western has 17 branches in Nevada, including 12 in the Las Vegas area and three in the Reno area. Other divisions are in Elko and Ely. Branches in Oregon and Washington bring First Western's total outlets to 21.

Guiding the association is Raymond J. Gregor, chairman of the board, president, and chief executive officer, who has been an officer in the association since 1971. Gregor is also president and chief executive officer of the holding company. He has served as president and director of the Savings and Loan League of Nevada, director of the Federal Home Loan Bank Board of San Francisco, director of the United Way of Southern Nevada, director of the Boulder Dam Area Council of Boy Scouts of America, member of the National Association of Home Builders, and member of the Las Vegas Chamber of Commerce.

Taylor founded the U.S. Air Force Fighter Center at Nellis Air Force Base, now called "the home of the fighter pilot." He served in the U.S. Air Force and the U.S. Army Air Corps for 30

▲ **First Western's headquarters building in Las Vegas.**

years before retiring as a major general. He serves on the boards of a number of community and charitable organizations and is a past director of the Federal Home Loan Bank Board of San Francisco, past president of the Las Vegas Chamber of Commerce, and past president of the United Way of Southern Nevada.

Senior executive vice-presidents are LuAnn Beadle, H. Bruce Francis, and Ronald D. Herr. Catherine A. Sourk serves as senior vice-president and controller.

Others on First Western's board of directors are Howard W. Cannon, former U.S. Senator and a retired U.S. Air Force major general; Frank N. Bender, a native Nevadan and president of Reno's Bender Warehouse Co.; J. Kell Houssels, Jr., a former Nevada assemblyman who has been president of the Tropicana Hotel and the El Cortez Hotel and serves on the boards of Showboat Hotel and the Union Plaza Hotel and Casino; Herbert W. Marache, Jr., first vice-president of Janney Montgomery Scott, Inc., stock-brokerage firm; Poul E. Moller, a veteran oilman who is president of International

Fuels Corp. and of Trans World Oil Co. and former head of USA Petroleum Corp; Charles L. Ruthe, chief administrative officer of The Boyd Group of casinos; and Roger S. Trounday, executive vice-president of John Ascuaga's Nugget Hotel and Casino in Sparks.

Under their leadership, First Western is moving ahead with an expansion strategy that will stretch into the 1990s. It was the first Nevada-based financial institution to add offices in other states, a move made possible in 1985, when the state legislature approved a new interstate banking law, under which banks and savings and loans can make acquisitions anywhere in the country.

The association acquired Metropolitan Savings of Portland, Oregon, in 1987, and the following year opened a metropolitan office in Eugene, Oregon. In 1989, in a purchase of Eastern Washington Savings and Loan Association, First Western acquired an office in Wenatchee and subsequently opened an

office in Tacoma, Washington.

"These troubled times offer good opportunities for strong and healthy savings and loans to expand," Taylor says. "We studied all the western states and found the Northwest to be the best place for us to grow. When a troubled institution such as Eastern Washington Savings and Loan became available, it fit our plan."

First Western is targeting other small metropolitan areas for expansion instead of cities such as San Francisco, San Diego, or Los Angeles, according to Gregor. The association is studying markets in Utah, New Mexico, and Arizona, as well as additional outlets in the Northwest. New branches are also in the works for Las Vegas.

First Western Savings Association, which currently is financing approximately 10,000 homes in Nevada, also plans to set up home-lending operations in its new territory. "We don't forget that home loans are still our primary job," says Taylor. "They are why we are one of the strongest savings and loans in the nation. First Western stuck to the savings and loan business."

VALLEY BANK OF NEVADA

Valley Bank of Nevada may be Nevada's largest state-based financial institution, but its growth is based on a tradition of service to individuals and small businesses and its response to the financial needs of Nevada's unique business community.

Valley Bank is a story of yesterday, today, and tomorrow.

YESTERDAY

Valley Bank's predecessor, the Bank of Las Vegas, proclaimed itself "a Western Bank for a Western City," when it opened in the 1950s.

It was the first bank that took the time to understand the gaming business and recognize it as a legitimate industry, according to E. Parry Thomas, now chairman of the board and chief executive officer of Valley Capital Corporation, Valley Bank's parent company.

The group of prominent Las Vegans who opened the Bank of Las Vegas on January 18, 1954, in a building on Maryland Parkway at East Charleston Boulevard, were shortly joined by Thomas and Jerome D. Mack, who still contribute leadership to the bank as well as to the state itself.

Competing against two existing banks in town, both controlled by the same organization, the Bank of Las Vegas became the only financial institution to show faith in the growth of gaming, the industry that would become Nevada's number-one business. For the first time, Las Vegas resort/hotels were able, with Bank of Las Vegas loans, to finance their growth.

"Nobody was servicing that market (gaming)," recalls Valley Bank's chief executive officer, Richard A. Etter. "It was a tiny, mom-and-pop industry; they financed themselves because banks wouldn't finance them. They were uncomfortable with gaming. They didn't understand it," Etter adds. "We invested

the time to learn the industry. We decided they were responsible business people. We are still a major lender to casinos."

As the bank helped give gaming legitimacy and helped it mature, gaming helped the bank mature. Valley Bank

has maintained a steady growth rate achieved by few banks in America. In its first two years assets grew to $14 million. It has become the nation's 150th-largest bank, with assets of $2.9 billion.

In the 1960s the Bank of Las Vegas opened branches rapidly throughout southern Nevada, and in 1968 it merged with Valley Bank of Nevada, then headquartered in Reno. Valley Bank, with branches throughout the north, opened in 1964. The merger created a statewide banking institution, with headquarters in Las Vegas.

Another component of Valley Bank is the much older Security National Bank of Reno, started in 1939 on East Second Street with three employees and $100,000 capital. Its first branch was

◀ Valley Bank of Nevada's downtown Reno Plaza building at 401 South Virginia Street is headquarters for the bank's northern Nevada operations.

▼ Valley Bank of Nevada is headquartered at 300 South Fourth Street in downtown Las Vegas. The 17-story bank office building is located in the heart of the fastest-growing city in the country.

opened in 1943 to serve the Naval Ammunition Depot in Hawthorne. In 1951, when it moved into new headquarters along the Truckee River, Security introduced the state's first drive-up banking window. In 1980 Security became the state-chartered Security Bank of Nevada and opened its first Las Vegas office in 1982.

By 1987 Security Bank was Nevada's fourth-largest commercial bank, with 18 branches and $500 million in assets. At the close of business on the last day of that year, Security merged with Valley Bank to create the largest bank based in Nevada. Ernie Martinelli, formerly chairman of the board of Security Bank of Nevada and now vice-chairman of the

▶ The bank's hot-air balloon participates in many statewide events every year, including The Great Reno Balloon Race.

▼ The Las Vegas Symphony's Picnic Pops concert series is among the many community and cultural events sponsored by Valley Bank.

Credit makes available a full range of SBA loan products on a direct basis to Arizona businesses and through other financial institutions that do not have SBA programs of their own.

TODAY

With offices in its high-rise headquarters building on South Fourth Street in Las Vegas, Valley Bank is the largest division of its parent, Valley Capital Corporation. Its Corporate Banking Department handles large commercial and real estate loans and has developed other specialized banking services for Nevada's cash-oriented economy. In addition to serving the needs of small businesses, its Retail Banking Department is putting increasing emphasis on new product development and better customer service programs.

The bank's Trust Division manages $7 billion in assets for clients, and is rapidly becoming a nationally known provider of trust services. It is now the largest provider of such services in Nevada, Arizona, Utah, and Idaho.

Valley Bank is the largest preferred SBA lender in Nevada, and for many years the bank has been number one in both number and dollar amount of SBA loan activity. It is among the top 25 banks nationally in dollar volume of SBA loans.

Valley Bank grants SBA-backed loans through its Commercial Lending Centers throughout Nevada and Priority Lending Centers in Reno and Las Vegas. The bank's local management teams have broad authority to approve small business loans. Authority at that level has allowed the bank to improve service, develop more personal relationships with its customers, and keep a closer watch on the pulse of the marketplace.

In addition to financing businesses not able to tap the national credit mar-

board of Valley Bank, has responsibility for the bank's operations in the northern part of the state. Valley Bank now serves the businesses and people of Nevada with approximately 60 branch offices and more than 2,000 employees.

Valley Bank's first out-of-state venture occurred in 1989, when it opened Valley Business Credit in Phoenix, an extension of its commercial lending operation that specializes in Small-Business Administration (SBA) lending. Valley Business

kets, Valley Bank's increased focus is on individuals' banking needs. Valley Bank was the state's first bank to open with extended hours at its 56 branches statewide, which are open from 9 a.m. to 6 p.m., five days per week. Likewise, Valley Bank as among the first banks in Nevada to open on Saturdays from 9 a.m. to 1 p.m., at selected branch locations throughout the state. "Since we live in a 24-hour environment, it's crucial to many of our customers that we offer more nontraditional banking hours," says Etter.

Developing the supermarket, full-service banking concept is also at the forefront of Valley Bank's growing customer service program. The bank is

▶ **Valley Bank's Partners for Nevada's Future cooperative education programs provide high-school seniors with part-time employment at the bank while continuing their education at the college level. The statewide program also gives students a chance to secure a four-year scholarship to state universities in Reno and Las Vegas.**

▼ **Frank Kim Elementary's academically talented fourth and fifth graders collected one million pennies as part of the bank-sponsored Penny Power program. Students studied the value of the penny and whether it should remain as part of the nation's monetary system.**

opening full-service branches in supermarkets throughout Nevada, providing customers with a new level of customer service and convenience.

Through increased formal training for employees and expanded computer capabilities, the bank has been able to shorten transaction times and make more banking products available to its customers. In a recent development, Valley Bank, which has more Automated Teller Machines (ATMs) than any other Nevada bank, has installed multilingual ATMs, which include Chinese characters.

At Valley Bank, everything and everyone is focused on the goal of better customer service. "People used to select a bank for its location," says Valley Bank president Peter M. Thomas. "Now it's for service. The financial industry is pretty much the same when it comes to bank products, but when it comes to

customer service, we believe it's the quality of service that sets one bank apart from another. We believe the customer will see a noticeable difference between us and our competition."

Planning such programs and guiding Valley Bank's policies is the job of an eight-person executive committee, consisting of Richard A. Etter, chairman of the board and chief executive officer; Peter M. Thomas, president and chief operating officer; Ernest Martinelli, vice-chairman of the board; Richard H. Taggart, senior executive vice-president; Kenneth E. Miller, executive vice-president, chief financial officer, cashier, and treasurer; Douglas M. Todoroff, executive vice-president and senior credit officer; Roger F. Gornichec, executive vice-president and director of Retail Banking; and Jon A. Joseph, executive vice-president, assistant cashier, assistant secretary, and general counsel.

In addition to Valley Bank, Valley Capital's other subsidiaries include Valley Leasing Company, Inc. (VLC), which leases a wide variety of equipment to a wide variety of businesses. VLC offers business customers several leasing options, including lease/purchase, lease financing, and true leases, with up to 100-percent fixed-rate financing.

Valley Electronic Services Inc., (VESI) was created to develop, sell, install, and service electronic transaction devices, such as ATMs and credit card terminals for the casino industry and retail merchants nationwide. A new product, a debit card point-of-sale service, allows customers to buy goods with ATM cards while speeding up the check-out process and reducing check handling by merchants.

Valley Bank has three other affiliates: Valley Mortgage Co., Inc., is one of the largest originators and servicers of residential mortgage loans; Valley Financial Services offers competitive insurance-premium financing to insurance agencies statewide; and Valley Capital Life

▲ Area scouts distribute thousands of food-collection bags every year in an effort to help needy and homeless people. More than 200,000 food bags are donated by Valley Bank for the annual Scouting for Food drive.

▶ University athletics are among the many community events sponsored by the bank. The nationally recognized University of Nevada, Las Vegas, Runnin' Rebels play in front of home crowds of 18,000 in the Thomas and Mack Center.

Insurance Company provides life and disability credit insurance to the bank's customers.

TOMORROW
From its start as "a Western Bank for a Western City," Valley Bank of Nevada has become a western bank for a western state. Now its projected growth across state lines will make Valley a western bank for the entire West.

Through the bank's parent company, Valley Capital Corporation, a strong banking presence has been established in the Arizona market. The acquisitions of Century Bank of Arizona and First Business Bank of Arizona allow the corporation to specialize in banking products and services designed to meet the financial needs of small- to medium-size business customers—"The same type of customer Valley Bank is working with in Nevada," says Peter Thomas.

The company is also currently involved in expansion plans that include new SBA loan offices in San Diego, Sacramento, Phoenix, and Seattle, and a Valley Mortgage office in Sacramento. Other areas under study include southern Utah, Denver, New Mexico, and Tucson.

Thomas and Etter also cite growth

plans within Nevada, placing their faith on Nevada's geographic advantages and its robust economy that benefits all banks. Las Vegas is in the heart of the Southwest, closer to Los Angeles and San Diego than are cities in Northern California; Reno sits astride the major interstate and rail lines to the East. An increasing number of companies are finding Nevada an ideal place to relocate their regional headquarters. Furthermore, the state's recreation and leisure industry continues its phenomenal growth.

Community Service: The Tradition of Thomas and Mack

Valley Bank of Nevada is synonymous with community service, especially youth work—a continuation of the tradition set by a pair of its early leaders. In addition to guiding the early and rapid growth of the Bank of Las Vegas, E. Parry Thomas and Jerome D. Mack were constant participants in civic projects.

They helped turn the tiny Nevada Southern University into the University of Nevada, Las Vegas. Their continuing financial commitment and that of the bank have helped build UNLV into a major institution of higher learning.

In addition to the support of higher learning, Valley Bank sponsors other such community events as economic seminars for schoolteachers, Juvenile Diabetes Foundation walk-a-thons, Partnership in Education for 11th and 12th graders throughout Nevada, Youth Leadership programs that involve youngsters in community service projects, Scouting for Food drives that help collect food for the homeless, and a nationally recognized project called Penny Power that teaches elementary schoolchildren about business and marketing concepts as well as how to handle money.

"It's important that our young people be given every opportunity to learn about economic issues and how their lives will eventually be affected by our economy," says Peter Thomas. "The teaching of economic ideas and concepts must become more of a focal point in our elementary, junior high, and high schools if we're to better prepare our kids for tomorrow's financial marketplace."

Thomas adds that perhaps the programs best describing the bank's commitment to education and the community are Financial Freeway and Children's Discovery Museum. Says Thomas, "These two bank-sponsored projects teach our children the importance of responsibility and independent living."

AMERICAN BANK OF COMMERCE

Niche banking is a modern term for one of the oldest principles of business: finding a need and filling it.

Las Vegas-based American Bank of Commerce has been successfully filling the niche it carved out for itself—servicing the financial needs of small businesses—ever since its founding in 1979.

At that time American was the first bank organized in Las Vegas in 23 years. "There was a real belief that our community was growing, and there was certainly room for additional banks," recalls the institution's president and chief executive officer, James V. Bradham.

"Our thought was, we will pick an area that we will specialize in, and in that area we will be better than anybody else," Bradham says. "The specialty we took was small business. We call ourselves the business bank."

The sign of success for that policy is that today American Bank has more business checking accounts than personal accounts—unusual for a bank.

At its four branches around Las Vegas, American Bank of Commerce has no drive-up windows, no walk-up windows, no automatic teller machines. "These are consumer-driven conveniences," explains Bradham. "There's something else we don't have at our bank. That's long lines in our lobbies. It is not the highlight of a businessman's week to wait in a teller line for 15 minutes."

Instead of long lines, business customers of American Bank of Commerce face friendly tellers who know their first names and loan officers who know how their businesses operate. For depositors who do not have time to come to the bank, the bank sends messengers to their places of business to make daily pickups. "The rush hour in our lobby is when our armored transport comes by in the afternoon and drops off 80 or 85 bags," Bradham says.

"Ours is a smaller bank with fewer layers of bureaucracy," says the bank's president. "We know your name, we know your business, we know your spouse, we know the clerk who brings in your deposit. The small businessman likes to be acknowledged as a person, rather than as a number."

Because American Bank of Commerce is a smaller organization, deci-

▼ **Claudine Williams, chairman of the board.**

sions come more quickly than at larger banks. There also is a low personnel turnover. Of 27 corporate officers, 23 have been with American Bank more than five years. Bradham explains the importance of that: "You're in business, and you've got a banker who understands your business. You've been with this bank for many years, but your banker gets promoted or transferred. So when you come in next week, there's a new person sitting there who says, 'Who are you?' It is just like you're a new kid on the block again. It is important to our banking clients that we have continuity, that the lenders are on a first-name basis and have a good understanding of their businesses."

A good example of knowing the business is Bradham himself. Much of his bank's loan portfolio is in the real estate construction business. Bradham admits construction loans are riskier than other kinds of loans, but he says, "Because it's riskier, your yield goes up, and you cut the risk by having knowledgeable lenders." Bradham should know—he has been a licensed general contractor himself.

In addition to developers, American Bank of Commerce also makes loans to contractors and subcontractors and to individual owners of larger homes.

Bradham runs the bank, which has total assets of more than $120 million, with the help of almost 80 employees and three executive vice-presidents who make up the management team: Bruce

▲ American Bank of Commerce's managing officers, from left: James Zurbriggen, executive vice-president; James Bradham, president and chief executive officer; Robert E. Olson, executive vice-president; and Bruce Hendricks, executive vice-president.

Hendricks, senior loan officer; Robert E. Olson, chief financial officer; and James Zurbriggen, in charge of branch administration.

Bradham also credits his board of directors with taking interest in the bank's management and for the bank's success. "They are a good cross section of Las Vegas business people," he says.

The board's chairman, Claudine Williams, formerly headed the Holiday Inn and Casino and is 1990 president of

the Las Vegas Chamber of Commerce. Board members also include Keith Ashworth, former state senator and executive of Nevada Power Co.; R. W. Bugbee, a longtime builder; Dr. Elias F. Ghanem, a prominent Las Vegas physician; Murray Gennis, vice-chairman of the board of Caesars Palace; leading businessmen such as Vern J. Christensen, Nasser F. Ghanem, and Edward D. Smith; and Lu Lehman, a psychotherapist married to District Judge Jack Lehman, who was one of the American Bank of Commerce founding directors.

"These are bright, knowledgeable business people who bring us direct input from the business community," says Bradham. "It is extremely rare that we get a new customer who one of our directors does not know."

PRIMERIT BANK

When Las Vegas-based Nevada Savings changed its name to PriMerit Bank in 1988, its plans were to stimulate home building and business expansion and serve the retail banking needs of the Southwest, just as it had served families in Nevada for 32 years. Since then PriMerit's story has been the continuation of the Nevada Savings success story.

Today PriMerit is the second-largest financial institution based in Nevada, according to Kenny C. Guinn, chairman of the board and chief executive officer. It is helping to finance some of Las Vegas' largest residential developments, as well as others in California. And it plans rapid expansion of its branch system in

▼ At the November 14, 1988, unveiling of PriMerit Bank's new name and logo in Las Vegas are (from left): Mayor Ron Lurie; Sherman Miller, PriMerit's retired chairman of the board; and Kenny C. Guinn, PriMerit's chairman and chief executive officer.

Arizona and possibly other states, as well as in its home state.

Profitable for 22 consecutive years, PriMerit Bank is also a major contributor to the financial health of its parent company, Southwest Gas Corp. And safety for its retail customers' deposits is a prime concern, Guinn adds.

PriMerit was born out of the post-Korean War boom that hit Las Vegas in the mid-1950s. When the bank opened in 1956 as a state-chartered savings and loan association, PriMerit's predecessor, Nevada Savings, was the first association in southern Nevada to offer insured accounts. Always looking out for the individual, Nevada Savings was owned and operated by Las Vegas residents and offered savings accounts that earned 3.5 percent interest and were insured up to $10,000.

Nevada Savings, under its then-president Sherman Miller, survived those tumultuous years of building booms and busts and roller-coaster profits, until it had become the largest savings and loan association in the state— as its memorable slogan proclaimed—"Big, Safe, Friendly." Miller's reforms made Nevada Savings a model for the savings and loan industry.

The first northern Nevada branch opened on Reno's Plumb Lane in 1972. Nine years later Nevada Savings entered the consumer credit market, adding credit-card services; today PriMerit participates in the INN Network, PLUS System, and Star System automatic teller machines. And with the acquisition of Home Savings Association of Reno in 1982, Nevada Savings developed a statewide branch network.

The association moved into its beautiful financial center and cor-

porate headquarters at Spanish Oaks in Las Vegas in 1986—a landmark year in many ways. That was also the year that Nevada Savings was purchased by Southwest Gas—a move that gave the public utility company a new source of cash flow and gave the savings and loan association the financial strength to expand beyond Nevada's borders. The foundation for that growth came in 1988, when Nevada Savings purchased a small Phoenix-based association named Union Savings.

With the Arizona expansion, Nevada Savings outgrew its name. After 32 years as a state-chartered association, it became a federally chartered savings bank and changed its name to PriMerit Bank, Federal Savings Bank.

"The choice of the name was not easy," recalls David H. Rogers, PriMerit's president and chief operating officer.

"PriMerit's root words, 'prime' and 'merit,' are positive words evoking images of strength and high quality. These characteristics were important features of Nevada Savings and will continue to be so with PriMerit Bank."

In the tradition established by Nevada Savings, PriMerit is a bank that serves its community wherever it operates, according to Rogers. As a retail bank, its emphasis is on promoting accounts and services for individual depositors. As a lender, PriMerit helps to make housing more affordable.

PriMerit is already a heavy participant in the burgeoning real estate markets of Las Vegas and Southern California, helping families finance homes of their own. An example is Desert Shores, a 680-acre lakeside community of homes and shops in northwest Las Vegas, jointly developed by PriMerit Bank and R.A. Homes. Other

Las Vegas residential communities whose construction was aided by PriMerit financing include Painted Desert and The Lakes. The bank also develops apartment projects in the Las Vegas Valley.

Outside of Nevada, PriMerit is involved in community building projects in California's Riverside, Orange, San Diego, and Los Angeles counties, and it plans others in Arizona.

With projects in the form of profit-sharing ventures, PriMerit Bank and its venture partners take responsibility for developing the infrastructure of a project—roads, curbs and gutters, and utilities—and then either build single-family homes or sell the developed land to other builders for the same purpose.

To provide the needed resources, PriMerit puts an emphasis on customer loyalty in its retail banking branches. By the end of 1990 PriMerit expects to have

more than 25 branch offices in Nevada, including those in Carson City and Gardnerville in the north, and seven in Arizona, including newly constructed offices in the upscale communities of Scottsdale, Sun City West, and Mesa.

The bank trains its 600 employees to appreciate and care for its individual depositors "because a bank expands by building a great customer loyalty," Rogers says. PriMerit Bank also provides various customer-service packages tailored for depositors' individual needs.

And, says chief executive officer Guinn, "At PriMerit we want to be the premier retail bank in Nevada and the Southwest—the consumer's bank."

CITIBANK (NEVADA), NATIONAL ASSOCIATION

Citibank (Nevada), National Association, is a subsidiary of Citicorp, a worldwide financial services company offering a broad array of products to consumers, businesses, governments, and financial institutions through the efforts of more than 90,000 employees in 90 countries around the globe. The corporation's bankcard business in Nevada, part of Citicorp's U.S. Card Products Group, began customer service operations in October 1984 for just over one million cardmembers, and has grown in five years to more than 8 million cardmember accounts serviced at The Lakes site. Citibank's business in Nevada, through its bankcard products, provides services to cardmembers in 14 western states and, through its Diners Club products, provides services to cardmembers in all 50 states.

Citibank Nevada's mission is to provide superior financial services to consumer households for its MasterCard, VISA, Preferred Cards, and Diners Club products. The business at The Lakes handles customer telephone calls and correspondence, produces and issues

▼ Citibank Nevada's 250,000-square-foot facility in southern Nevada features two cafeterias and a fitness facility to serve its 1,200 employees.

credit cards, prints and mails statements, and receives and processes cardmembers' payments. During 1989 employees answered 10.5 million customer calls, responded to 1.3 million customer letters, mailed 94 million customer statements, produced 9.5 million new cards, and processed 78 million payments.

Citibank has succeeded in Nevada because of the investment it has made in people and the focus it has made in hiring Nevadans to implement its business proposition. There are currently 1,200 Nevadans employed at Citibank Nevada, with an investment in training and management development of 257,000 hours. An investment in innovative technology and continual retraining on new technology has broadened the horizons of employees by providing new and advanced career opportunities. Since 1984, $92 million in salaries and benefits have been paid to Citibank Nevada employees.

Citibank measures quality and productivity through daily monitoring of 127 key indicators, and has honored more than 500 staff members for extraordinary quality performance through a variety of service recognition programs. Employees received Nevada's highest honor in 1989, when Citibank won the U.S. Senate Productivity Award in Nevada in the ser-

▲ Citibank Nevada employees won the 1989 U.S. Senate Productivity Award in the service category.

vice category. Citibank's combination of a "Perfect Service Every Day" mentality with a "How May I Help You?" attitude has been the key ingredient in this outstanding service organization. The company provides a broad spectrum of employee benefits, a tuition assistance program, an employee fitness center, and an employee cafeteria in each building.

As a corporate citizen, Citibank has sponsored an aggressive program of charitable contributions, totaling more than one million dollars, to 55 charitable and civic organizations to support educational, cultural, civic, and medical efforts statewide. Citicorp's Small Change financial education program provided fifth-grade students in the Clark County and Washoe County School districts with classroom materials, as well as a Teachers Guide and a video produced in partnership with KLAS-TV. The program has become part of the fifth-grade math curriculum with more than 10,000 students per year having some fun learning about money.

The Citibank Computer Center at the Boys and Girls Clubs of Las Vegas is providing after-school tutoring and study time for children who are bused to the club after school. The

additional computer skills training allows students to be better equipped for future education and the work force.

Since 1988 Citicorp has sponsored the Helping You-Helping Me mentoring program in the Clark County School District. The project, conceived by two teachers, Bobbie Cartwright and Donna Barber, matches high school students with elementary students for volunteer after-school tutoring three days per week throughout the school year. Citibank awards the annual Citicorp Success Scholarships to four high school students who excel as mentors. This heartfelt program, now being sponsored in all 16 high schools, has raised the reading and math grades of the elementary students, and raised the self-esteem of everyone in the program. In addition, Citibank awarded Teacher Mini-Grants to the two founders of the program in honor of their innovative achievement.

Citibank employees actively participate in the community as volunteers for 31 different organizations in Nevada. The staff is encouraged to "get involved," and Citibank supports volunteer efforts by allowing employees to meet volunteer commitments during business hours. Citibankers organize food and clothing drives for HELP of Southern Nevada, an information and referral agency that directs people in need to those who can help them.

"Citibankers always show up, roll up their sleeves, and get the job done," says HELP executive director Sharon Beatty. Employees also compete in the City of Las Vegas Corporate Challenge, a weeklong event that raises money for senior citizens and recreation programs in Clark County. In addition, Citibank's contributions to United Way since 1984 have totaled $535,000, with more than 96 percent of the staff participating in the program. Employees participate in the annual Opportunity Village Gift Wrap and deliver teddy bears to sick and needy children.

As a corporation doing business in Nevada, Citibank has kept its pledge to support economic diversification efforts with contributions of more than

$200,000 to the Nevada Development Authority, and plays a major role in attracting new business to the state. Visits to The Lakes site and the opportunity for prospective business leaders to meet with Citibank officials has resulted in important new economic development in Nevada. By 1989 the corporation's presence in the state had resulted in a cumulative regional output of $1.1 billion and induced the creation of more than 7,000 jobs.

"Citibank Nevada is a proud partner in Nevada's economic development," states Richard McCrossen, "and we're excited about a future that holds more of the same."

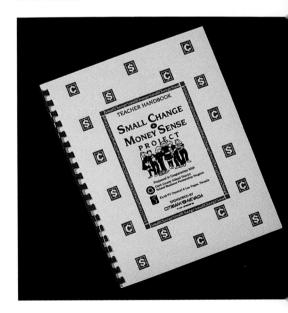

.11.

THE BAR

◇◇◇◇

Behind the scenes or before the court, Nevada's distinguished legal firms represent their clients with expertise and experience.

◆◆◆◆

Beckley, Singleton, DeLanoy, Jemison & List, Chtd.: 232

Vargas & Bartlett: 234

McDonald, Carano, Wilson, McCune, Bergin, Frankovich and Hicks: 236

Woodburn, Wedge and Jeppson: 238

Crowell, Susich, Owen & Tackes, Ltd.: 240

Keefer, O'Reilly, Ferrario & Eskin: 241

Allison, MacKenzie, Hartman, Soumbeniotis & Russell, Ltd.: 242

Jones, Jones, Close & Brown: 244

**Photo by
Douglas E. Walker/Masterfile**

BECKLEY, SINGLETON, DE LANOY, JEMISON & LIST, CHTD.

▲ **Robert List, a senior shareholder of the firm, is a former Nevada governor.**

Beckley, Singleton, De Lanoy, Jemison & List, Chtd., takes a positive approach to clients' problems. Former governor of Nevada Robert List, who oversees the firm's Reno office and maintains offices in both Las Vegas and Reno, calls it "our can-do approach.

"Many lawyers have been perceived—and rightly so—in a negative light," List explains. "To some, the lawyer is the bad guy. We find our clients a way to meet their objectives. We take the can-do approach to a client's problem."

This approach helps make Beckley, Singleton one of Nevada's largest and most influential firms, and continues to contribute toward its growing national and international reputation.

More than 50 attorneys, aided by approximately 80 support employees, staff the firm's Las Vegas and Reno offices, and offer clients a full range of legal counsel and technical and technological resources. "In a state as fast growing and dynamic as Nevada," says Drake De Lanoy, the firm's president, "nothing less will suffice."

"Today's client," says List, "relies upon the fact that he can walk through the doors of Beckley, Singleton in Reno or Las Vegas—whether he wants to buy a hotel-casino, needs tax advice, has a major piece of litigation, wants to buy a piece of land, or wants to sell a business—and find a legal specialist to handle the problem. That's why we're attracting clients here . . . There's a measure of effectiveness that flows from being a full-service law firm."

Beckley, Singleton's national and multinational corporate clients similarly depend upon the firm's full range of services for top representation in a wide array of transactions. "Corporate clients," says List, "more so than ever before, need a law firm that can handle all of their needs—everything from tax matters and mergers and acquisitions to environmental permitting, mining, natural resources law, or the complexities of putting the financial package together for a major project. As the U.S. and international business environment has grown more complex and exacting, we've adapted and stayed a step ahead."

Beckley, Singleton was founded in 1962 by Drake De Lanoy, then a Washoe County deputy district attorney, and Bruce Beckley, a leading business attorney whose family was one of the oldest in southern Nevada. They were joined by gaming attorney William Singleton and litigator Rex Jemison. In 1967 the firm became the first professional law corporation in Nevada.

In the beginning the firm's practice centered primarily around corporate law, litigation, probate, and gaming. But as the state and its economic base expanded, so too did the firm.

Today the Las Vegas office occupies a four-story building and an adjoining brand-new tower with a connected parking garage a block from the courthouse in the commercial center of the city. The firm's Reno offices occupy the second floor of the PriMerit Bank Building at 50 West Liberty Street, within close proximity to both the state and federal courts. The Las Vegas and Reno offices are linked by state-of-the-art computers and telephone equipment, and are equipped with computerized data bases that allow the firm's attorneys access to up-to-the-minute statutory amendments and case precedents. The firm has the largest private law library in Las Vegas.

"While technology is crucial," says List, "we do not let it overshadow a personal touch to the work we do. We stress teamwork and personal attention to client satisfaction. We have all kinds of people and personalities. We recruit people with varied backgrounds and interests." This is one reason that the

▲ **The Beckley, Singleton Building at 411 East Bonneville is home to the firm's Las Vegas offices.**

firm is considered by young lawyers to be a good place to work and to train for the profession.

The firm's attorneys are considered to be some of the best in the country. Drake De Lanoy, a nationally recognized litigator, is one of the state's top business attorneys. Rex Jemison is nationally recognized as one of Nevada's leading appellate lawyers. Mitch Cobeaga—"a litigator's litigator," says List—is a former fighter pilot and former president of the Clark County Bar Association. Robert Saint-Aubin, the head of the firm's natural resources unit, is an MIT-educated Philadelphia lawyer who relocated to

Nevada. List, in addition to having served as governor of Nevada, also served as Nevada attorney general and helped shape modern public policy and law in Nevada. List primarily represents a number of the largest companies in the world before both state and federal agencies, and maintains a broad-based administrative and commercial law practice.

Although List is a Republican, the

firm's political range is bipartisan. Firm alumni include Democrat U.S. Senator Harry Reid, now the senior United States Senator from Nevada, and Democrat Robert Miller, currently serving as governor of Nevada.

"We like to think that successful service to our clients has played an important role in the development of Nevada," says De Lanoy. "We're proud of that. We value the trust level that we have established over the years with our clientele, and we strive to create that same level of trust in our relationship with new clients. Law is, after all, a people business."

VARGAS & BARTLETT

As one of Nevada's oldest law firms, with a record of competency and integrity going back to the 1920s, Vargas & Bartlett is also one of the most modern law firms.

Its partners and associates over the years have included governors, state bar presidents, governors of the American Bar Association, and future casino executives. Its list of clients has included some of the most distinguished individual and corporate names in Nevada, such as Howard Hughes, William F. Harrah, Don Laughlin, Valley Bank of Nevada, Harrah's, and Showboat Casino.

Vargas & Bartlett was one of the first law firms to go statewide, with offices in both Reno and Las Vegas. It was also one of the state's first law firms to use computers.

Today Vargas & Bartlett is a full-service law firm with clients such as banks, insurance companies, oil and mining companies, casinos, developers, out-of-state corporations, and individuals. As Mead Dixon, a former senior partner and now of counsel to the firm, ob-

serves, "We know how to get things done in Nevada."

The firm's roots are in Elko, Nevada, a northern Nevada community known for mining and cattle ranching, where Milton Reinhart and Morley Griswold set up law practice in the 1920s. Shortly after Griswold was elected Nevada lieutenant governor in 1926, he opened the firm's first branch in Reno. Reelected in 1930, Griswold became the state's chief executive in 1934, upon the death of then Governor Balzar. That same year George Vargas became the firm's first associate.

After the retirement of Reinhart in the early 1940s, the firm closed its Elko

▲ Members of Vargas & Bartlett's Reno commercial department (from left): Linda A. Bowman, L. Mead Dixon (of counsel), and John P. Sande III.

◀ The firm's senior partners (back row): Albert F. Pagni and Frederic R. Starich, and (front row) Robert W. Marshall and John C. Renshaw. Together they bring 100 years of legal service to the firm.

▼ Las Vegas office partners (back row): Martha J. Ashcraft, Michael J. Bonner, and Mark A. Kemp, and (front row) Thomas F. Kummer, H. Gregory Nasky, and Christopher L. Kaempfer.

office, and George Vargas became a partner. He became sole partner upon the death of Griswold in 1951 and undertook to build the firm to what it is today.

John C. Bartlett was a young attorney when he faced Vargas in a jury trial in 1952. According to Vargas, after Bartlett soundly won the case, Vargas offered the winning Bartlett a position with the firm. Bartlett became a partner in 1953 and the firm became Griswold, Vargas & Bartlett. In 1962 John Bartlett was elected president of the State Bar Association, a position that was later held by two other partners, James P. Logan in 1975 and Albert F. Pagni in 1986.

Mead Dixon's long association with Vargas & Bartlett began in 1963, when he joined the firm as a partner along with Kenneth P. Dillon. "The firm was principally an insurance defense firm then," recalls Dixon.

Under the leadership and guidance of the partners of Vargas, Dillon, Bartlett

◀ **The First Interstate Tower is home to Vargas & Bartlett's Las Vegas office.**

rectly, Vargas & Bartlett's. "Harrah was guided by this own inner conviction—he always did what he thought he should do," says Dixon. "He was a guy who carried himself with class and believed that the needs of his customers came first. He helped us understand value-based decision making, rather than doing what might have been expedient at the moment."

As the firm grew and prospered, it realized that more of its time was devoted to servicing clients statewide and not just in the Reno area. "There was a change in Nevada," recalls Dixon. "Reno was the gateway to Nevada in the 1950s—the financial and business capital of the state. Later you could see that it was shifting to Las Vegas. We reasoned that a law firm could be well positioned if it were in both communities."

That was in 1972, and today almost all major Nevada law firms, following the footsteps of Vargas & Bartlett, maintain offices in both cities. In September 1989 the firm moved its quarters in Las Vegas to the First Interstate Tower on Hughes Parkway. Like the Reno office, the Las Vegas office handles a full range of legal services.

The firm's litigation has also broadened its emphasis. It now has a full-service litigation department, directed by partner John C. Renshaw, who works out of both Reno and Las Vegas. Litigation expertise includes aviation, professional liability, bonding, securities, insurance, construction, trademark and patent infringement, environmental, tax, and complex litigation. The firm also has an appellate department.

"Long years of integrity and competency are the key to the firm's success," observes the firm's managing partner, Albert F. Pagni. "That is the heritage of the firm. Our professional competency and integrity reflects in our ability to retain clients for years. As we learned from Bill Harrah, the needs of the client always come first. This is the philosophy of Vargas & Bartlett's approach to problems and cases."

& Dixon, the firm broadened its emphasis and became prominent in the fields of corporate, securities, real estate, mining, oil and gas, probate law, and litigation. Later Robert W. Marshall was to bring expertise in the field of utilities to the firm. The firm also, through George Vargas, developed expertise in the lobbying area, appearing regularly before Nevada's legislature and numerous state and local boards and agencies. This tradition of legislative advocacy has contin-

ued after the death of Vargas and is now headed by John Sande, with clients including major oil companies doing business in Nevada and the Nevada Bankers' Association.

William F. Harrah and his casino properties, doing business as Harrah's, were a few of the clients that Mead Dixon brought to Vargas & Bartlett when he joined the firm. Dixon credits Bill Harrah with shaping his philosophy and approach to problems, and so, indi-

McDonald, Carano, Wilson, McCune, Bergin, Frankovich and Hicks

Poised to tackle complex legal issues in a dynamic environment, the law firm of McDonald, Carano, Wilson, McCune, Bergin, Frankovich and Hicks has grown to more than 30 attorneys with offices in Reno and Las Vegas to better serve the needs of its clients in northern and southern Nevada.

The law firm was established in Reno in 1952 as Bible and McDonald by the late Alan Bible and Robert L. McDonald. In 1952 Bible was elected to the U.S. Senate, where he served for 20 years before returning to the firm in an of counsel role. Robert McDonald, a native Nevadan and former deputy U.S. attorney, continues as the firm's senior partner, providing his colleagues with the wisdom of long and hard-won experience.

McDonald, Carano's greatest strengths are the quality and diversity of its attorneys and their ability to work as a team. Its attorneys come from across the United States and represent a broad spectrum of backgrounds. Many McDonald, Carano attorneys have served as clerks for federal and state judges. Others have pursued careers in other fields, including education, accounting, and military service before practicing law.

The firm is committed to providing superior, timely, and economical legal services to its clients, developing new areas of expertise and integrating new technology into its practice.

The firm's rapidly expanding Las Vegas office was opened in 1986 by merger with the law firm of Boyd and Huff, whose principals remain of counsel to the firm. In early 1989 the firm moved its Las Vegas office into the new Security

Pacific Bank building, located at the corner of Rancho and West Sahara. Its Las Vegas office services the needs of the firm's southern Nevada clientele and their involvement in the unprecedented growth of the Las Vegas area.

While the firm's early years were devoted largely to a general business, corporate, trial, and gaming practice, the firm's practice covers a broad range of civil law.

Its corporate practice consists of assisting clients in major acquisitions and mergers, dissolutions, federal securities filings, formation and operation of corporations, and corporate litigation. The firm has served as associate counsel for Bally Manufacturing Company in its $500-million acquisition of MGM Hotels, Inc.; Holiday Corporation in its acquisition of Harrah's Corporation; the Boyd Group in its acquisition of the Stardust and Fremont hotels; Martin Sosnoff in an attempted acquisition of Caesars World, Inc.; and BATUS, Inc.,

in its takeover of Farmer's Insurance Group.

An inherent part of McDonald, Carano's practice is to serve all of the legal needs of large hotels and casinos in the areas of gaming and commercial matters. Many of the firm's corporate clients are involved in the gaming and hospitality industry, and the firm assists them in all facets of their business operations.

Representing clients in all types of civil litigation is an integral part of the firm's practice. The firm's litigation experience includes representation in disputes in the areas of construction, personal injury, landlord/tenant, real estate, wrongful discharge, lender liability, securities law, corporate takeovers, debt collection, and administrative law. The cases handled by the firm range from small lawsuits to complex multistate transactions. The firm also represents general contractors, developers, and landholders in both arbitration and litigation involving construction disputes.

McDonald, Carano represents clients in a wide variety of real estate transaction, including development of commercial and residential properties. Its work in these areas includes real estate-based financing, acquisition, sales, land use, project approvals, title matters, and foreclosures. It also has extensive experience before planning commissions and similar government agencies in obtaining zoning, plan approvals, and variances.

The probate and estate planning department advises individuals and institu-

▲ Founding partner Robert L. McDonald (third from left) with partners resident in the Reno office of the firm (left to right): Leo P. Bergin, Larry R. Hicks, Robert L. McDonald, Thomas R.C. "Spike" Wilson, William A.S. Magrath, John J. McCune, Robert E. Armstrong, John Frankovich, A.J. "Bud" Hicks, and Timothy Rowe. Absent from photo are Lenard T. Ormsby, Valerie Strandell, and Deborah Schumacher.

tions in a wide array of legal problems in probate, trust administration, and pre-postmortem tax planning. The firm has special experience in complex estates and multistate probates.

McDonald, Carano's tax practice represents clients in all aspects of federal and state taxation. The firm performs tax planning for individuals, partnerships, tax- exempt organizations, and corporations.

In its bankruptcy practice, the firm principally represents secured creditors and lessors in Chapter 11 reorganizations and liquidations, work-out arrangements, court-appointed creditors' committees, trustees, and debtors in possession. It also serves clients' business planning needs regarding the potential bankruptcies of third parties. The firm's clients utilizing the firm's bankruptcy counsel include institutional lenders, real property developers, manufacturers, and distributors.

To face the significant challenges in employee/employer relations, the firm's labor and employment practice encompasses litigation, administrative proceedings, and counseling of clients. It represents employers in all types of legal disputes, including wrongful discharge; age, sex, and race discrimination; workmen's and unemployment compensation; and claims arising from the employment relationship, including trade secret disputes. Firm attorneys have experience before state and federal agencies that regulate labor and employment, and regularly assist clients in the preparation of employment manuals in review of personnel problems and conduct seminars covering the hiring and discharge of employees.

As the firm encourages active participation of its lawyers in civic, professional, and political activities, partners of the firm have served on the state bar board of governors, as president of the Washoe County Bar Association, as Washoe County district attorney, and as Nevada state senator. They include a former chief deputy attorney general, two former assistant U.S. attorneys, the founding trustee and president of the International Association of Gaming Attorneys, the former chairman of the state bar's Section of Taxation, and the chairman of the American Bar Association's Gaming Law Committee. Many of the firm's attorneys donate substantial time to charitable causes and the representation of people with limited financial means.

McDonald, Carano is proud of its successful past. The firm also realizes that to continue to prosper, it must continue to adapt to the changing needs of its clients and maintain staffing, administration, and support services to provide superior service. The firm looks with confidence to the future and these challenges.

▼ The firm's Las Vegas resident lawyers (standing): Tom F. Twesme, Leslie A. Nielsen, Sean T. McGowan, and James W. Bradshaw. Sitting (left to right) are Robert W. Freeman, Sal C. Gugino, and T. Art Ritchie.

WOODBURN, WEDGE AND JEPPSON

Longevity and reputation are important factors to clients selecting legal representation. Nevada's oldest law firm, Woodburn, Wedge and Jeppson, has enjoyed a superior reputation for more than 80 years. Virgil H. Wedge, a senior partner, credits the firm's longevity and record of excellence for its present success.

Even before the formation of the firm, the name Woodburn was an important part of Nevada's early development. William Woodburn, father of the firm's founder, then residing in Virginia City, Nevada, served in the United States Congress in 1868 and again in 1872. In 1918 George Thatcher was winding up his term as Nevada attorney general and William Woodburn, Sr., was retiring as the Washoe County district attorney. Frank Norcross invited them to join him in law practice in Reno. Norcross was then chief attorney for banker George Wingfield, Sr., and the new firm of Thatcher and Woodburn opened offices in Wingfield's bank building, still standing at Second and Virginia streets.

Since its formation, the Reno-based firm has developed a strong corporate and business clientele, especially among mining and utilities companies—as be-

▲ Left to right: Kirk S. Schumacher, Charles A. Jeannes, and Roger W. Jeppson.

fits a pioneer Nevada law firm. Today, with 24 lawyers and a support staff of 26, Woodburn, Wedge provides full services for a wide variety of clients from its location in the top three floors of the First Interstate Bank Building in downtown Reno.

Though Woodburn, Wedge maintains a general law practice, its attorneys concentrate on litigation, corporate law, commercial law, real estate law, mining law, water law, environmental law, and public and private land-use law. The firm also has broad experience in administrative law, estate planning, probate, and tax law.

The firm is organized into various practice areas. Attorneys William E. Peterson, Suellen E. Fulstone, W. Chris Wicker, and Steven C. Malvey are the firm's principal litiga-

tors. The firm also has a special strength in natural resources and mining, occupying a three-attorney team almost full time: Roger W. Jeppson, Charles A. Jeannes, and Gregory V. Etter. Indicative of the team's practical knowledge, Etter worked as an exploration geologist for Exxon before going to law school and joining the firm.

Roger H. Elton and Michael E. Kearney are the foundation of the firm's tax division. James J. Halley is active in estate planning and health law. Halley is general counsel for Saint Mary's Regional Medical Center, a major regional health care provider.

Water law is the specialty of Gordon H. DePaoli who "knows more about water litigation than any other person in Nevada," according to senior partner Virgil Wedge. DePaoli is deeply involved in negotiations to reach a favorable compromise on use of Truckee River waters. The proposed compromise would resolve competing interests between the Paiute Indians trying to nurture hatcheries for the prehistoric cuiui

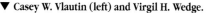

▼ Casey W. Vlautin (left) and Virgil H. Wedge.

▲ From left: **Gordon H. DePaoli, Patrick J. Joyce, Richard O. Kwapil, Jr., and G. David Robertson.**

and cutthroat trout and the cities of Reno and Sparks, which need water for new growth.

The firm's litigation excellence is evidenced by the number of former members who have gone to serve in the judiciary. After founding the firm, Frank Norcross served 18 years as a United States District Judge for the District of Nevada. Proctor Hug, Jr., was appointed by President Jimmy Carter to the Ninth Circuit Court of Appeals in 1977. Gordon R. Thompson was appointed to the Nevada Supreme Court in 1961 and served two terms as the state's chief justice before retiring. And in 1974 William N. Forman was appointed to the state district court, the trial court of general jurisdiction in Nevada, and has since been reelected three times.

Despite its deep Nevada roots, Woodburn, Wedge tries to recruit the best young attorneys from law schools all over America to carry on its reputation for excellence. That's one of the firm's cornerstones for success, according to Wedge. "Such diversity gives our attorneys contacts everywhere," he explains. "Often our attorneys will receive referrals from old classmates across the country for clients that need matters handled in Nevada. Conversely, this informal national affiliation allows our Nevada clients to have a national representation."

Longevity and reputation are other cornerstones, says Wedge, adding, "I frequently get calls from people who select us because their people did business with the firm's partners years ago. That continuity is important."

"A final test of a law firm is the quality of clients it repre- sents," says Wedge. The firm's nationwide base of clients includes Ford Motor Company, Chrysler Corporation, IBM, Atlantic Richfield, Donrey Media Group, Freeport Minerals Company, Cyprus Minerals Company, Nevada Bell, Sierra Pacific Power Company and its Westpac subsidiary, Western Union Telegraph Company, the Prudential Insurance Company, and many others.

Woodburn, Wedge is one of the few private law firms ever retained to represent the United States Air Force. The firm assisted the Air Force in acquiring necessary water rights for its MX Missile project, which was later abandoned. The firm also advised the Air Force on Nevada's environmental, water, and land-use laws.

Woodburn, Wedge has the largest law firm in Reno. "After 1980 other firms began hiring and growing until several have approached our size," recalls Wedge. "We have grown, too, but we select out attorneys and our clients carefully. We wanted to grow with quality people for quality clients. Any young lawyer can develop a very busy practice in a very short time—but that's not quality." Managing partner Casey Woodburn Vlautin adds, "Our lawyers have a great sense of pride in their work and a great disdain for failure. Our lawyers strive to turn out the best work possible and that drives everybody here pretty hard."

▼ Standing are **Lynne K. Jones and Michael E. Kearney. Seated from left are John F. Murtha and Shawn B Meador.**

CROWELL, SUSICH, OWEN & TACKES, LTD.

The law firm of Crowell, Susich, Owen & Tackes, Ltd., proudly traces its origin to William J. Crowell, Sr., its founder, who began practicing law in 1937 at Tonopah in central Nevada, then the hub of the Silver State's growing mining industry.

In 1950 the firm was relocated to Carson City, the center of state government and economic development, where Crowell was joined by his sons, William Jr. and Robert, and later by the other present members. William J. Crowell, Sr., died in July 1988, having practiced law for more than 50 years.

Crowell, Susich, Owen & Tackes,

Ltd., continues a tradition of excellence by providing the highest caliber of representation to a diverse client base. Various members of the firm are admitted to practice in the U.S. Supreme Court, the U.S. Tax Court, and other federal and district appellate courts, as well as before the highest state courts in Nevada, California, Arizona, Utah, and Washington. Experienced trial and appellate attorneys, they pride themselves on their aggressive approach and negotiating skills essential to solving the complex legal problems encountered by clients throughout Nevada and around the country.

Serving the corporate community, the firm provides representation in the formation of corporations, as well as their consolidations, mergers, and dissolutions. With the help of an exceptional support staff, the firm acts as resident agent for a long list of clients who have taken advantage of Nevada's favorable incorporation and tax laws.

In addition, members of the firm have in-depth skills in the areas of water and mineral rights and environmental law—key issues in Nevada. Appointed by the Nevada governor, Robert Crowell serves as chairman of the Colorado River Commission, which allocates the waters of the Colorado River for use in Nevada. Gary Owen is litigation counsel for the Tahoe Regional Planning Agency.

Crowell, Susich, Owen & Tackes, Ltd., is highly involved in governmental affairs, even in the highly specialized fields of regulating utilities and obtaining certificates of public convenience. The firm has represented a variety of state agencies, including the State Industrial Insurance System, the Nevada Industrial Commission, and the Employment Security Department. The firm also lobbies before the state legislature on behalf of a number of clients, including Anheuser-Busch and Farmers Insurance Group of Companies. A captain in the U.S. Naval Reserve, Robert Crowell also serves as naval aide to the Nevada governor.

Members of the firm have successfully represented clients in matters of real estate law, estate planning and administration, personal injury, domestic relations, and criminal law.

Clients include Omneco, Inc., a division of Morton Thiokol; the Nevada Motor Transport Association; the Las Vegas Transit System; Gray Line Tours of Southern Nevada; the Utility Shareholders Association of Nevada; MCI Telecommunications, Inc.; the Tahoe Regional Planning Agency; and Idaho Power Co. (Nevada).

◀ From their Carson City headquarters, the attorneys and staff of Crowell, Susich, Owen & Tackes maintain a tradition of excellence.

KEEFER, O'REILLY, FERRARIO & ESKIN

▲ Left to Right: Mark E. Ferrario, Jeffrey L. Eskin, Milton W. Keefer, and John F. O'Reilly.

Keefer, O'Reilly, Ferrario & Eskin has a reputation for thorough, complete, and aggressive legal representation. The firm provides a full range of legal services for its roster of clients, which include many successful businesses and individuals whose problems have ranged from multimillion-dollar complex litigation, real estate, and other legal matters to less complicated legal problems.

The background and experience of the members of the firm enable Keefer, O'Reilly, Ferrario & Eskin to be effective, creative, and economical in the delivery of legal services. It is because of these characteristics that the firm has been retained by some of the largest corporations in the state, as well as thousands of individuals through the years.

The firm's practice includes all litigation matters, civil and criminal, and virtually all other areas of the law, including, for example, corporate, business, bankruptcy, real property, entertainment, personal injury, administrative, labor, construction, commercial, contract, family, probate, insurance defense, and other insurance-related representation.

The collective experience of the attorneys in the firm includes service as judge, accountant in the tax and audit fields with international certified public accounting firms, agent with the Federal

Bureau of Investigation, real estate broker, licensed contractor, special prosecutor for the state of Nevada, general counsel to U.S. Senate campaign, editor, bar association president, educator, instructor, hearing officers, member of the Local Government Employee-Management Relations Board, district attorney, deputy attorney general, and adviser to gubernatorial candidates.

In addition, two of the firm's members, Milton W. Keefer and John F. O'Reilly, have been appointed by governors of the state of Nevada to serve as chairmen of the Nevada Gaming Commission. The experience of the firm's members with the Nevada Gaming Commission dates back to the year in which the commission was formed and continues actively through the present day. Members of the firm have served in various other capacities at the request of the governors of the state of Nevada and have been associated with various agencies of the state government.

The educational backgrounds of the members of the firm as well as their work experience have enabled the firm to develop a statewide and worldwide network of contacts to assist in provid-

ing services to clients. The firm's attorneys have attended universities located on the East Coast, including Washington D.C.; on the West Coast, including the Los Angeles area; the South, including Atlanta; the Midwest, including Chicago and St. Louis; and the Southwest, as well as other areas throughout the country. Their degrees include juris doctor degrees in law and master's degrees in business administration, as well as degrees in accounting. Members and associates have attended prestigious universities, and have received academic honors and accolades that, when combined with the firm's legal successes, explain why, in addition to its other clients, many fellow attorneys have turned to the firm for representation and legal services.

The philosophy of Keefer, O'Reilly, Ferrario & Eskin is to provide tight case management, close client contact, and the ability to serve virtually all of its clients' legal needs. The firm has provided effective legal representation through its principals and its staff of attorneys, paralegals, and secretaries for many years. As the state of Nevada continues to experience unprecedented growth, Keefer, O'Reilly, Ferrario & Eskin looks forward to providing quality legal service in an aggressive manner for years to come.

ALLISON, MACKENZIE, HARTMAN, SOUMBENIOTIS & RUSSELL, LTD.

Walk in to the Carson City law offices of Allison, MacKenzie, Hartman, Soumbeniotis & Russell, Ltd., and immediately one sees a display of Nevada memorabilia—from the mines and early railroads of the nearby Comstock to the political history of this state capital. The firm's deep roots in Nevada are not only represented in the office foyer but in the firm's members.

George Allison, a native Nevadan and the most senior of the firm's shareholders, is conscious of the firm's strong ties to both Nevada and the state capital. James T. "Todd" Russell recalls growing up in the nearby governor's mansion as the son of former Governor Charles Russell. Other partners hail from Nevada's broad expanse and from old-line Nevada families: Andrew MacKenzie from Yerington, Steve Hartman from Las Vegas, Mike Soumbeniotis and Mike Pavlakis from

▲ The firm's eight partners are (from left): Stephen D. Hartman, Patrick V. Fagan, Joan C. Wright, James T. Russell, Andrew MacKenzie, George V. Allison, Mike Soumbeniotis, and Mike Pavlakis.

Ely, and Pat Fagan from Reno. Only one of the firm's real estate partners, Joan Wright, hails from a neighboring state and a long family line of attorneys, but after a decade her roots are firmly in Nevada.

Even the land occupied by the firm's distinctive two-story, Spanish-style headquarters building, which occupies most of a block in Carson City, is rich in this capital city's heritage, in that it was formerly the site of a historic church and a 100-year-old boardinghouse.

The firm is very proud of the accomplishments of its former members, such as former United States Senator Paul

Laxalt, United States Ninth Circuit Court of Appeals Judge Melvin Brunetti, and former Interstate Commerce Commission chairman Reese Taylor.

The firm is what the shareholders modestly refer to as a very traditional, business-oriented firm, with substantial involvement in both local and state government, in addition to the general practice needs of the firm's clients. The firm provides its clients with a diversity of legal experience not customary in moderate-size firms. Though the firm's office is in Carson City, its work ranges from one end of the state to the other—and, indeed, across the country. Its clients include substantial corporate firms, insurance companies, gaming establishments, major project developers, public utilities, trucking firms, and regulatory agencies.

The firm handles litigation and administrative hearings throughout Nevada in both the state and federal legal and administrative systems.

In addition to providing general legal work, which includes estate planning, state agency and regulatory work, and insurance defense, Allison, MacKenzie attorneys, as registered lobbyists, represent various clients before the state legislature and interim committees. The firm has represented various development projects and has helped draft state laws and regulations governing interval resort projects and membership campground projects. Members of the firm have also participated in drafting state regulations governing trucking, public utilities, municipal incorporation, geothermal exploration, Nevada's unclaimed property act, and myriad other matters involving state regulation.

The firm has been involved in a number of large projects throughout northern Nevada. A major interval resort development in Lake Tahoe has involved the firm in land-use planning, development, and other legal representation over the past several years. Another is a proposed ski resort and hotel-casino project with commercial and multifamily residential development that is planned for a site near Mount Rose, high above Reno and Lake Tahoe. Yet another new development project involving the firm's expertise features nearly 1,000 residential units, an Arnold Palmer-designed golf course, and business and industrial parks adjacent to the project's general aviation airport in Dayton, Nevada.

The firm's members are actively involved in professional and other organizations in their community. Attorneys within the firm hold or have held positions on the state judicial selection committee, the state board of bar examiners, the state continuing legal education committee, the state practice and procedure committee, disciplinary committee, local bar administrative and fee dispute committee, and executive counsel of the young lawyers section of the state bar. Members of the firm serve or have served on the Carson City Redevelopment Authority, Historical Architectural Review Committee, the Carson City Airport Advisory Committee,

▶ Formerly the site of a historic church and a century-old boardinghouse, the two-story headquarters of Allison, MacKenzie, Hartman, Soumbeniotis & Russell, Ltd., occupies almost a whole Carson City block.

▼ The firm's partners and associates pose at the company headquarters. They are (from left) Karen A. Peterson, Patrick V. Fagan, David R. Lloyd, James T. Russell, Joan C. Wright, Stanley J. Steiber, Stephen D. Hartman, Mike Pavlakis, Mark E. Amodei, George V. Allison, Mike Soumbeniotis, Andrew MacKenzie, and Thomas J. Ray.

Saferide, Rotary, Masonic Lodge, Special Olympics, Soroptomists, Carson Water Management Board, Carson City Childrens Museum, and a variety of other charitable and community-involved programs. The firm is involved in the state and the community, and through that involvement it has the pulse of northern Nevada and the state capital.

The firm serves a relatively large number of clients without sacrificing the personal relationship of attorney and client with its present complement of 14 lawyers. There is little turnover in attorneys, Allison says, because of the firm's "family feeling and the quality of both the attorneys and staff we have. That is important not only for the firm,

but also provides the stability most clients are looking for. We are very selective when bringing in new associates," he explains. "We look for people who aren't afraid to earn their credentials through hard work and who are willing to spend time learning the practice of law. We couldn't serve our clients very well if we hired individuals who are not philosophically compatible and dedicated to hard work."

Allison, MacKenzie, Hartman, Soumbeniotis & Russell, Ltd., is looking forward to a period of continued growth in the economy of the state of Nevada, and will be prepared to address the challenges of the coming years by continuing to grow to meet the needs of its clients.

JONES, JONES, CLOSE & BROWN

One of the oldest and most respected law firms in Nevada, Jones, Jones, Close & Brown serves clients having a challenge requiring intimate knowledge of the law as well as the state and how it works. The firm's problem-solving approach to the law has been winning repeat clients since 1938.

The firm's four original partners are still practicing law. Clifford and Herbert Jones came to Nevada from their native Missouri in the early 1930s to work on the construction of Boulder Dam. Cliff Jones, one of five lawyers admitted to the bar in 1938, opened an office in tiny Las Vegas that same year. Shortly after World War II he was joined by his brother, Herb. Mergers with Melvin Close and his partners and with Joseph W. Brown and his partners in the early 1970s produced the present firm.

Members of the firm have distinguished themselves in Nevada affairs. Cliff Jones is a former district court judge, a former majority leader of the state assembly, and a lieutenant governor.

Herb Jones, a former state senator, has served as deputy district attorney, president of the Clark County Bar Association, and president of the State Bar of Nevada.

Melvin Close spent many years in the state legislature and served as both speaker of the assembly and president

▲ The firm's stockholders: (seated from left) Clifford A. Jones, Herbert M. Jones, Melvin D. Close, Jr., Joseph W. Brown, (standing from left) J. Randall Jones, Janet L. Chubb, Richard F. Jost, Michael E. Buckley, Kirk R. Harrison, Gary R. Goodheart, Charles H. McCrea, Sr., and Douglas G. Crosby. Not pictured: Will Kemp and William A. Prezant.

▶ The firm's Las Vegas office is located in the city's premier high-rise office building, which is also the headquarters for Nevada's largest state-chartered bank. Valley Bank of Nevada has been a client of Jones, Jones, Close & Brown since 1954, when Herbert M. Jones and other community business leaders obtained a charter for the bank.

pro tem of the senate. He serves as chairman of the State Environmental Commission.

Joseph Brown was appointed by President Ronald Reagan to the State Justice Institute, of which he is presently a member. He also served during the Reagan Administration as a member of the U.S. Foreign Claims Settlement Commission. He recently completed a two-year term as chairman of the Nevada Development Authority, an organization devoted to attracting new businesses to southern Nevada.

With approximately 35 attorneys and

a staff of almost 80, Jones, Jones, Close & Brown has offices in both Las Vegas and Reno. Because of its size the firm can offer its clients areas of specialization not available in smaller firms—an advantage for attorneys who can become experts in a particular field of law and an advantage for clients needing the assistance of an experienced and highly capable legal team.

◀ Members of Jones, Jones, Close & Brown's Reno office (from left): Janet L. Chubb, Richard F. Holley, Brian E. Holthus, and (seated) William A. Prezant.

▲ Attorneys Kirk B. Lenhard and Mary Kay Sinicki review a case.

The firm's practice is divided among five basic departments: Litigation; Real Estate, Commercial, and Banking; Administrative; Probate and Estate Planning; and Municipal Finance.

The attorneys in the Litigation Department routinely participate in complex business-related litigation. In addition to its business litigation, the firm also has an active personal injury practice. Jones, Jones was one of the leading firms representing claimants in the litigation arising from the MGM Grand Hotel fire in Las Vegas. The firm currently participates as a member of the Plaintiffs' Steering Committee on behalf of claimants in the Du Pont Plaza Hotel fire litigation in Puerto Rico.

Lawyers assigned to the Commercial, Real Estate, and Banking Department represent a wide variety of corporate, partnership, and individual clients in sophisticated business transactions. The firm does work for two of the largest banks in the state, Valley Bank of Nevada and First Interstate Bank, both major lenders playing significant roles in the state's rapidly growing economy.

Jones, Jones' administrative lawyers routinely practice before the state gaming agencies, local planning and zoning boards, the Public Service Commission of Nevada, and other administrative agencies. The firm also appears on behalf of clients at the biennial sessions of the state legislature.

Jones, Jones was the first Nevada law firm to qualify for listing as recognized municipal bond attorneys in the *Directory of Municipal Bond Dealers of the United States* (the "Red Book"). The firm's municipal bond lawyers have represented a variety of state and local agencies as both bond counsel and issuer's counsel as well as serving as underwriter's counsel in numerous municipal bond issues.

Nevada is one of the nation's fastest growing states, and Jones, Jones, Close & Brown is committed to being a part of that growth. The firm annually recruits at some of the nation's leading law schools for the purpose of expanding the firm with graduates who have demonstrated superior academic and extracurricular achievement. The firm has an active summer associate program in which second-year law students spend approximately three months clerking for the firm. Many of the firm's attorneys are products of the summer associate program.

Jones, Jones, Close & Brown has a strong tradition of community service, providing free legal assistance for needy clients and nonprofit organizations. The firm regularly helps organizations such as The Nature Conservancy, the United Way, Boys and Girls Clubs, the YMCA, and HELP of Southern Nevada. Individual attorneys have served on the boards of various organizations such as the Nevada Taxpayers Association and the Desert Research Institute. "My partners and I have always been sensitive to the need to give something back to the community that has been so good to us," says Gary Goodheart, the firm's managing partner.

Herb Jones attributes the success of the firm to "our ability to work effectively together for the benefit of our clients." As he looks out over Las Vegas from the firm's offices in the Valley Bank Plaza, Jones admits that he never thought either the city or the firm would be so successful—or so big. "Our greatest contribution to the growth of this city has been the practice of law with integrity."

.12.

FROM THE GROUND UP

◆◆◆◆

Spectacular resorts and casinos,
sleek industrial and office parks,
and quality housing—developers,
architectural engineers, and
construction companies are all
making it happen in Nevada.

◆◆◆◆

Photo by
Toby Rankin/Masterfile

DERMODY PROPERTIES

Reno's quality of life reflects the quality of service given to its customers by Dermody Properties, a full-service, turnkey development company with 8 million square feet of industrial space and 1,000 acres of developable land in its inventory.

Living in a recreational paradise that includes Lake Tahoe, Reno residents celebrate their vast opportunities to ski, hike, boat, hunt, fish, raft, golf, and play tennis. Clean air, outstanding schools, premier cultural offerings and good neighbors attract and keep an energetic and skilled work force committed to the community.

Reno's location at the hub of the West's best transportation system gives easy access to goods and markets worldwide and helps to explain why Nevada's second-largest city leads the state in industrial development.

Another part of the explanation is the top priority given to service and customer satisfaction practiced by Dermody Properties. "In an attempt to better serve our clients, we continually research our products and constantly review our approach to not only construction but also landlord/tenant management. By constantly striving to improve our product, we hope that we provide the best service possible to our customers," says Michael C. Dermody, the company's president.

Dermody Properties' business is divided into three categories: building and renting retail space such as Airport Square, developing service-oriented warehouse facilities, and building and leasing customized structures for national and international companies such as RCA Records, Sherwin-Williams Paint Co., US Air, Thomas & Betts Co., Boehringer Ingelheim Co., and Shinko Micronics.

Dermody Properties serves these customers with innovative designs and pioneering technology. One innovative Dermody design is a 100,000-square-foot circular building in Dermody Air Center that separates industrial loading docks from office and customer entrances,

▶ **The headquarters of Dermody Properties is located in Dermody Business Park, a 200-acre development in Reno.**

◀ Dermody Air Center, situated on a 187-acre site, is linked with one of the West's best highway, rail, and transportation networks adjacent to Reno Cannon International Airport, with direct taxiway access. Courtesy, Davis Visual Communications

▼ A unique multi-tenant building at 4790 Longley Lane is part of the expansive Dermody Air Center. Photo by Valerie Clark

thereby providing each of the building's several tenants their own windows.

In the 1960s Dermody Properties pioneered concrete tilt-up construction and brought the first New York Stock Exchange company—Bigelow Sanford Carpet Company—to northern Nevada.

In the 1970s Dermody Properties was among the first developers to incorporate energy-saving techniques such as radiant heat, sodium vapor lights, and dual-pane windows. By creating alignments with support companies, Dermody Properties worked toward a more efficient growth plan. Dermody Properties' partners in progress are United Construction Co., Inc., D&D Contractors, Ponderosa Wholesale, and Gallagher Sheet Metal.

In the 1980s many companies used Dermody Properties' unique customer-service program and enabled the firm to gain national recognition as one of the top 100 development companies in America. For example, S.T. Imaging Technology, a domestic Japanese manufacturer, built its North American headquarters in Reno because of Dermody Properties' complete customer-service package. S.T. Imaging Technology moved into its 58,000-square-foot building four short months after ground breaking.

In the 1990s Dermody Properties will service its growing customer base by opening a new Las Vegas office, by developing the second phase of Dermody Business Park in Reno, and by expanding into other areas of the country: a 140,000-foot facility for Certified Grocery Co. in Fresno, California, and a 300,000-foot building for Sherwin-Williams Paint Co. in Atlanta, Georgia.

Dermody Business Park, which provides space for office, manufacturing, and service companies, is Nevada's first to include a child-care facility and a private one-acre park to serve the people who work there.

Dermody Properties believes in meeting the social needs of the people and communities where it operates. It has created Dermody Properties Foundation devoted to education, children, and the elderly. Dermody Properties' president is also founder and chairman of the Children's Cabinet, a nonprofit organization that coordinates community services available to children and families.

Dermody Properties' growth has been consistent from its 1949 founding to its 1989 position as the nation's 81st-largest developer.

Michael Dermody is quick to give credit for his company's growth to his staff. "What makes this company grow and prosper is the foresight of my father and the dedication and efforts of the people at Dermody Properties," he says. "We expect Nevada to continue its position as the fastest-growing state. And we would hope to have our business support that growth while maintaining the same good quality of life that we enjoy in our state."

▼ The Reno-Sparks Foreign Trade Zone, located on a 23-acre site, is part of Dermody Properties' 8-million-square-foot roster of industrial properties. Photo by Valerie Clark

SEA CONSULTING ENGINEERS, INCORPORATED

Sparks was just a little railroad town next door to Reno when the firm that was to become SEA Consulting Engineers, Incorporated, opened there in 1958. As Sparks grew to become an important partner in the Reno metropolitan area, SEA became one of Nevada's largest design and engineering firms.

SEA was an important factor in Sparks' growth: The firm designed most of the town's new subdivisions, did site engineering for many of its new companies, and designed the infrastructure to support those facilities.

Indeed, SEA has participated in the growth of cities all over Nevada. For example: SEA supervised site selection, planning, and construction of the sprawling JCPenney Distribution Center at Stead—one of the largest warehouses under a single roof west of the Mississippi, enclosing 43 acres. SEA laid out the original boundaries of the University of Nevada campus in Las Vegas. SEA has planned and engineered most of the Reno area's other giant warehouses and distribution centers for S.S. Kresge's, General Motors, Thrifty Drug, and many others. SEA planned the Highland Industrial Park in Las Vegas, as well as other industrial, commercial, and residential facilities.

Recently, SEA performed traffic studies for major Las Vegas projects, such as the Excaliber and Mirage, slated to be two of the world's largest casino-hotels.

With full-time offices in Las Vegas and Phoenix, Sparks-based SEA is one of the Nevada companies in *Engineering News-Record*'s listing of the nation's top 500 design firms, an honor it has had since 1976. The organization's new 9,500-square-foot Las Vegas office building is in the Hughes Industrial Park.
SEA's partners have been with the firm since the early 1960s: Ronald D. Byrd, Joe W. Howard, Harry R. Ericson, Steven G. Argyris, and Richard W. Arden, who is president. Also on SEA's board of directors are Larry Johnson and Mike Koizumi, manager of the Las

Vegas office.

With its computers and state-of-the-art laboratories, SEA produces soil profiles and other engineering studies, does advanced design work to match the soil conditions it finds, and tests material used by construction firms to make sure specifications are met.

SEA is involved in more than 1,000 projects each year, varying in size from several hundred dollars to millions of dollars in value. They include water and irrigation projects, feasibility studies, utilities, all kinds of surveys, urban and regional planning, environmental impact studies, soil and foundation investigations, computer studies, and construction inspection.

The firm takes a team approach to its projects. For each project a multidisciplined team is assembled—civil engineers, hydrologists, surveyors, geologists,

▲ An arterial highway and residential development in southern Nevada typifies SEA's design excellence.

planners, construction services, and more—whatever skills are needed for the project. Key people stay with the team until a project is completed.

"This gives our clients the best end product possible," says SEA Consulting Engineers' president, Arden, "an insurance for continuity and quality control."

▶ A large-scale commercial, industrial, and residential development in northern Nevada illustrates SEA's diversity.

KITTRELL GARLOCK AND ASSOCIATES, ARCHITECTS, AIA

▲ Kittrell Garlock and Associates has promoted its endeavors into public architecture with the completion of McCarran International Airport's existing terminal remodeling and expansion (the "McCarran 2000" project).

"There are two causes of beauty— natural and customary. Natural is from geometry consisting in uniformity, that is equality and proportion. Customary beauty is begotten by the use, as familiarity breeds a love for things not in themselves lovely." —Sir Christopher Wren, *Parentalia*

Architecture is a continuing exploration of the expression of man in time and place. Its expression is perceived as a search for beauty, and beauty, as Sir Christopher Wren writes, is twofold. These essential ideas are fundamental to the current architecture of Las Vegas.

For decades the architecture of Las Vegas revolved around the casino-lined street affectionately known as "The Strip." Indeed this single road is the image of Las Vegas found in the minds of most people; the glitzy stagefronts that led Robert Venturi to pronounce it the "decorated shed" epitomized Las Vegas architecture. It is ironic that the

▲ Taking an active part in the marriage of Las Vegas' past with its future, the new Downtown Transportation Facility is an integral link in the area's mass transit system. Its architectural expression creates a link to the neighboring historic structures.

majority of those early buildings are the works of architects who are not from Nevada. Today in Las Vegas local architects are designing new casinos with an understanding of their context and the people who use them. With this under-

standing a new, mature language of expression has evolved, one that is truly Las Vegas.

Away from the ever-growing casino boulevards, the urban dialectic that faces most cities is being addressed. Leading in this area of development is the creation of university buildings and civic structures with careful attention to local climatic and historic considerations, in addition to formal and aesthetic concerns.

Since 1980 Kittrell Garlock and Associates, Architects, AIA, has proudly assumed its place in the progressing architectual community by playing an active role in the development of Las Vegas, with an emphasis on the pursuit of a new architecture for Nevada.

▶ From assisting in the master planning of the University of Nevada, Las Vegas, to designing the Howard R. Hughes School of Engineering and the new College of Health Sciences, the firm focuses on centers of education in Las Vegas.

SUMMA CORPORATION

Buying up casinos, airlines, television stations, mining claims, and almost anything else that came his way, Howard Hughes had a greater impact on southern Nevada than any other person in the last half of the twentieth century. Hughes, a perennial visionary, bought land as eagerly as he bought companies. As a result, he "cast the die" for a new progressive Las Vegas, which is being recognized as one of this country's urban centers of the future.

Located on property acquired by Hughes are a master-planned community projected to house almost a quarter-million southern Nevadans, a corporate center planned to provide more than 1.5 million square feet of prime office space, Las Vegas' premier business and industrial park adjacent to McCarran International Airport, the leading retail center in Las Vegas, and other impressive real estate developments. Hughes' influence extends into Southern California, where the upscale Howard Hughes Center and Playa Vista properties are being developed into two of the finest mixed-use environments in the country.

Making these projects happen is Summa Corporation and its primary operating arm, Howard Hughes Properties. Summa is a far cry from the company Hughes nurtured until his death in 1976. Gone is the vast array of casinos, airlines, TV stations, manufacturing operations, and other businesses throughout Nevada and other western states that were part of the Hughes estate. Now focused entirely on real estate activities, Summa is rapidly becoming one of the largest real estate investment and development companies in America. And today Summa is reorganized to meet the challenges of the twenty-first century.

Managed by a team of talented real estate professionals, Summa is well positioned to be a leader, in Nevada and Southern California, in planning and creating a new standard for real estate development.

The new Summerlin community is more than just another real estate development. It is a new community—a new town and a new way of life. Given the family name of Hughes' grandmother, Summerlin is a real estate development for the twenty-first century, incorporating the best in planning, design, and construction, resulting in an unparalleled environment for living. The 25,000-acre property stretches northwest from Las Vegas to the foot of the Red Rock Mountains. Master planned to be developed in phases over the next 40 to 50 years, Summerlin will contain almost 85,000 single and multifamily homes. It also will be a setting for landmark office parks, major retail centers, and outstanding educational, civic, and cultural facilities. The residents also will be able to enjoy its many community centers, parks, and golf courses.

Summerlin is planned as a group of 30 villages organized around a central business core, The Town Center. Each village will be distinctive—some primary commercial, some residential, oth-

▼ Playa Vista conveys a powerful presence in the Los Angeles area, close to Marina del Rey and all major transportation networks.

▶ The Howard Hughes Center in West Los Angeles has attracted many high-profile tenants, including the computer giant Wang, whose distinctive Wang Tower, adjacent to the San Diego Freeway catches the eyes of thousands of motorists every day.

▼ Located in the heart of Las Vegas, Hughes Center features an oasis landscape and highlights the First Interstate Tower, home to Summa's executive offices.

ers mixed use. Housing will range from starter homes and apartments to town houses, deluxe golf-course condominiums, and executive estates. Protective restrictions ensure the master plan will be followed faithfully and the quality of development maintained.

Balanced land use will be achieved at Summerlin, with a significant percentage of the land reserved for open space. Residential neighborhoods, schools, recreational amenities, and retail centers are being connected with a community-wide system of parks and trails.

The first village developed is Del E. Webb's Sun City Summerlin, a new international prototype for successful, active adult communities. The first phase of Sun City will house 5,600 residents in 3,100 homes situated around a champi-

onship golf course and a major recreation center.

Another village at Summerlin will have a destination resort with its own dedicated golf course. Each village will be a real neighborhood with an image of its own.

A feature that will draw national attention to Summerlin is southern Nevada's only Tournament Players Club, a 36-hole complex that features a stadium golf course and clubhouse where PGA pros, as well as club members, will play. The stadium concept uses natural amphitheaters and earthen mounds to provide tournament-goers better views of the play.

In an innovative move to preserve the area's natural desert habitat and unique scenery and protect its wildlife,

Summa gave the Bureau of Land Management more than 5,000 acres on Summerlin's western edge to be added to the Red Rock Canyon National Recreation area. In return, Summa received a smaller parcel of BLM land adjacent to another portion of Summerlin. This exchange ensures that urban development will not mar the beauty of the Red Rock Canyon area. This illustrates that public and private interests can work together effectively to realize conservation goals while fostering economic growth.

Concern for the human environment also is present in all master planning. Summerlin's master plan projects acreage for recreation centers, libraries, churches and synagogues, health care centers, fire and police stations, and arts and cultural facilities. Schools are sited close to open spaces to buffer them from high-traffic areas. One of Summerlin's first developments was the Meadows School, a private, college-preparatory school on a campus donated by Summa. The Hebrew Academy, another private school, is also on a Summa-donated Summerlin campus.

Bringing Summerlin only 10 minutes from downtown Las Vegas is the high-speed Summerlin Parkway, leading from southern Nevada's first three-level interchange on Interstate 95 into the heart of the community. The four-lane, limited-access parkway developed by Summa, landscaped with shrubs, groves of mesquite, palo verde, and other desert varieties, is a visitor's first view of Summerlin.

East of Summerlin, in the heart of Las Vegas, lies Hughes Center. The unique location of Hughes Center, a 120-acre site at Paradise and Flamingo roads, central to the Strip, downtown, and McCarran International Airport, makes it ideal as the new central business district of Las Vegas.

Hughes Center is anchored by the

◀ Del Webb's Sun City Summerlin, a new international prototype community geared toward active adults, boasts 3,100 homes situated around a championship golf course and a major recreation center.

First Interstate Tower, which also houses the executive offices of Summa Corporation. The elegant 18-story granite building is a landmark in the glittering Las Vegas skyline. Tenants include many of the leading corporations and professional firms in the region. When completed, Hughes Center will include at least eight office buildings with 1.5 to 2 million square feet of space, plus restaurants, apartments, hotels, and service amenities. The grounds, with palm trees and shrubs, are planned to project the image of an oasis in the Las Vegas desert setting. A unique work environment with growth potential is a key to attract business and industry.

In Hughes Center, which is the business address of Las Vegas, Summa saw

● The 350-acre Hughes Airport Center, a master-planned business and industrial park, is strategically located near McCarran International Airport, an on-site rail line, Interstate 15, a foreign trade zone, and a regional post office distribution facility.

an opportunity to develop a planned, mixed-use environment that appeals to a broad segment of the market, far superior to the existing downtown area, a mixture of casinos, government, and offices. Its central location, proximity to McCarran International Airport, the size of the property, and excellent access create the opportunity for a truly master-planned central business district.

Within minutes of Hughes Center is Hughes Airport Center, a 350-acre master-planned business and industrial park. Located adjacent of McCarran International Airport, Hughes Airport Center is at a transportation crossroads with an on-site rail line and convenient

▲ A shopping mecca for residents and tourists alike, the Fashion Show Mall is home to Neiman Marcus, Saks Fifth Avenue, Bullock's, Dillards, and May Co.

◄ Park 2000, located to the east of McCarran International Airport, is a deluxe 118-acre mixed-use development.

roadway access to Interstate 15, the principal artery from Southern California to Salt Lake City. The center includes a 25-acre foreign trade zone and a regional U.S. Postal Service distribution facility. When completed, around the turn of the century, the center will provide 4.5 million square feet of office and research facilities, light industrial, and warehouse space.

Hughes Airport Center is tailored for a variety of users, including scientific engineering/research, warehousing/distribution, light manufacturing, and other diversified uses. Similar to other Summa developments, strong landscape features, proper planning, and attention to

details have made Hughes Airport Center the standard for industrial and office developments in Las Vegas. It also has been the choice location for companies relocating from various areas in the country because of the quality of environment provided.

Other Summa projects in Nevada include the 820,000-square-foot Fashion Show Mall and Park 2000, a mixed-use center on 118 acres located east of McCarran International Airport.

The Fashion Show Mall is a nationally acclaimed regional shopping center that is a landmark on the Las Vegas Strip. The enclosed mall, a joint venture with Earnest W. Hahn, Inc., is on a 33-acre site at the corner of Spring Mountain Road and Las Vegas Boulevard. Its major tenants are Neiman Marcus, Saks Fifth Avenue, Bullock's, Dillards, and May Co.

North of the Fashion Show Mall on the Strip, HHP made the decision to lease vacant land and encourage the development of Wet n' Wild as a continuing effort to create more family-based entertainment in Las Vegas.

In California, Summa is developing Playa Vista with Maguire Thomas Partners and JMB Realty. It is a 957-acre mixed-use community in West Los Angeles on one of the largest and most valuable parcels of real estate in an urban setting. This impressive property extends from the Pacific Ocean to the San Diego Freeway and lies between Marina Del Rey and Los Angeles International Airport. Howard Hughes Center, which will ultimately have 3 million square feet of office space and 600 hotel rooms, also in West Los Angeles, is the other major California development.

While Hughes and Summa have had visible impact on the economy and face of southern Nevada, there is an underlying commitment to contribute to a richer community as well. Continuing a tradition initiated by Hughes when he made a $3-million gift to the University of Nevada Medical School, Summa's $2-million gift to the University of Nevada, Las Vegas, helped fund the new Howard R. Hughes College of Engineering and Computer Science. Summa continues to be a leader in contributing to cultural, arts, and educational programs.

Howard Hughes saw Las Vegas as the city of America's future. Summa still believes in that through its commitment to the development of quality environments for living and working in one of the best locations in the country.

JMA ARCHITECTS AND ENGINEERS, INC.

▲ Lincoln Square in Las Vegas is a deluxe office tower with a sophisticated urban design.

In Las Vegas or Reno, one can pick out those buildings designed by JMA Architects and Engineers, Inc. They are created especially for their desert environment—stark lines and sun-shaded windows, mostly built of materials from the desert, and always appropriate for their surroundings. JMA is leading the field in contemporary desert architecture.

JMA, one of the oldest and largest Nevada architectural firms, has been meeting the challenges of the Las Vegas Valley's desert environment since 1943, when it was incorporated as Jack Miller Associates. With almost 65 employees, the firm now specializes in complex, multidisciplinary projects ranging from major administrative headquarters to regional convention centers. Buildings JMA has designed have earned numerous awards from groups like the American Institute of Architects, American Association of School Administration, and the National Association of Industrial and Office Parks.

JMA, as project architect, has planned the major convention center expansions in Las Vegas and Reno, the Clark County Detention Center, the new prototype for Clark County's elementary schools, hospitals, and academic buildings for the University of Nevada, Las Vegas.

With its own interdisciplinary team on staff, JMA studies the way a client operates, learns the client's needs, and matches them to design strategies.

Understanding how a building fits into Nevada's own desert environment is the key to JMA's successful designs, according to JMA president Thomas J. Schoeman, AIA. "Southern Nevada is unique from other desert communities in that it doesn't have a long history of development. You have an opportunity to establish and utilize contemporary materials in a passive and desert-responsive approach.

"Things that I think are appropriate to the desert are concrete block and ceramic tiles that may not tie in with historical recall, but certainly tie in with the desert coloration."

The detention center's deeply recessed horizontal windows that protect against the intense sun, the earth covering that protects students at Gibson Elementary School from the desert heat, and the use of indirect outside light at Gibson and at the Nevada Power Co. Operations Center are things that mark JMA's desert-style architecture.

JMA designed a park atop the Gibson Elementary School to make maximum use of the site, Schoeman says. The earth covering keeps the building cool. To avoid a feeling of being underground, JMA wrapped classrooms and multipurpose spaces around a central courtyard that diffuses natural light into the building. Now Gibson is the prototype design for Clark County earth-sheltered elementary schools in the 1990s.

JMA's designs also feature a contemporary look, with what Schoeman calls "timeless interiors." "The things I like the best change very little," he says. "A Rolls Royce doesn't have to change. A good design has timelessness to it. We try to design our buildings to have that timelessness."

JMA buildings are based on simplicity, Schoeman explains, "and not a particular frill or fad of the moment. The interior has to function well, it has to be organized well, it has to coordinate well." JMA doesn't stop at the interior design. To make sure the design works, the firm also provides space-planning services, right down to the design of employee work stations.

Another tenet of JMA design is emphasis on design for growth: master planning for a building's future. "Master planning should reflect the dynamics of the company and its own ability to want to change," says Schoeman, "and the trick is designing to allow that future to occur."

▼ The post office's 260,000-square-foot General Mail and Vehicle Maintenance Facility in Las Vegas has a government image and a low-maintenance sand-blasted concrete masonry exterior.

▲ JMA planned the expansion for the ultra-modern Las Vegas Convention Center.

JMA designed the 40,000-square-foot Desert Research Institute building so it could grow eventually to 350,000 square feet on its 11-acre site on the UNLV campus. The Citicorp Credit Services headquarters west of Las Vegas was designed in three phases. Phases I and II, with

▼ The St. Rose de Lima Hospital in Henderson was designed by JMA for the addition of up to five additional stories should the hospital's growth warrant further construction.

250,000 square feet, are completed. When Phase III is finished, the total structure will contain 400,000 square feet, with parking for 1,800 vehicles. JMA planned the two-story St. Rose de Lima Hospital in Henderson to rise five more stories, as the need justifies additional construction.

JMA recognizes the needs of a client

and tries to meet them with its designs, says Schoeman. The local post office wanted a government image and a low-maintenance building for its 260,000-square-foot General Mail and Vehicle Maintenance Facility in Las Vegas, Schoeman recalls. "We used sand-blasted concrete masonry, which is a wonderful desert material, and ceramic tile. It gave the building a tailored look, which is appropriate for the government, yet is easy to maintain. They never have to paint it; they never have to do anything with it. They think it is their most successful facility in the country."

Citicorp's primary consideration, on the other hand, was time—the bank-services company needed a building in six months. "They also wanted a high-tech image," says Schoeman. "For the building material we chose a metal skin, because we can prefab and erect that much quicker than with any other material, and it looks great."

Those projects, and hundreds of others, illustrate JMA Architects and Engineers, Inc.'s, philosophy. As Schoeman puts it: "Good architecture is problem solving."

AMERICAN ASPHALT, INC.

Though the work is referred to as excavating, it is rare for American Asphalt, Inc., to be called on to dig a hole in the ground. Rather, excavating means moving millions of tons of dirt to match a builder's plans.

The company, started in 1976, was purchased in 1983 by Don Andress and David Gubler. With eight pieces of equipment, its only capability then was asphalting parking lots, Gubler recalls. Andress, president of the firm, and Gubler, secretary/treasurer, are both native Las Vegans.

Today American Asphalt, with more than 70 pieces of heavy earth-moving equipment that it owns outright and more than 100 employees, has helped develop some of the valley's largest pieces of property.

Working only with private developers, American Asphalt specializes in turnkey operations—installing a giant

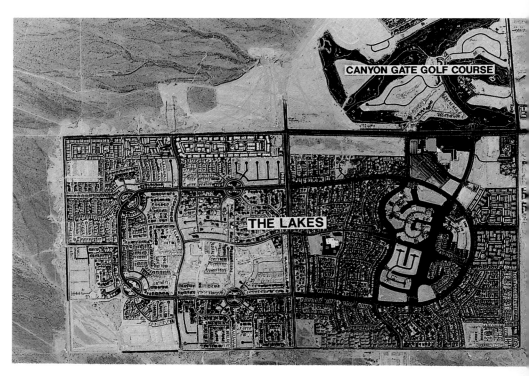

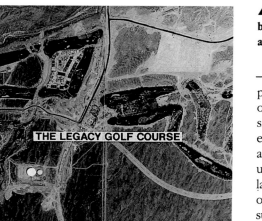

▲ Four million cubic yards of soil were moved by American Asphalt in order to create the lake at The Lakes at West Sahara.

---

parcel's infrastructure, then turning it over to individual builders for subdivision. American Asphalt grades a property; installs curbs and gutters, sewers and water mains, electrical hookups and utilities, and street lots and signs; and landscapes common areas. New developers in the Las Vegas area often consult with American Asphalt to find reputable subcontractors. "We take total responsibility for a project from the initial earth work through completion," says Andress.

At Summerlin, the enormous development by Howard Hughes Properties northwest of Las Vegas where a quarter-million people will live, American Asphalt did initial site work and is building a Tournament Players Course where the world's top golf pros, as well as resi-

---

● American Asphalt changes the face of Nevada to make the landscape more livable. The Legacy Golf Course landscape (top) was formed by the company, as was the Third Nine at Spanish Trails Country Club (bottom).

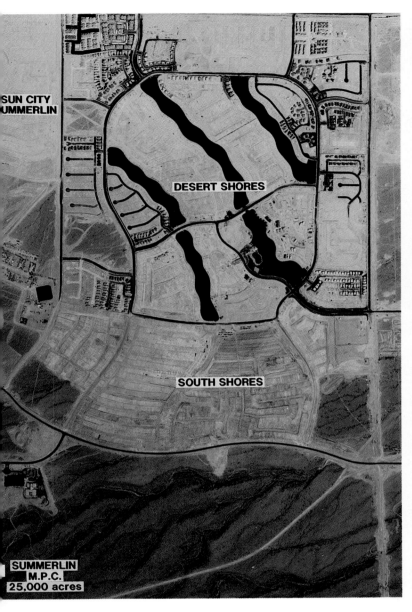

SUN CITY
SUMMERLIN

DESERT SHORES

SOUTH SHORES

SUMMERLIN
M.P.C.
25,000 acres

WHITNEY RANCH

▲ The four lakes at Desert Shores were made with the hard work and expertise of American Asphalt.

▲ American Asphalt paved the way for development at the premier community Whitney Ranch.

dents and visitors, will play regularly.

At Del Webb's Sun City, one of Summerlin's villages, American Asphalt graded the first 300 building sites and moved 1.5 million cubic yards of dirt for another golf course.

American Asphalt built the lake at The Lakes on West Sahara. To build the 36-acre lake, the firm moved 4 million cubic yards of soil, building up one side of the open-ended arroyo and contour-

ing and sealing the bottom.

Among other projects, American Asphalt built four lakes at Desert Shores, and performed work on communities such as Stonegate, Whitney Ranch, Lakes at West Sahara, and Green Valley South. In addition, American Asphalt graded the Legacy Golf Club in Green Valley, Canyongate Country Club, and the Third Nine at Spanish Trails Country Club.

It regularly works with developers such as A.G. Spanos, Del E. Webb, Lewis Homes, DiLoreto Construction, American West Development, B.H.P. Development, Collins-Graves Homes, Homes by Dave Brown, Paradise Development, Pacific

Properties, Plaster Development, R.A. Homes, Richmond-American, and Torino Development.

American Asphalt was general contractor for the developer of the planned community of South Shores, with 1,590 units ranging from single-family homes to town houses and apartments.

Soon American Asphalt, Inc., plans to begin developing business parks for medium to heavy industry.

A.G. SPANOS CONSTRUCTION, INC.

Almost 40 years ago, when Alex G. Spanos first took out an $800 bank loan to start his own catering business, he had little inkling that it would eventually turn into a construction empire. But that's exactly what happened: Today A.G. Spanos Construction, Inc., is one of the nation's top 10 home builders and a predominant force in the residential growth of Nevada.

The story of this Stockton, California-based company is the story of the man behind it—a classic rags-to-riches saga of hard work, dedication, and fiery competitiveness. Spanos, the son of poor Greek immigrants, worked in his father's bakery and small restaurant almost from the time he could walk.

But in 1951, with $800 borrowed from a local bank, Spanos left his father's business, bought a panel truck, and became the sole proprietor of the A.G. Spanos Catering Company. Over the next few years Alex and his wife, Faye, worked 16 hours per day, seven days per week, to supply meals to hundreds of farmworkers in California's Central Valley.

The work was hard, but in less than a year Spanos had built one of the most profitable catering businesses in California. In 1954, with the money he had saved from his catering business, Alex bought office buildings in Stockton, San Francisco, and San Jose—the first seeds

▲ Alex Spanos with sons Michael (seated), Dean, and son-in-law Barry Ruhl (right).

▶ George Filios, executive vice-president of A.G. Spanos Construction, Inc., has served the company for more than 20 years and is responsible for operations in Nevada, Kansas, and Oklahoma.

▼ Chelsea Park, completed in 1987 and located in Atlanta, Georgia, is typical of Spanos' residential developments in growing metropolitan areas across the United States.

of what would later become one of the largest fortunes in the United States.

The turning point came in 1960. With no previous knowledge of the construction business and against the advice of friends and associates, Spanos formed his own construction company. In the following years he proceeded cautiously, erecting a few commercial and residential buildings in the Stockton area. Encouraged by these modest yet successful efforts, Spanos set his sights across the state border where Nevada's promising economy and population growth beckoned the visionary entrepreneur.

In 1972 A.G. Spanos Construction broke ground on its first Nevada property—an apartment building in Reno. It was the city of Las Vegas, however, that

◀ As a result of his purchase of the San Diego Chargers, Alex Spanos became aware of the development opportunities in the team's home city. A.G. Spanos Construction, Inc., developed the Mission Trails project there in 1986.

Plaza Professional Offices, Topaz Village, Springs Pointe, Westwood Pointe, and Somerset Pointe. During its first 12 years in Nevada, A.G. Spanos Construction built more than 10,000 apartment units and 500,000 square feet of commercial property in Las Vegas and Reno.

As Las Vegas grew in size, so did the fortunes of the Spanos construction interests. For seven straight years AGS was the number-one apartment builder in the state of Nevada. Corporate revenues, $51 million in 1974, increased by almost 200 percent to $143 million in 1978. That same year the company was named the nation's number-one builder of attached apartment units and has held that ranking ever since.

The growth of the business has continued throughout the 1980s, as Spanos projects spread throughout the West, Midwest, and South: Colorado, Kansas, Oklahoma, Washington, Missouri, Kentucky, Utah, Tennessee, New Mexico, Georgia, Florida, Texas, and Arizona. In all, the firm has developed and built more than 60,000 apartment units and 2.4 million square feet of commercial property in 15 states from coast to coast.

Nine regional divisions administer this far-flung building empire—among them, the dynamic Las Vegas Division, which foresaw the promising growth of the Las Vegas market and helped propel the organization to its leadership position in the apartment housing industry.

Today the Spanos enterprises have diversified into real estate syndication, securities, aviation, and professional sports. More than 500 people are employed in 10 companies: A.G. Spanos Construction, Inc., A.G. Spanos Development, Inc., A.G. Spanos Enterprises, Inc., A.G. Spanos Management, Inc., A.G.S. Financial Corporation, A.G. Spanos Jet Center, A.G. Spanos Properties, A.G. Spanos Realty, A.G.

really intrigued him. At the time Las Vegas was in the throes of economic revival. Local planners, led by the Las Vegas-based Nevada Development Authority, were expending a great deal of effort to diversify the area's economy, which in turn was sparking a population spiral. Spanos recognized that these new residents would need affordable, quality housing.

In 1974 the firm established its Nevada headquarters in Las Vegas. While Alex himself took charge of the plan-

ning, he entrusted the supervision of new construction to his son, Dean A. Spanos, president, and George Filios, executive vice-president of the company.

When Spanos' confidence in the Las Vegas housing market was quickly rewarded with brisk sales, the firm plunged into a flurry of construction activity. The AGS logo began to appear on apartment and office complexes all over Las Vegas' residential neighborhoods—first the Tropicana Village, then the Canyon Club, and then the Tropicana

Spanos Securities, and A.G. Spanos Land Company.

The confidence of investors in the firm's performance prompted Spanos to create the AGS Financial Corporation to facilitate individual investments in the company's apartment complexes. This Spanos venture is also initiating full-service syndication and financial services.

The A.G. Spanos Jet Center was built in 1981 at the Stockton Airport to facilitate the demanding travel schedule of its founder and other corporate executives. One of the most modern private facilities of its kind in Northern California, the jet center accommodates private aircraft from throughout the United States and offers sales, rental, maintenance, and repair services.

Spanos, a study in perpetual motion, takes a hands-on approach to all his business endeavors. He, his two sons, and son-in-law each travel 4,000 miles per week in the company jets to oversee the wide array of corporate projects and explore new opportunities. Only

● Whispering Lakes, completed in 1989, offers Las Vegans luxury apartment living with poolside recreation.

Bob Hope travels more, and it is no accident that Hope and Spanos are longtime friends. "Without a doubt," Hope has said, "Alex Spanos is one of the most successful and hardworking individuals I know."

The company jets are also used eight Sundays during the fall and winter months to fly Spanos, family, employees, and friends to San Diego to watch the Chargers play football. An avid sports fan, Spanos fulfilled a lifelong dream in 1984 when he purchased the National Football League team.

Ownership of the team not only re-flects Spanos' love of football but also his intense competitive spirit. "Winning is instinctive with me," says Spanos. "I don't know anything else that is greater than winning."

Spanos is a noted philanthropist, donating millions of dollars to benefit numerous charities, educational institutions, hospitals, churches, civic organizations, and athletic associations—many of them in Nevada. In recognition of his business and philanthropic activities, Spanos has received many honors and awards, including the Statue of Liberty-Ellis Island Medal of Honor, the Horatio

Alger Award, and the AHEPA's Aristotelian Award.

Spano's personal life has been as rewarding as his extraordinary career. Alex met his wife, Faye, also the progeny of Greek immigrants, at the Greek church in her hometown of Tarpon Springs, Florida, in 1945, when he was stationed there with the Air Force. They were married three years later.

"The most important influence in my life has been my wife," says Spanos today. "Her unfaltering support and love have given me the peace of mind that is so essential to my total success."

The marriage has produced two sons, two daughters, and seven grandchildren, and Spanos credits a skilled use of nepotism with much of his company's success. In addition to Alex Spanos, the corporate officers include sons Dean A. and Michael A. Spanos, and son-in-law Dr. Barry Ruhl.

Two other keys to the company's

● Rancho Del Sol, completed in 1988, is one of
many quality luxury apartment complexes in
Las Vegas bearing the AGS logo.

success are the founder's willingness to
take risks and tenacious goal setting.
"I've never known a successful person
who hasn't been a risk taker," Spanos
points out. "And if you don't set goals,
and just exist, you aren't striving for anything, and the world just sort of passes
you by."

But perhaps the overriding factor in
the company's success has been its confidence in its employees. George Filios,
vice-president of A.G. Spanos Construction, has served the Spanos companies
for more than 20 years and is in charge of
projects in the states of Nevada, Kansas,
and Oklahoma. "We are a company that
relies on its people and their initiative,"
Filios acknowledges. "As employees, we
have the latitude to explore new methods, and are encouraged to adopt pro-

gressive and creative approaches."

Sixteen years ago the Spanos group
of companies established permanent
roots in the city of Las Vegas. The firm's
goal is to continue working with the
state and local communities to best serve
Nevada's population needs.

And that means creating the best in

apartment living—luxury garden apartments and condominiums, Nevada's
most active housing market. "Our projects are tops because we take the time
to see that quality, aesthetics, and function blend together," Alex Spanos explains. "We build with one goal in
mind—to be the best at what we do."

INVESTMENT EQUITY

The rapidly expanding southern Nevada market is a place that naturally produces business success stories—but few of them match the story of the meteoric rise of Investment Equity. Established in 1985 by David and Michelle Inman, Investment Equity has become a very diverse company with an ever-expanding list of interests and holdings.

Headquartered in one of its earlier business developments, The Festival Professional Office Park, on the corner of East Flamingo and Decatur, Invest-

▲ A palm-lined entryway with a spectacular fountain greets guests and residents of Ritz Cove, Investment Equity's new residential development at Desert Shores in Las Vegas.

ment Equity is currently involved with the construction of a new office complex, two apartment projects, and two upscale housing developments, with more projects in various stages of planning.

Over the past few years Investment

▲ Marbeya Business Park features a waterscaped courtyard with streams, pools, and fountains visible from every office.

Equity has also developed several successful retail projects. From the 30,000-square-foot Mercado del Sol at West Charlston and Rainbow, to the 160,000-square-foot Sahara Towne Square at Maryland Parkway and East Sahara, Investment Equity has built, leased, and managed five retail shopping centers, all of which have been acclaimed for their architectural style, location, and professional leasing and management staff.

Recently the company has ventured into the single-family housing market with two developments at Desert Shores on the fast-growing west side of Las Vegas. Ritz Cove and Mediterranean Cove represent the upper end of homes available at Desert Shores.

Ritz Cove homes start in the upper

◀ Investment Equity, in a joint venture with Ferguson Partners of Irvine, California, is building Marbeya Business Park, located near Rainboy and West Sahara in Las Vegas.

Those features include a special media room available to all tenants. The room will incorporate state-of-the-art audio and video equipment in a theater-style arrangement. The media room will be available to all firms located at Marbeya for presentations, meetings, or seminars.

With all of these projects and more in the planning stages, it is easy to see why Investment Equity has soared to the top as one of the successful new companies of the 1980s. This success has come about due to hard work, good management techniques, and a willingness to take chances in new areas.

"We do have a lot of 'irons in the fire' right now," Inman smiles. "But that's the way we like it. We believe

▼ Ritz Cove and Mediterranean Cove are just across from the club house and beach club at Desert Shores. Both developments are by Investment Equity.

$200,000 range, with 20 waterfront locations among its 61 home sites. Mediterranean Cove, located adjacent to Ritz Cove, will have 58 homes, many with waterfront and view locations.

Another Investment Equity project under way is the Marbeya Business Park on West Sahara Boulevard at Sorrell, near Rainbow. Marbeya is a joint venture with Ferguson Partners of Irvine, California. It is a 108,000-square-foot office complex that features a lush 40,000-square-foot waterscaped courtyard.

Marbeya marks the second joint venture between Investment Equity and Ferguson Partners. The other venture is the 256-unit Catalina Shores luxury apartments. "Ferguson Partners has been involved in some of the largest and most prestigious developments in Southern California," Inman explains. "When we had the opportunity to get into a deal with them, we knew we really had a winning team."

The two firms have designed a beautiful yet functional office environment in Marbeya Business Park. The Spanish Mediterranean theme is carried out architecturally and is highlighted by the spectacular waterscaped courtyard. "Marbeya

will provide a wonderful working environment in which to conduct business," Inman beams. "The streams, waterfalls, and fountains will have a relaxing and soothing effect that can only enhance any business climate. In addition, we have added some very innovative features that will be attractive to everyone who has an office at Marbeya."

southern Nevada is a very hot market, and we want to continue to be involved with it. That's why we are constantly looking for new projects. We have some exciting ideas for the future, and all of us can't wait to get started."

If Investment Equity's first productive years are any indication, its future will be very bright indeed.

CFA, INC.

▲ The attractive Mountain Shadow apartment complex in southeast Reno demonstrates CFA's attention to aesthetic principles.

Over the past decade the Reno-Sparks area has been one of the nation's fastest growing urban areas. Such growth and the consequent changes in the character of the community demand a thoughtful and comprehensive approach to planning and engineering. This is the motivation of CFA, a well-known Reno-based consulting firm.

CFA offers planning, civil engineering, landscape architecture, and surveying services to public and private clients. Founded in 1981, the company has grown from two people to nearly 20. Although still relatively small in size, this multidisciplinary design firm is impressive in the range of projects undertaken. They run the gamut from major public facilities and commercial centers to small subdivisions and neighborhood parks. The client list is equally diverse and includes some of the most well known names in development and major national corporations, as well as smaller, local development entities.

What makes CFA different in the field of consulting firms? Part of the answer to this question lies in the fact that the Reno area is the focus of the organization. CFA has concentrated on learning everything possible about the Truckee Meadows and vicinity rather than seeking far-flung projects outside

its sphere of knowledge. With a few exceptions CFA's projects are all within minutes of the office.

Knowing a place means knowing the people and the aspirations of a community. CFA's approach to any job is to assess the goals of the client in relation to the social, economic, and psychological climate currently prevalent in the Truckee Meadows. As Alex Fittinghoff,

the company's president, states, "The most important thing we can offer a client is local knowledge. We deal with most of the local officials on a first-name basis." This local knowledge means that a CFA can supply to its clients a realistic assessment of what the community's concerns about a proposed project are likely to be and what can be done by the potential developer to blend his project into the fabric of the community.

Keeping abreast of community attitudes means talking to the citizens as well as meeting with elected and appointed officials. CFA has a strong record of meeting with neighborhood groups and home owners' associations to work through objections to various aspects of a development proposal. Significantly, the principals of CFA pioneered in the use of neighborhood design workshops for design of neighborhood parks—a technique that has been used successfully for parks in Reno and Sparks.

▼ Rolling hills provide a backdrop for the 200,000-square-foot Baring Village Shopping Center in Sparks.

Environmental awareness is another trademark of CFA's work. The firm recognizes its obligation to find development solutions that meet the client's economic objectives without "butchering" the land. Because CFA identifies so closely with the community, it realizes the importance of keeping this area a beautiful and desirable place in which to live and work.

CFA relies on the latest in computers and related technology to provide the highest level of accuracy and efficiency in the production of engineering documents. For instance, CFA's surveying system includes an electronic "total station" to record field data that is automatically fed into the engineering computer system. This data, after manipulation by CFA's engineering staff, is automatically plotted onto mylar sheets to produce accurate topographic and boundary base maps for planning and engineering uses. This computer capability extends to the preparation of grading and drainage plans and the calculation of earthwork quantities.

To supplement CFA's in-house capabilities, CFA planners and engineers assemble and coordinate specialized project teams to meet the particular requirements of any project. Geotechnical

● **The Edgewater subdivision on the Truckee River in Reno blends harmoniously with its natural surroundings.**

engineers, air-quality specialists, architects, and archaeologists are among the many types of experts enlisted by the firm to address specific project issues. These experts are those known by CFA to adhere to the same high standards of thoroughness and accuracy.

The CFA difference is one of total project consideration, from conceptual design to construction and return on investment. Any engineering firm can produce a set of plans. CFA believes that its responsibility to clients goes beyond the mechanics of engineering. How appropriate is a project? Is this the most cost-efficient design? Can the project be approved? If not, are there alternative solutions that meet the client's and the community's needs? Seeking these answers and reflecting them in its work makes CFA positively different.

DI LORETO CONSTRUCTION AND DEVELOPMENT, INC.

What is the key factor involved when a small Reno-based construction company expands to the point of achieving an enviable place in the home-builder market? Something is obviously being done right.

While Perry Di Loreto may or may not see his company become the largest home builder in the state of Nevada, he is definitely working toward making it the best. His 300 employees are reminded of this dedication to quality every time they pull out a business card, which has this slogan printed on the back: "The difference between mediocrity and excellence is attention to detail."

Perhaps that is why Di Loreto Construction and Development has grown to become Reno's largest home builder and is giving other builders in Las Vegas a run for their money as well.

Perry Di Loreto and his brother Tom began the company in the summer of 1976 by building a single 3,000-square-foot home in California's Bay Area, which they then sold to get the money to build two more houses, and so on. Over the years, through the difficult period of high inflation and double-digit interest rates, Di Loreto continued to sell homes to a public that demanded top quality.

As the firm continues to plan new

developments in both Reno and Las Vegas, the pace of construction is well in excess of 300 homes per year in Reno and zeroing in on 600 statewide. Di Loreto always has two or three subdivisions under construction in each city at any one time. In addition, the company has developments at Plumas Pines Golf Course, high in the California mountains, and in the Sacramento area.

To accommodate a rapidly growing number of young families who needed affordable housing, Di Loreto pioneered the idea of patio homes in Nevada, by developing The Shadows in northwest Reno. Di Loreto's Cape Cod-style Millstream patio homes in Las Vegas won the Southern Nevada Homebuilders Association award for Best Single-Family Attached Home in its category.

▲ Di Loreto's plush lobby at the corporate headquarters in Reno demonstrates the upbeat, modern construction for which the firm is known.

Di Loreto also builds large luxury homes, picturesque riverfront town houses and condominiums, and apartment developments. The firm has entered the area of commercial development and plans to continue in that vein, according to Di Loreto.

Rather than the term *subdivisions*, Di Loreto likes to think of his projects as *communities*. He begins each project by finding the ideal location, with proximity to freeways, transportation, parks, shopping, and good schools. With this convenient access to needed services, the company then strives to give its projects the feel of a complete community by adding special finishing touches.

"Incorporated into many of our communities are thoughtfully designed recreational facilities that cater to the life-styles of the very active to the leisurely," explains Di Loreto. "We want our home owners to live in places they can proudly call home."

As for the company's emphasis on attention to detail and quality construction, Di Loreto comments: "My dad taught me the purpose of a hammer and a saw at a very young age. I know the pain of missing a nail and slamming my thumb—I also know the deep pleasure of building something to cherish forever."

▼ Di Loreto's The Virginian model home, built in Las Vegas, Reno, and Sparks, is a popular choice for discriminating home buyers.

AMERICAN NEVADA CORPORATION

▲ Rain or shine, this life-size bronze sculpture never puts down his newspaper. This work by sculptor J. Seward Johnson, Jr., is one of eight owned by Green Valley, which boasts the largest collection of Johnson's pieces. This and many other works comprise Green Valley's outdoor sculpture museum collection.

Before the edges of the Las Vegas Valley began filling with master-planned communities, there was Green Valley, still southern Nevada's showcase community, used by home buyers and home builders to measure all the rest.

"We wanted to build a new town," says Mark Fine, president of American Nevada Corporation, Green Valley's developer, "a place where people could feel, 'This is home.'"

With about half of its 8,400 acres still to be developed, Green Valley's 20,000 residents take part in community activities such as plays, picnics, and Little League baseball; golf at The Legacy, a new public golf course; swim, play tennis and squash, and work out at the new 112,000-square-foot Green Valley Athletic Club; and enjoy a wide range of well-developed parks, churches, schools, and a public library.

Known in Las Vegas as "the place where the statues are," Green Valley is a community where children play on artist Lloyd Hamrol's *Serpent Mound* sculpture in front of the public library, or pause to talk to a lifelike J. Seward Johnson, Jr., a figure sitting on a bench, apparently waiting for a bus in front of the Green Valley Civic Center Plaza. Set carefully in place around the development's parks and other greenbelt areas are 16 lifelike human-figure sculptures, America's largest collection of Johnson's work. Other public sculptures at Green Valley

are by Alan Osborne, Lita Albuquerque, and Lee Sido.

The Green Valley library features rotating art exhibits in its public gallery and, in conjunction with American Nevada Corporation, sponsors several shows each year. American Nevada has even set up a sculpture information center outside its headquarters.

"We have Shakespeare in the park, races on Memorial Day, community picnics, and a Green Valley home owners' association—neighborhood reps who meet with us," says Fine. "We want residents to know that Green Valley is not just another subdivision where they live, but one where they can identify and have a sense of place."

Other developments in Green Valley include a 112-acre business park with tenants such as Ethel M Chocolates and Meredith Broadcasting; several office complexes including a new 32,000-square-foot Civic Center office building and the Green Valley Professional Center garden office complex; several retail centers, including the Athenian Specialty Retail Center, the Gateway Plaza convenience center, and the 100,000-square-foot Green Valley Plaza Shopping Center; and the 75-acre Community Center.

As part of the Green Valley community, American Nevada Corporation is also developing the Village of Silver Springs and a 705-acre golf course community.

Green Valley homes range from houses and apartments for first-time buyers to luxury executive homes and condos. "We can't be an elitist community," says Fine. "We can't just sell the upper end. We don't want to be an entry-level community, either. We want people to know that they can move into an entry-level home and be proud that they're part of this community, and know that they can move up as their income level moves up. We want them to be Green Valley residents from the beginning to the end."

▼ Sprawling over an impressive 10 acres, the Green Valley Athletic Club is one of the largest athletic clubs in the country. This modern facility boasts the latest in fitness technology within an expansive 112,000-square-foot building.

G.C. WALLACE, INC.

G.C. Wallace, Inc., is proud to be a part of the growing Las Vegas community. Since its founding in 1969, the engineering and architectural design firm has had a major impact on some of the largest developments in the Las Vegas Valley. The GCW touch is found in master-planned communities such as Spring Valley, Summerlin, and Sun City; public works projects such as McCarran International Airport; transportation projects such as the three-tier Summerlin Parkway interchange that gives Summerlin access to U.S. Highway 95; and water-related projects, including water reservoirs, pipelines, sewerage, and flood-control facilities.

"We work closely with our clients to translate their objectives into reality," says G.C. "Scott" Wallace, the firm's chief executive officer and founder. "We are well versed in the technical and procedural requirements of land development projects and believe in responsiveness to our clients' needs and in quality service."

Scott Wallace, a graduate of the University of Illinois with a degree in civil engineering, moved to Las Vegas in 1961 and founded G.C. Wallace Consulting Engineers, Inc., in 1969. In the early years the firm participated in joint-venture projects that enabled it to gain experience in large projects and achieve quick recognition among developers and governmental agencies. Through a joint venture with another engineering company, the young firm won planning and engineering contracts for Pardee Construction Company's Spring Valley

Community and a large family-housing project at Nellis Air Force Base. Pardee, GCW's first major client, remains a client today. At present approximately 90 percent of GCW's business is repeat business from satisfied clients. The firm's policy is to serve existing clients before trying to acquire new clients.

In contrast from the one-man operation launched in 1969, to the largest engineering-architectural firm headquartered in Nevada, Scott Wallace points with pride to the firm's attractive new 40,000-square-foot desert-style office building and its 170-plus employees. GCW handles municipal and private projects statewide, but the firm's real mark on the southern Nevada landscape is in master-planned communities. In 1985 GCW became the first southern Nevada-based design firm to be included in *Engineering News-Record*'s annual list of the top 500 design firms

in the United States.

Wallace credits the firm's success to well-qualified staff—from the engineers, architects, and designers to the supporting personnel. "They provide a service that is timely and they demonstrate a sincere concern for the welfare of the client," he says.

Leading the firm is a management team made up of Wallace, once named Nevada's Small Business Person of the Year by the U.S. Small Business Administration; Michael Radojevich, president; and Kay Adams and Gary Spinkelink, senior vice-presidents.

The firm has planned and designed more than 100 flood-control projects, major water storage and distribution facilities, sewage collection and treatment projects, and more than 500 miles of road projects, including Rainbow Boulevard, Tropicana Avenue, Cheyenne Avenue, Sunset Road, Pecos Road, Maryland Parkway, and Lake Mead Boulevard.

Architecture projects include institutional works such as fire stations and a church, commercial assignments for office buildings and shopping centers, and the full range of housing types from apartments and moderately priced houses to luxury homes.

The firm's capabilities include land planning, civil engineering for land development, traffic engineering, transportation (roads, railroads, airport runways, and bridges), water and wastewater projects, hydrology, drainage, flood control, structural engineering, architecture, land surveying, and construc-

tion administration.

Its hundreds of clients include some of the most prominent names in development in Nevada: Pardee, Lewis Homes, Howard Hughes Properties, Del Webb Communities, Community Construction, Metropolitan Development, Hilton Hotels Inc., R.A. Homes, Pacific Properties, Spanish Trails Associates, and Peccole. Public clients include McCarran International Airport; the cities of Las Vegas, North Las Vegas, Boulder City, and Henderson; Nellis Air Force Base; and other state and local government bodies such as the Nevada Department of Transportation, Nevada State Public Works Board, Clark County Public Works, Las Vegas Valley Water District, Clark County Sanitation District, Clark County Regional Flood Control District, and the Regional Transportation Commission.

GCW's largest project to date has been Howard Hughes Properties' (HHP) Summerlin development. Comprised of master-planned villages of approximately 500 to 1,000 acres each, the 22,000-plus-acre development will be the home of more than 200,000 people by the early twenty-first century. Since 1986 GCW has been involved in the master planning of Summerlin as well as planning, design, and construction management duties for the roadways, drainage improvements, and utility infrastructure to serve the total development.

GCW provides similar services for village development within Summerlin, such as Del Webb's Sun City Summerlin, and Summerlin's villages one, two, three, and seven. GCW designed Summerlin Parkway and the steel bridges on the parkway's U.S. Highway 95 interchange that will ensure Summerlin residents access to and from downtown Las Vegas within relatively few minutes.

GCW provided the land planning, and engineering and architectural designs for Desert Shores, a 986-acre water-oriented community featuring five lakes and a swimming lagoon.

Other projects in which GCW has been involved include Spring Valley, South Shores, Painted Desert (with a target golf course), Canyon Gate (with a 7,000-yard PGA course), Towne Square (with a casino/hotel, shopping center, RV park, and apartments), Ocotillo Condominiums (with golf course and country club), Meadow Valley, Sunrise Valley, Rainbow Vista, Las Palmas, Hughes Airport Center (an industrial park), Hughes Center (a business park), and Spanish Trail (with a 7,088-yard PGA course).

G.C. Wallace, Inc., is dedicated to providing high-quality and efficient land planning, engineering, architectural, and construction administration services, from project planning through design and construction for clients in Nevada and the Southwest.

VTN NEVADA

▲ VTN's offices are located within The Plazas, a master-planned office and commercial development engineered by VTN.

With more than 3,000 projects to its credit, VTN Nevada has helped map the growth of Clark County for more than 20 years. The projects range from public works to residential and commercial developments to land-use planning.

Using the newest computer technology, this civil engineering and land-surveying firm is a specialist in water supply, flood control, and traffic management projects. And whenever a government agency, developer, or group of home owners needs boundary expertise, it calls on VTN.

Among projects to VTN's credit are Sam's Town Gold River in Laughlin, the planned community of El Mirage, an 8,000-acre Green Valley master plan and development, the Meadows Mall, the City of Las Vegas Sewer Action Plan, and the Angel Park detention basin.

VTN is one of the most highly regarded firms in its field in Clark County because of the training and experience of its people. David Weir, senior partner, has been with the firm since 1963. Charley Johnson is a Clark County planning commissioner, a director of the

Southern Nevada Homebuilders Association, and past president of the state Consulting Engineers Council. J.L. MacFarlane, also a past president of the Consulting Engineers Council and active in the Southern Nevada Homebuilders Association, serves on the Governor's

Advisory Committee for Transportation Funding and the Citizens Advisory Committee to the Clark County Flood Control District.

VTN's experienced engineering managers oversee every aspect of a project: coordinating the often complicated approval process with government agencies, mapping and planning, and ground breaking. VTN's 80-plus employees include traffic engineers, flood control analysts, hydraulics engineers, and civil engineers, as well as licensed land surveyors, draftsmen, and computer specialists.

The firm came to Nevada in 1961, when Voorheis-Trindle Engineering Co., a successful Southern California company, opened an office in Las Vegas. In 1969 the name was changed to VTN Nevada, and two years later VTN Nevada became an autonomous operation, wholly owned by its present managers and able to

▶ VTN's engineering and surveying divisions oversee land preparation and grading operations for projects such as Rock Springs Vista, Las Vegas' best-selling condominiums.

concentrate its efforts on giving personalized service to the southern Nevada community.

VTN's goal, says MacFarlane, is to improve the raw land, planning so the developer's zoning problems and costs of working the land are at a minimum, and the environment and aesthetic factors are protected.

After its preliminary proposal is accepted by a client and VTN becomes project manager, the firm goes to work—planning, surveying, doing drainage and traffic studies, and drafting preliminary design—coordinating the developer's needs with the land conditions. VTN's itemized engineering estimates enable the developer to make accurate financial projections and get a quick start on financing proposals.

Backed by its long record of amicable relations and fair dealing with local and regional government officials, VTN is able to shepherd most projects quickly through the approval process.

After final planning and detailed drawings, VTN provides bid specifications, helps developers select contractors, and, if required, provides contact administration. VTN stakes out public improvements, such as roads, sidewalks, sewer, water lines, and building sites as construction moves along. And the firm provides consultation for the on-site needs of the builder.

In Clark County, VTN has applied these practices to regional and local shopping centers, office complexes, industrial parks, and mixed-use and residential developments of all sizes.

Supported by the latest computer technology, VTN's experience in public works is extensive. Its highway engineering team provides a total package of

▲ **Angel Park Detention Basin was designed to protect the city from flooding by containing runoff from major storms and releasing it slowly.**

traffic control, lighting, drainage structures design, and landscaping for projects large and small—ranging from local and arterial street improvement to regional highways and major bridges.

Computer technology enables VTN to do water-system modeling to simulate peak-hour demand and fire-flow analysis that helps compute water pressure for any size water system. The same kind of modeling analyses helps VTN design sewer-collection and flood-control projects, computing peak runoffs and determining flood-hazard areas. VTN's other hydrology capabilities include design of detention basins, flood channels and culverts, and drop inlets and storm sewers.

VTN has several registered water rights surveyors on its staff to handle all kinds of services related to the appropriation of water and changes in its place and use.

With its sophisticated computers and the latest in surveying equipment—laser geodimeters, theodolites, and electronic distance-measuring equipment—a VTN specialty is boundary control.

When fences and roads wander,

when ancient survey markers are destroyed and where typography changes, there is often need for a boundary detective, explains MacFarlane.

The professional land surveyor uses old maps and charts, diaries, field notes, descriptions of land features, and common sense to refix boundaries fairly and help settle disputes, he adds. Sometimes MacFarlane is called upon to testify as an expert witness in court trials.

VTN spent eight months mapping the conflicts of one potential boundary dispute affecting 700 land owners near Las Vegas. It was a situation in which property lines were off by as much as several hundred feet within an eight-square-mile area, and early records had been destroyed. "There were none of the usual clues," recalls MacFarlane. "There was no way we could find out where the true corners were."

After months of aerial and field mapping and more months of public meetings and working with individual property owners, VTN Nevada worked out new lines that avoided cutting swimming pools or houses in two or shifting existing roads. "We tried to leave every owner with more or less the amount of land the deeds said they were entitled to," says MacFarlane.

"Land ownership is the key to democracy," he adds. "That goes back to the days of Thomas Jefferson, who developed our rectangular system of quarters and acres. It gives you peace of mind to know that your corner is fixed, that your little piece of land is inviolable."

▼ **Underground pipe is installed at the Tiffany Place apartment site. VTN's involvement with the project will continue until construction is complete.**

LEWIS HOMES

The Lewis Homes group of companies occupy a prominent position in the nation's building industry. With each new year its development projects—residential, commercial, office, and industrial—play a greater role in the economy of the West. The Lewis name has consistently represented sound decision making, stability, and, above all, quality.

The companies' success started in 1955, when an attorney and certified public accountant, Ralph M. Lewis, and his wife, Goldy, dedicated themselves to building homes of enduring value,

thoughtfully and honestly priced. To date, the Lewis Homes group of companies have built more than 30,000 single-family houses; 8,000 multi-family units; and developed more than 2 million square feet of office, commercial, and industrial space.

Year after year Lewis Homes of Nevada has been the state's largest and most respected home builder. It has maintained its reputation for excellence by its emphasis on quality and its insistence on fair dealings. "Excellence is achieved through a combination of an

in-house staff of real estate development professionals and leading outside consultants, who are all committed to a common goal," says Robert E. Lewis, president of Lewis Homes of Nevada.

"Listening and responding to the needs of an ever-changing market has placed Lewis Homes in the forefront of the building industry," comments Lewis. "Building styles change. Interior design trends change. One thing that has not changed is what people want in their homes—quality and excellence."

● In Nevada and California, quality-built Lewis homes, apartments, and shopping centers are beautiful additions to the communities in which they are built.

THE SCHULMAN GROUP

"Welcome Home," the trademark of The Schulman Group, are two words being heard more and more often by an ever-greater number of families and individuals as the firm becomes a leader in all phases of southern Nevada real estate development.

When Robert H. Schulman came to Nevada in 1983 to develop homes and commercial properties, he ignored conventional Las Vegas wisdom and did things his own way. Since then, his company has built and successfully operated the city's first nongaming resort/hotel, the internationally known Alexis Park, and is now operating its second one, the St. Tropez Resort Hotel.

The group is busy, along with other developers, creating a new central business district for Las Vegas along Paradise Road, east of the Strip. It is also concentrating its home-building activity on a wide range of housing projects throughout Clark County within the area's largest master-planned communities. "We build homes for the way people live, in places where they want to live," Schulman relates.

Schulman, in his quarter-century in Nevada and California real estate, is responsible for developing more than one billion dollars' worth of projects.

Originally based in Southern Cali-

fornia, The Schulman Group opened a branch office in Las Vegas in 1983. Says Schulman, "As we familiarized ourselves with the marketplace, we saw that Las Vegas was just beginning to grow. The more time we spent here, the more we liked it."

Schulman liked it so well that, after building and managing the Alexis Park Resort Hotel, the 150,000-square-foot Citibank Park office and retail center, and several smaller housing projects, he moved the firm's headquarters to Las Vegas in 1987.

The Schulman Group owns, operates, and manages all of its properties under a management team that has worked together for many years. The firm currently has five operating divisions.

The Hotel Division is the major developer of nongaming hotel properties in Las Vegas. In addition to the Alexis Park, it has developed the first phase of the expanding Ramada Suites-St. Tropez Hotel with additional rooms and commercial development under construction.

The Housing Division is a sales leader and builds in all of the major master-planned communities in southern Nevada. The Schulman Group is building homes in prestigious communities such as The Lakes, Desert Shores, Painted Desert, Silver Springs at Green Valley, and Rancho Del Norte, expecting to deliver more than 600 homes per year during the 1990s. The expertise garnered in building in planned communities has carried over to its own land development in the rapidly expanding northwest corridor of Las Vegas.

The Land Development Division as-

▲ CitiBank Park is a Schulman Group development and a Silver Award winner. Pictured here is the interior courtyard.

sembles both large and small parcels to sell either raw, fully developed, or to transfer to one of the other Schulman divisions for further improvement. This division has further development plans in the works for several master-planned communities in the exploding northwest area of the Las Vegas Valley. Preliminary studies are being conducted on Lake Las Vegas, a project to rival the world-famous Las Vegas Strip, which promises to be the most ambitious multiple-use master-planned community in Nevada and which will command the expertise of all The Schulman Group's impressive talent.

The Commercial Division develops and leases commercial and industrial properties such as Citibank Plaza, a mixed-use retail/office park; Sahara Paradise Plaza; and St. Tropez Shopping Plaza. Also under study for development during the 1990s are several industrial projects in North Las Vegas and Henderson, the fourth- and second-largest cities in the state, respectively.

Launching an impressive array of new projects each year, The Schulman Group enters into joint ventures with such leading financial institutions as Citicorp Real Estate and Pacific First Federal.

"We're committed to Las Vegas," says Schulman. And his goal is to be not only one of Las Vegas' biggest builders, but its best. The words "Welcome Home" will become ever more recognized as The Schulman Group realizes this goal.

▼ The Schulman Group develops homes and commercial properties. A maverick, Robert H. Schulman built and successfully operated the nongaming resort/hotel St. Tropez (pictured here). It was the company's second nongaming hotel.

SILVER CANYON
A DIVISION OF COSMO WORLD OF NEVADA, INC.

Nevada's first destination golf resort, Silver Canyon, is under development high in the south hills overlooking the Las Vegas Valley. At the destination resort developed by Cosmo World of Nevada, Inc., guests will be able to play 27 holes of a Jack Nicklaus championship golf course featuring dramatic views of the mountains and the city skyline.

Serious golf students will also be able to hone their skills at a high-technology Jack Nicklaus Golf Academy. Residents of the master-planned community will have an exclusive Reese Jones golf course of their own. Indeed, golf courses will cover more than 40 percent of the 1,288-acre resort community.

"The community is primarily golf oriented with some gaming associated with the resort hotel," according to Ronald Kopf, Cosmo's Las Vegas project manager.

The venture is one of three destination resort golf-course developments in the United States by Cosmo World Corp., a leading developer of such resorts in France, Austria, and Japan. Headquartered in Tokyo, Cosmo World Corp. is a multinational company involved in photography, restaurants, and sports-equipment manufacturing in Japan and the United States. Among its products are Mamiya cameras, Ben Hogan golf equipment, and Olympic golf shafts and fishing gear.

Operating 14 golf resorts in Japan, Cosmo is developing similar resorts in Los Angeles and on the island of Kona in Hawaii. The firm commissioned legendary golfer Jack Nicklaus to design

▲ The Nevada desert landscape will complement the lush feel of the golf course.

▼ From the Silver Canyon community's vantage point, the Las Vegas city lights glow warmly to form a wonderful twilight view.

the course for a European resort in Salzburg, Austria, and the company is developing another Nicklaus course near Paris, France.

Jack Nicklaus' 27-hole championship course for the Cosmo World Silver Canyon community will be the resort's centerpiece. His golf academy will feature three challenging holes, plus putting greens and sand traps, exclusively for the use of academy students. The students will stay at the resort during their four- to seven-day seminars designed for all skill levels—beginners to touring professionals. They will practice on a driving range with video teaching facilities and have use of the resort's many other amenities.

The main Nicklaus course will wrap around the 700-room resort hotel that project/construction manager Yasushi Nara anticipates to be "a four-star property." Facilities will include restaurants, swimming, tennis, gaming, meeting facilities, and a health club.

A tennis center operated by the

Association of Tennis Professionals (ATP) will host the world's best tennis players, and it will include a 2,000-seat tournament stadium facility, a learning center, a practice area, clubhouse facilities, and 11 additional courts with various types of playing surfaces—grass, European clay, asphalt, and composite.

Also planned for the resort community are approximately 2,500 homes, ranging from resort condominiums to custom-designed estates, located around the private 18-hole golf course designed by Reese Jones.

The Cosmo World Silver Canyon resort, 600 feet above the valley floor, accessed by the southern extension of Maryland Parkway and Eastern Avenue, is a 10-mile drive from McCarran International Airport. The community is anticipating start of construction by mid-1990.

LAKE LAS VEGAS

With the same flare and attention to detail that it brought to projects such as McCormick Ranch in Scottsdale, Arizona, and The Shores at Waikoloa Beach Resort in Hawaii, Transcontinental Properties, Inc., has begun development of what will surely be Nevada's premier destination resort community of the 1990s—Lake Las Vegas.

Currently under construction on 2,200 acres in the City of Henderson, bordering Lake Mead National Recreation Area, the Lake Las Vegas development is a master-planned community of destination resorts, luxury homes, and supporting commercial properties located just 12 miles east of the Strip and McCarran International Airport. When completed in the late 1990s, the development is planned to include as many as 8 destination resort hotels and casinos, more than 2,000 new homes, and a Resort Village commercial complex all overlooking two-mile long, 320-acre Lake Las Vegas, the largest private man-made recreational lake in Nevada.

While casino gambling will be an important magnet for Lake Las Vegas visitors, it will certainly not be the only attraction. Transcontinental Properties has planned four 18-hole championship golf courses on the resort-oriented, north shore of the lake plus a fifth course on the residential south shore. Other planned amenities include restaurants, retail shopping facilities, several lakeshore marinas, an equestrian center, and a major tennis complex.

Led by chairman Ronald F. Boeddeker

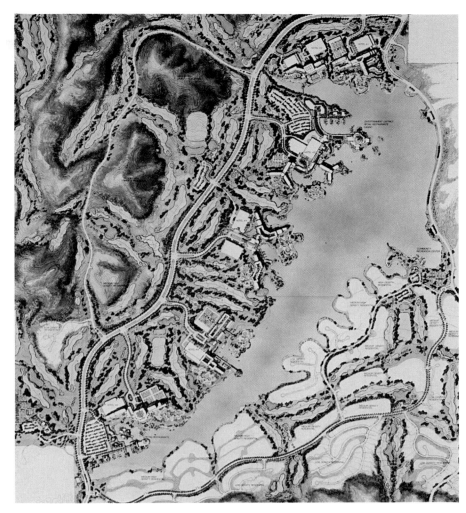

▲ Lake Las Vegas promises to be one of the most unique land development projects in southern Nevada. This illustrative concept plan gives an overall view of the 2,200-acre resort community upon completion.

and chief executive officer Gregory G. Kreizenbeck, Transcontinental Properties, Inc., was formed in 1980 and is headquartered in Scottsdale, Arizona. It is the successor to Aetna Diversified Properties, Inc., the original developer of McCormick Ranch. Transcontinental operates as the managing general partner of several real estate investment and development joint ventures with projects throughout the United States.

McCormick Ranch, an award-winning 3,100-acre master-planned community featuring luxury resorts, golf courses, and more than 9,000 homes, has set the development standard for the Scottsdale area. Transcontinental's business parks near Baltimore, Phoenix, and outside Chicago provide more than 21 million square feet of office and industrial space. On the Kohala "Gold Coast" of the Big Island of Hawaii, Transcontinental developed The Shores at Waikoloa Beach Resort, a 120-unit luxury resort condominium complex located adjacent to the Hyatt Regency Waikoloa resort. Just outside San Juan, Puerto Rico, the company's CPK Homes affiliate has developed more than 2,000 single-family homes at Villas de Loiza.

Like each of these earlier Transcontinental projects, Lake Las Vegas reflects the firm's imagination, environmental sensitivity, financial strength, management expertise, and, most of all, its ongoing commitment to excellence.

▼ More than 20,000 lineal feet of massive piping has been installed to carry normal wash flows under Lake Las Vegas and through the dam structure.

.13.

RECREATION AND LEISURE

◆◆◆◆

Relaxing resorts and vibrant casinos attract millions each year with unparalleled excitement, glamour, and fun.

◆◆◆◆

Harrah's: 280

Eldorado Hotel-Casino: 284

Jackpot Enterprises, Inc.: 286

The Boyd Group: 287

Bally Manufacturing Corporation: 288

Circus Circus Enterprises, Inc.: 292

Photo by
Tom Campbell

HARRAH'S

When Harrah's became the first gaming company listed on the New York Stock Exchange in 1973, the *Wall Street Journal* examined the company's history, its performance, and its management and dubbed Harrah's "the Cadillac of casinos."

Started as a one-room bingo parlor by William F. Harrah in 1937, it is currently the only hotel/casino company with properties in every major U.S. gaming market. Now one of the oldest gaming companies in continuous operation in the United States and still based in Reno, Harrah's became a division of Holiday Corp., parent company of Holiday Inns, in 1980. In 1990 Harrah's became part of Promus Companies, Inc. Harrah's casinos contain almost a quarter-million square feet of casino space and account for almost 10 percent of the total gaming business in the United States.

Harrah's is Nevada's largest private employer, with more than 10,000 workers. Moreover, with the opening of its sixth major property in Laughlin, Harrah's also became Nevada's largest taxpayer, contributing more than 5 percent of the state's gross revenues.

Harrah's Reno, the company's original property, is located in downtown Reno where Bill Harrah parlayed his

● **A Mexican theme gives Harrah's Del Rio a south-of-the-border resort flavor. Situated on the banks of the Colorado River, it is the newest addition to Harrah's Nevada properties.**

bingo business into a gaming empire. Today it consists of a facility that covers almost two city blocks, has 565 hotel rooms, a 70,000-square-foot casino, a theater-restaurant, plus four other restaurants, a convention center, and a cabaret. Harrah's Reno has won both the *Mobil Travel Guide's* four-star rating and

▲ **Excellence in gaming has been the key to Harrah's success ever since the days of Bill Harrah's bingo business in the 1930s.**

the American Automobile Association's four-diamond rating each year for more than a decade. Its gourmet restaurant, the Steak House, consistently wins the *Travel/Holiday* Award for fine dining.

Harrah's Tahoe has won the *Mobil Travel Guide's* prestigious five-star award as well as AAA's five-diamond rating—the highest awards given by those organizations. It was one of only two hotels in the United States and Canada to be awarded both ratings. On the shore of America's largest mountain lake, Harrah's Lake Tahoe set standards for luxury and environmental responsibility from its first day. Its brown exterior was planned to blend with the mountains and not intrude on their beauty. The resort complex has 540 rooms and more than 65,000 square feet of casino floors in its 18 stories.

Bill's Casino, also at Lake Tahoe, is a laid-back place with lower-stakes games and loose slots in a little corner near Harrah's, under the shadow of Harrah's hotel tower. Bill's is designed to attract the first-time gamer. "We view it as a greenhouse," explains Harrah's president and chief operating officer, Phil Satre, "a place where we can introduce them to gaming, and a place where we can try out new ideas, perhaps ideas we can eventually use in our larger establishments." Named in honor of Bill Harrah, the three-story Bill's has 18,100 square feet of gaming area; Bennigan's,

▲ The massive Holiday Casino/Holiday Inn epitomizes gaming on the Las Vegas Strip. The "Ship on the Strip" casino is housed within a riverboat and has long been a Strip landmark.

a 5,500-square-foot restaurant owned by Pillsbury; and a McDonald's restaurant.

The Holiday Casino/Holiday Inn, in the heart of the Las Vegas Strip, is America's largest Holiday Inn, with 1,725 rooms. Called "the Ship on the Strip," the Holiday Casino is housed inside a big riverboat; it has been a prominent Strip landmark for many years. The property is the largest Holiday Inn hotel in the world.

Harrah's Del Rio features a Mexican theme and is the newest addition to Harrah's properties in Nevada. It is located on the banks of the Colorado River in the booming town of Laughlin. The new property includes a twin-tower,

1,000-room hotel and a 26,500-square-foot gaming area. Del Rio has 500 covered parking spaces for guests and a riverfront beach area, both firsts for a Laughlin hotel-casino.

Both the Holiday Casino/Holiday Inn in Las Vegas and Harrah's Del Rio reflect Satre's belief that "the gaming industry is moving toward highly themed properties," a trend that he says "is almost an

art form in Las Vegas."

The company's sixth property is Harrah's Marina Hotel/Casino, opened in Atlantic City, New Jersey, in 1980, the nation's first hotel-casino that offers boat-docking facilities in its 107-slip harbor on the Atlantic.

Before he died in 1978, William Fisk Harrah's insight and business savvy had made him a giant in Nevada gaming. He knew that people came to his casinos not to just gamble, but also to relax and be entertained. His formula was big-name entertainment in the showrooms, great restaurants, and personal service.

While other casinos' cocktail servers cried "Cocktails," waitresses at Harrah's

▲ Designed to blend harmoniously with its beautiful mountainous surroundings, Harrah's Lake Tahoe has set standards for luxury and environmental responsibility.

▲ Harrah's Lake Tahoe features well-appointed, comfortable rooms close to the excitement of the casino and the relaxation of the lakeside.

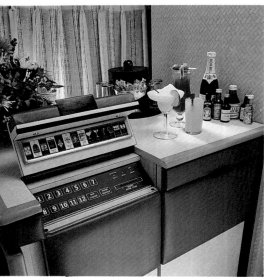

◄ Each of Harrah's Lake Tahoe's 540 rooms feature an automated bar that dispenses a variety of drinks.

would tell customers, "Bill Harrah would like to buy you a drink." Many of Bill Harrah's customers became his personal friends.

Harrah booked singer Eddie Fisher into the Headliner Room when it opened in 1966. Earlier, comedian Red Skelton helped open the South Shore Room at Harrah's Tahoe in 1959. After that, Harrah's set the pace for northern Nevada showrooms in showcasing the leading stars.

And Harrah logged many firsts. Few were more dramatic than the Rockettes' first performance outside of Radio City Music Hall, at Harrah's Tahoe, where they appeared during the winter of 1975. Another first at Tahoe was the back-to-back concept developed in 1975, with folk singer John Denver performing for dinner shows and Frank Sinatra entertaining at late shows.

The list of performers who first appeared at Harrah's as opening acts and then went on to stardom is a long one. It includes Wayne Newton, who was first introduced to Harrah's audiences by Jack Benny; Barbra Streisand, introduced by Liberace; and Bobby Darin, introduced by comedian George Burns. Harrah's was Jim Nabors' first live billing, and Kenny Rogers first came to Harrah's as a cabaret act.

Harrah's made history off the stage, too. For one thing, Bill Harrah built the first hotel skyscraper in Reno, opened in 1969. Now many hotel towers crowd the skyline. Harrah's was the first to put jackpot lights on the tops of slot machines. Harrah's pioneered multiple-coin slots and electronic keno. Harrah's introduced air curtains at casino entrances, making front doors unnecessary.

But Bill Harrah's greatest legacy to the gaming empire, according to Satre, is the philosophy that continues to guide the company's policies. "Bill Harrah brought some strong traditions to this company—in customer service, in attention to detail," relates Satre. "His policies have attracted top employees to the company."

That includes Satre himself. At age 36, when he became Harrah's top executive, Satre is one of America's youngest chief executive officers and is active in the Young President's Organization. He is also a corporate senior vice-president and a director of the parent Promus Companies, Inc. A native Californian, Satre trained as a lawyer and became familiar with Harrah's while he was representing the company.

A dedicated fisherman, Satre recalls an early visit to Reno when he hauled in a four-pound trout off a downtown bridge over the Truckee River. "I was so delighted, I told my wife that someday we would move to this town," he recalls.

Satre came to work for Harrah's in

▲ The sun sets and brings on the night at Harrah's Del Rio in Laughlin.

1980, moving through various senior management positions until he was elected to his present leadership posts in 1984. He takes an active role in the community, too—among other things, serving as a director of the National Judicial College, as a director of the Sierra Nevada Museum of Art, and as a member of the Governor's Commission on Tourism.

Satre has set four standards for Harrah's:

Customer relations—"We want to be a leader with our customers," he says. "We want them to recognize Harrah's for the highest levels of service. That's why we have the highest-rated casino at Tahoe."

Employee relations—"We maintain the best employee relations in the casino business. That makes us a very attractive employer." Satre encourages employee participation in company decision making, and often holds small round tables,

seeking employees' ideas.

Profitability—"We try to be competitive," Satre states. "We need a fair profit for our long-term survival."

Community service—"We want to be a good community participant. Our goal is to be a good corporate citizen."

Satre is proud that the company has helped keep Harrah's name alive in the communities it serves. His office high in Harrah's executive building overlooks the Truckee River and the new museum that houses the famous William F. Harrah automobile collection. Holiday Corp. donated 225 cars it acquired from Bill Harrah's estate to the foundation that runs the museum.

In Las Vegas, the firm honored Bill Harrah's name with the largest single gift ever made to the University of Nevada,

Las Vegas—a $5-million donation from the company and Harrah's widow, Verna, to establish the William F. Harrah College of Hotel Administration. The gift, administered through the UNLV Foundation, establishes three distinguished academic chairs and enhances academic programs in what was already one of the country's leading hotel schools.

"Harrah's believes that UNLV's College of Hotel Administration is one of the premier programs in the world," Satre related in announcing the gift in 1988. He adds: "Harrah's has been closely involved with the University of Nevada system for years. In northern Nevada, many of our Reno executives serve on University of Nevada, Reno, boards and committees. We sponsor the university's annual William F. Harrah Lecture Series, which raises funds for the UNR Foundation."

And the company's involvement in education is not limited to the college level. Harrah's spearheads the innovative Adopt-A-School program in northern Nevada, under which companies and individual schools form partnerships. Harrah's, for example, provides classroom speakers for its chosen high school, helps pay for special programs and equipment, offers career guidance to students, and hosts both students and teachers in tours and special seminars. Following Harrah's leadership, 75 other northern Nevada companies have now adopted schools.

Satre sees the future of gaming in Nevada as bright. "Gambling continues to be more and more acceptable as a form of recreation," he comments. "Growth is a fact of Nevada life—and even more in Las Vegas and Clark County than anywhere else. That will influence everything about Nevada living—education, our resources, and a broad range of public services.

"I call Los Angeles 'the city of the 1990s,'" he muses. "The nation's most important city, especially because of its relationship to the Pacific Rim. Las Vegas' proximity to Los Angeles makes a nice ride on those coattails."

And that trend, Satre adds, is bound to be good for Harrah's, as well as for Nevada.

ELDORADO HOTEL-CASINO

▲ The Caranos (back row, from left): Gary, Gregg, and Glenn, and (front row, from left) Cindy Carano-Wrentmore, Don, Rhonda, and Gene.

Typical of the new leaders shaping Nevada's gaming industry is the Carano family, whose Eldorado Hotel-Casino has altered the face of downtown Reno and become one of the city's most successful gaming properties in fewer than two decades.

Today, the Eldorado's spectacular 25-story hotel tower dominates the area north of the railroad tracks that before 1973 was a wasteland of parking lots and rundown stores well outside the crowded downtown. Now the downtown surrounds the Eldorado—a cleaner, more attractive downtown, thanks in good part to the leadership of Donald Carano.

The gleaming tower that opened in 1989 as the centerpiece of the Eldorado's $45-million expansion project is also a tribute to the leadership of Don Carano and the family he brought into the gaming business: his wife, Rhonda, who is Eldorado's advertising and public relations director; sons Gary, general manager, Glenn, director of marketing, Gene, director of gaming, and Gregg, food and beverage director; and daughter Cindy Carano-Wrentmore, hotel manager. "The customers can always find a Carano here, day or night. It gives it that personal touch," says Don Carano. "You can always talk to the boss."

The block-square Eldorado, with 12,000 square feet of convention facilities, eight restaurants, a 60,000-square-foot casino, and more than 800 hotel rooms, was designed by Carano's partner, architect Jerry Poncia. The hotel-casino employs more than 2,000 people.

Carano, a third-generation Renoite, practiced law for 20 years before entering gaming. In 1968, with Poncia and other partners, he opened the Pioneer Inn and Casino on South Virginia Street. Then he went into partnership with Bob Cashell and others to build the Boomtown Casino. In 1973 he opened the Eldorado, with a small casino and 282 rooms. In 1978 Carano gave up his legal practice to operate the casino full time, along with his oldest son, Gary.

Gary Carano, like the other Carano offspring, grew up in gaming, then studied a specialty in college. Gary was pumping gas at Boomtown when he was 18.

After that he dealt cards, tended bar and worked as a slot mechanic and casino cashier while earning a degree in business administration at the University of Nevada, Reno.

A special background is brought to the family business by Glenn Carano, former quarterback for the University of Nevada, Las Vegas, the Dallas Cowboys, and the Pittsburgh Maulers. It was not until Glenn retired from professional football that the Caranos opened a full-service race and sports book at the Eldorado—"to avoid any possible conflicts of interest," Don Carano explains. Articulate and outgoing, Glenn is a natural in his role as Eldorado's director of marketing, his father says. And he adds that his son's sports background "should open a lot of doors for us."

Even when they were youngsters, the Carano offspring competed in sports, Don Carano recalls, and today they still compete with each other over who runs the best department. "Never place second," says Gary Carano, adding that the competition, discipline, and teamwork taught in sports is a valuable preparation for business. "It taught us to set goals, work hard, and cooperate with others."

With family management, Gary Carano says, "you have people who care about the business because they

▼ Rhonda and Donald Carano survey the grounds of their beautiful Ferrari-Carano Vineyards. The 250-acre estate, located in California's Sonoma County wine country, produces several wine varietals, among them Chardonnay, Fumé Blanc, and Cabernet Sauvignon.

have a stake in the business. And there is a customer perception that family owned and operated is good. "As a family, we can also make business decisions quicker."

Great-grandson of Italian immigrants, Don Carano is proud of his heritage and makes it an important part of Eldorado's marketing program. The hotel's La Strada is a top Italian restaurant. Each fall the Eldorado hosts the Great Italian Festival that includes a spaghetti cook-off, a spaghetti-eating contest, pasta-making demonstrations, and a celebrity grape stomp.

The Caranos' strategy is to develop a gourmet cuisine from Old-Country recipes. "The Italians who came here . . . didn't come over with any money. They brought their peasant recipes. We're taking those basic recipes and expanding them," Don Carano explains.

It helps that his wife, Rhonda, is an accomplished cook who often plans menus—and occasionally cooks them—for both the family and visiting V.I.P. banquets. "The best Italian cook I ever knew," claims Don Carano, proudly.

Wine is an important part of the Caranos' Italian heritage, too. Don Carano talks about it all the time, drinks it after 5 p.m. (because, he says, he is watching his weight), and, with his wife, owns one of California's leading new wineries, Ferrari-Carano. (The family

▲ Eldorado's beautiful 25-story tower has brought new life to downtown Reno.

name "Ferrari" honors his immigrant great-grandparents, whose daughter married the first Carano.)

"It was just going to be our hide-away . . . to get away from here," says Don Carano of his growing winery. "We bought a little vineyard over in the Alexander Valley in California's Sonoma County—didn't even make any wine commercially. Then we got caught up in it and couldn't put it down." Today there are seven Carano vineyards, a modern winery and tasting room, and the Ferrari-Carano label is beginning to win medals.

The Eldorado has hosted the West Coast Wine Competition, Nevada's largest and one of the nation's most prestigious wine events, with more than 250 premium wineries represented. In 1989 the Eldorado gifted this event to the Reno-Sparks Convention Authority in hopes of developing it into a city-wide festival where the whole town will benefit.

Supporting the community is important to Don Carano. His leadership promoting downtown beautification helped get that renovation project moving. He has served as local chairman of the March of Dimes and as a director of the Reno/Sparks Tourist and Convention Authority. Rhonda Carano has been on the board of the Reno Philharmonic, the Sierra Museum of Art, YWCA, and the Nevada Women's Fund. Gary Carano sits on the YMCA Board of Directors. And the Eldorado has "adopted" Reno's Wooster High School as part of the business community's new Partners in Education program.

"We enjoy living here," explains Don Carano. "And you have to give back to the community something it's given you."

▼ Patrons try for 21 at one of Eldorado's black-jack tables.

JACKPOT ENTERPRISES, INC.

To most people, the word "jackpot" means a torrent of coins gushing from the hopper of a slot machine. But there is another meaning for the word: Jackpot also stands for a well-run company that operates coin-operated gaming device routes in every major city in Nevada—and in many of the smaller towns as well.

Jackpot Enterprises, Inc., owns, installs, operates, and services coin-operated gaming devices (such as reel-spinning slots and video poker machines) located in high-volume national drug and supermarket retail chains, as well as in bars and taverns. In addition the company operates and services smaller and diversified local retail locations throughout the state.

Jackpot Enterprises, Inc., was organized in 1980 to acquire Cardivan Company and Corral United Inc., two of

● Jackpot operates gaming devices in retail locations throughout the state of Nevada.

Nevada's oldest coin-operated gaming device route operators. Today Jackpot is one of the largest operators in the state and is expanding its focus into diversified casino operations, the majority of the revenues of which will be generated by coin-operated gaming devices such as The Nugget, operated by Jackpot in

Reno, Nevada.

Because of the size and scope of the state of Nevada, the logistics of doing business 365 days per year, 24 hours per day as a route operator, especially outside the major population areas such as Las Vegas and Reno, presents a tremendous challenge. Jackpot strives to

provide the best possible service and maintenance and to provide sufficient personnel in all of its locations.

J. Emmett Sullivan, executive vice-president of Jackpot and a Nevada resident since 1933, commented that "the company has regarded itself as an integral part of the growing Nevada economy, and to that end the company pays substantial gaming taxes to the state and participates in charitable community activities. Employees are provided with health care, retirement benefits, and options to purchase stock in the company. It is the company's policy to have its employees participate in its growth."

Robert L. McDonald, Sr., a longtime resident of Reno, Nevada, who has been a director of the company since its founding and is a member of the board of directors of Valley Bank of Nevada, notes that "Jackpot has worked extensively within the gaming industry to assemble a team of upper and middle management that encompasses hundreds of years of experience."

Jackpot Enterprises, Inc., is a publicly traded company listed on the New York Exchange under the symbol "J."

THE BOYD GROUP

With five major hotel/casinos, The Boyd Group is one of the largest players in Nevada's gaming industry and one of the state's few remaining family-operated gaming companies.

The family's patriarch, Sam Boyd, has been leaving his mark on Las Vegas since 1941, when he moved to the young town with his wife and son, Bill, and $30 in his pocket. Boyd, a self-made millionaire in the classic Nevada tradition, learned the gaming business from the ground up and built his first property in downtown Las Vegas in 1975. As a community leader, Boyd was founder of the Clark County Boys Club, president of the chamber of commerce, and director of the Nevada Safety Council. In 1985 the University of Nevada, Las Vegas, renamed its stadium the Sam Boyd Silver Bowl, in tribute to the Boyd family's strong support.

Though Sam Boyd remains honorary chairman of The Boyd Group board, the company today is headed by William S. "Bill" Boyd, chairman of the board and chief executive officer, and Charles L. Ruthe, president and chief operating officer.

The Boyd Group operates many properties, including the California Hotel, Casino, and RV Park. Newly remodeled and expanded, this high-rise hotel was the first to bear the Boyd name. Opened by Sam Boyd in 1975, the California boasts 650 rooms and suites and downtown Las Vegas' only recreational vehicle park, with full hookups for 222 campers.

The Boyd Group also owns the Stardust Hotel and Casino. When the Stardust opened on the Las Vegas Strip in 1958, it was one of the largest hotels in the world, with 1,354 rooms. The firm spent $60 million remodeling the Stardust after buying it in 1985. Home of the long-playing Lido de Paris show and now headquarters for The Boyd Group, the Stardust features an 83,000-square-foot casino area, a 234-space recreational-vehicle park, and a Sports Handicapper's Library, a feature that has made its sports book world renowned.

Sam's Town Hotel and Gambling Hall is a western-theme gaming resort on the eastern edge of town, catering to both visitors and Las Vegas residents. Now featuring two recreational-vehicle parks with 500 spaces total, 200 guest rooms, a 56-lane bowling center, and one of the largest western-oriented department stores this side of the Mississippi, Boyd's Sam's Town was the first major hotel/casino along the Boulder Highway entrance to Las Vegas.

Sam Boyd's Fremont Hotel and Casino, built in 1956, was Nevada's first high-rise building and one of the anchors of Glitter Gulch's well-known "four corners." Boyd's name was added to the title when his company purchased the downtown Las Vegas hotel in 1985. The remodeled Fremont has 452 rooms and suites and 36,000 square feet of gaming space.

Sam's Town Gold River Hotel and Casino, themed to resemble an old mining smelting plant, was built in 1985 on the banks of the Colorado River in Laughlin, where boats ferry visitors across the river to gamble from Bullhead City, Arizona, and up the river to other Laughlin resorts. The hotel, with 225 rooms and suites and three floors of gaming, has a romantic walkway along the Colorado. An 800-room addition to the facility is currently under construction.

The Boyd family also operates The Eldorado, a neighborhood casino under expansion in Henderson.

▼ **Heading The Boyd Group are Bill Boyd (seated), chairman of the board and chief executive officer, and Chuck Ruthe, president and chief operating officer.**

BALLY MANUFACTURING CORPORATION

There was a time in America when the name "Bally" stirred the competitive spirit in every youngster who found a nickel in his pocket. Through the magic of Bally's pinball machines in drugstores, ice cream shops, and penny arcades, American youth fought World War II, won the West, and, with keen eye and quick hands, impressed their high school sweethearts.

It was Bally that gave the word "tilt" a special meaning all its own.

It was a simpler time for America. Since then, both the nation and Bally Manufacturing Corporation have come of age, ready to tackle the challenges of the next century.

Founded in Chicago in 1930, Bally is now the worldwide gaming industry's largest player, is one of the leading companies serving health-conscious America, and has a full-service lottery division.

With its growing operations in

Nevada, Bally is one of the state's largest manufacturing employers, annually exporting millions of dollars worth of gaming throughout the world, and operates two of the largest casino hotels in Las Vegas and Reno. Still headquartered in Chicago and headed by Robert E. Mullane, chairman of the board and chief executive officer, and Roger N. Keesee, president and chief operating officer, Bally Manufacturing Co. has three operating units.

The casino division owns and manages Bally's Casino Resort in Las Vegas,

Bally's Casino Resort in Reno, and Bally's Park Place and Bally's Grand in Atlantic City, New Jersey.

The gaming equipment and services division designs, builds, and sells equipment such as slot machines, video gaming machines, and German wall machines.

Through its Scientific Games, Inc., subsidiary, Bally produces a wide range of products and consulting services for a growing number of state lotteries.

The health and fitness division builds and sells exercise equipment for home,

● **Bally's is a strong presence in Atlantic City, New Jersey.** Featuring a 45,500-square-foot gaming area and more than 500 well-appointed rooms and suites, Bally's Grand (below) is a familiar stop on the Boardwalk. Also on the Boardwalk is Bally's Park Place (right), a giant casino hotel featuring 13,000 rooms and suites, an expansive gaming area, convention and meeting facilities, and a deluxe health spa.

club, and other commercial markets, and operates fitness centers worldwide, offering amenities such as running tracks, swimming, work-out equipment, and instruction.

One of the pioneer casino hotel operators in Atlantic City, Bally Manufacturing purchased the two giant MGM Grand Hotels in Nevada in 1986, refurbished and modernized them, and changed their names to Bally's Casino Resorts.

In dollar volume, Bally's four casino hotels make the company the world's largest casino operator. The trademark of Bally's casino hotel operations, according to chairman Robert Mullane, is "opulence and elegance."

Bally's establishments in Reno and Las Vegas define casino gaming in

Nevada—the epitomes of the glamour, the excitement, the entertainment, fine dining, and gracious service that make the Silver State a place where all the world plays.

Virtually a city within a city, the 26-story Bally's Casino Resort in Las Vegas contains 3.25 million square feet on its 71-acre site at the intersection of Flamingo Road and Las Vegas Avenue, the very center of the famed Las Vegas Strip. Bally's has 2,832 luxurious rooms and suites and 4,500 employees.

The Clark County Fire Chiefs Association has declared Bally's "the safest hotel in the world" as a result of a multimil-

lion-dollar Life Safety System. Guests are protected by a central computer, programmed to detect fire or smoke anywhere in the building and initiate up to 1,000 safety measures, including activating 30,000 fire sprinkler heads and automatically notifying the fire department.

The hotel has one of the world's largest casino floors—substantially larger than a football field—with more than 56,000 square feet devoted to slot machines, video games, a race and sports book, keno, poker, pai gow, and table games such as blackjack, craps, roulette, and baccarat. More than 1,500 casino employees keep the action going 24 hours per day.

Bally's is the only hotel in Las Vegas offering world-class entertainment in two major showrooms. International su-

perstars such as Frank Sinatra, Dean Martin, Sammy Davis, Jr., Jerry Lewis, Barbara Mandrell, Johnny Mathis, and a host of others perform at dinner and cocktail shows in the 1,400-seat Celebrity Room.

Next door is the 1,100-seat Ziegfeld Theatre, home to Donn Arden's spectacular, long-running production "Jubilee!" Staged at a cost of more than $10 million and with a cast of more than 100 singers and dancers, Las Vegas' biggest show features 60 musical numbers.

Catch A Rising Star in Bally's Theatre is the city's most exciting new comedy club, and the Celebrity Lounge just off

▲ Bally's Casino Resort in Reno features its own lagoon as part of its 148-acre site. The towering 26-story hotel offers 2,001 rooms, a 50-lane bowling center, convention facilities, and a deluxe shopping mall.

◄ A city within a city, the 3.25-million-square-foot Bally's Casino Resort in Las Vegas is "the safest hotel in the world." The gaming floor is larger than a football field; a work force of 1,500 employees keeps the action going 24 hours per day. Superstars regularly entertain audiences of 1,400 in the celebrity room.

the casino features nonstop musical entertainment.

Bally's Las Vegas resort, on average, serves more than 18,000 meals per day in its six restaurants that include four gourmet rooms. As many as 4,000 people in one sitting have been served in one of its massive banquet rooms. Las Vegas residents as well as visitors come to Bally's to dine on French cuisine at Gigi's, Italian fare at Caruso's, steaks and chops at Barrymores', or Chinese food at Tracy's. Other restaurants are

the Orleans Coffee Shop and Swensen's Old Fashioned Ice Cream Parlor.

With more than 200,000 square feet of convention space, Bally's is one of Las Vegas' premier meeting facilities. In addition to 43 convention meeting rooms, larger conventions also can use supplemental space such as the Celebrity Room and Ziegfeld Theatre.

A bonus to conventioneers is Bally's Business Theatre, a unique way to present products, services, companies, or associations through entertainment. Bally's takes the concept of the industrial show and refines it to an art form, a powerful way to unify and motivate a convention group. Bally's also arranges and produces theme parties for luncheons, banquets, and receptions, complete with appropriate sets, menus, and entertainment.

Visitors to Bally's browse through the largest luxury shopping mall of any hotel in Las Vegas, where more than 40 stores offer everything from art to zebras. There are men's and women's health spas, 10 championship tennis

▲ Bally is America's leading owner-operator of health clubs. Holiday Spa, popular in California and Florida, is a comprehensive fitness center featuring Life Fitness equipment.

▶ The popular Lifecycle, manufactured by Bally's subsidiary Life Fitness, Inc., allows users to read and ride.

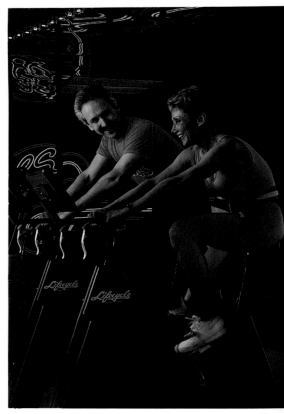

courts (seven lighted for play at night), and a landscaped outdoor pool and cabana area.

Bally's Casino Resort in Reno, because of its scale and amenities, is also one of that city's leading gaming facilities. Similar in appearance to Bally's Las Vegas hotel, Bally's Reno hotel dominates the northern and eastern approaches to the city—whether by plane, rail, or auto. On a 148-acre site, complete with a lagoon, the 26-story Bally's offers 2,001 rooms, each with unobstructed panoramic views.

Bally's Reno Lanes, a 50-lane bowling center with state-of-the-art electronic scoring, a pro shop, and snack bar, makes the resort a popular location for regional and national tournaments. Bally's recently was the site of the Women's International Bowling Congress tournament, which drew 60,000 bowlers and their families to Reno.

Behind its hotel building, Bally's operates Camperland, Reno's largest recreational vehicle park, with hookups for 452 recreational vehicles, showers, a gas station, a convenience store, and a laundry. And Bally's Mall, with 40 high-quality shops similar to those in Bally's Las Vegas mall, is the largest hotel shopping area in Reno.

With its own 50,000-square-foot casino, seven fine restaurants, 200,000 square feet of convention space, 2,000-seat Ziegfeld Theatre showroom, and a 192-seat movie theater, where classic and art films are shown, Bally's Reno resort, like its Las Vegas counterpart, is

▶ Bally's subsidiary Scientific Games, Inc., dominates the lottery ticket printing industry.

▼ Slot machines and video games made by Bally's gaming equipment division set the standard in the Silver State and beyond.

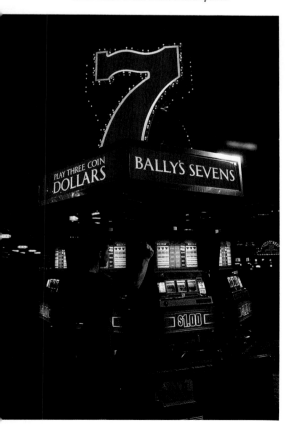

also a city within a city.

Bally's Park Place has been one of the largest casino hotels in Atlantic City since its opening in 1979. The hotel has 1,300 rooms and suites, 60,000 square feet of casino space, 50,000 square feet of convention and meeting space, and a 38,000-square-foot health spa. At Park Place and the Boardwalk, Bally's is within four blocks of the city's Convention Hall.

Bally's Grand, also located on Atlantic City's Boardwalk, has more than 500 deluxe rooms and suites and a 45,500-square-foot gaming area.

Bally Manufacturing Co. soon will become one of Nevada's largest manufacturing employers with its new high-technology facility in Las Vegas' Hughes Airport Center industrial park, where the company produces gaming machines and lottery equipment and exports them worldwide.

Employing 300 workers, Bally will move the plant from the Chicago area in the fall of 1990 to take advantage of Nevada's location and favorable business climate, according to Bally's president Roger Keesee. "It makes sense to be a gaming manufacturer in a gaming state," he said at the time. "Opening the Nevada plant brings our manufacturing closer to our customers, enabling us to serve them quickly and efficiently."

In addition to conventional electronic

slot machines and video games for the casino industry, Bally's gaming equipment division makes things such as video poker machines for U.S. military bases worldwide, slot machines for Taiwanese customers, a video Keno game that complies with new Montana law, wall machines for gambling in German bistros, and an electronic bill changer coupled with a slot machine that eliminates the need for players to leave their machines to make change.

Bally's Scientific Games, Inc., subsidiary prints instant lottery tickets for more than half of the states that conduct lotteries. In addition, it provides lottery consulting services in several offshore jurisdictions.

Bally Manufacturing Corporation has become a leader in the fitness movement. Its Life Fitness, Inc., subsidiary specializes in research, manufacturing, and marketing computerized exercise machinery for commercial and consumer use. The company's aerobic and strength-training equipment is sold to health clubs, hotels and resorts, hospitals and medical facilities, team-training rooms, military and government facilities, and private homes. In addition, Bally is the largest owner-operator of health clubs in the United States, with more than 300 Health & Tennis Corporation of America clubs, where more than 3 million members work out weekly.

"There has been a radical change in the way people think about taking care of themselves," explains Bally's chairman Mullane. "Fitness is one method by which people prepare for a healthier old age. Bally's fitness clubs appeal to a wide range of age groups, and the number of people interested in fitness is growing at an astonishing rate.

"Taking a prominent position in this movement fits Bally's role as one of the largest entertainment and recreation companies in America."

CIRCUS CIRCUS ENTERPRISES, INC.

Fantasy becomes reality at Circus Circus Enterprises, Inc., Nevada resorts and casinos.

Along the Las Vegas Strip and in downtown Reno, Circus Circus hotel/casinos stand out as the world's only gaming establishments offering entertainment for fun seekers of all ages. Under the pink-and-white big tops are

---

▼ A pink-and-white big top crowns the gigantic Circus Circus Hotel/Casino on the Las Vegas Strip, offering entertainment for fun seekers of all ages.

luxury accommodations (2,800 rooms in Las Vegas, 1,625 rooms in Reno), varied dining, multiple casinos, celebrated circus acts presented free 13 hours each day, glittering carnival midways, and, in Las Vegas, the adjacent 421-space Circusland recreational-vehicle park.

New on the Las Vegas Strip is Circus Circus's Excalibur Hotel/Casino, bringing to life the legend of King Arthur and the Knights of the Round Table. With 4,032 rooms and more than 100,000 square feet of casino area, it is the world's largest resort.

Also on the Las Vegas Strip are Circus

▼ The elaborate Colorado Belle Hotel/Casino in Laughlin features a riverboat theme.

▲ The world's largest resort—Circus Circus' Excalibur—combines first-class gaming and resort amenities with an Arthurian theme.

Circus's Slots-A-Fun Casino and the Silver City Casino, offering a rare brand of old-west friendliness and hospitality.

Circus Circus properties in Laughlin, on the Colorado River—the 1,500-room Edgewater Hotel/Casino and the 1,235-room, riverboat-theme Colorado Belle Hotel/Casino—blend gaming action with desert serenity.

Rich in amenities, yet affordable to all, the properties of Circus Circus Enterprises, Inc., encompass all the excitement, glamour, and beauty to be found throughout the Silver State.

Photo by Tom Cambell

.14.

QUALITY
OF
LIFE

◆◆◆◆

*Nevadans enjoy the quality of life
afforded by educational
institutions, quality medical care,
and arts and culture.*

◆◆◆◆

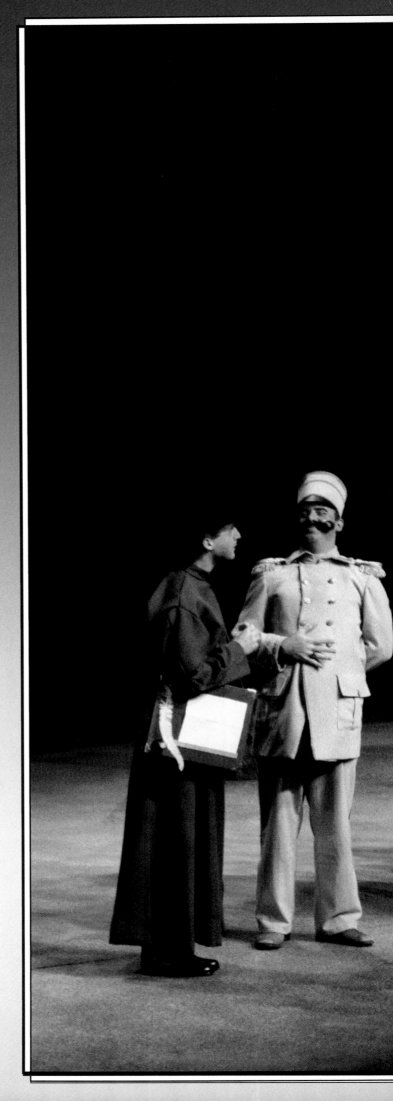

University of Nevada, Reno: 296

University of Nevada, Las Vegas: 300

The Desert Research Institute: 304

Saint Mary's Regional Medical Center: 306

Sierra Health Services: 308

Blue Cross and Blue Shield of Nevada: 312

Laura Spitzer: 313

Nevada Arts: 314

Photo by
Tom Campbell

UNIVERSITY OF NEVADA, RENO

The bronze statue of John Mackay stares thoughtfully across the historic Jeffersonian Quadrangle at the University of Nevada, Reno. The legendary mine superintendent, one of the famous Kings of the Comstock, leans on a pick for support, his right hand clutching a lump of silver that was the reward of his hard work. The Mackay statue, created by Mount Rushmore's sculptor, Gutzon Borglum, is an appropriate symbol for the University of Nevada, Reno. To Nevada, the university is the supportive tool that helps fulfill the promise of reward for hard work.

Looking to the next century with characteristic vision and vitality, the university is steeped in the rich tradition of its first 100 years. The University of Nevada was established as Nevada's land-grant state university in 1864 and opened its doors in Elko 10 years later. In 1885 the university moved to its permanent location in Reno and constructed its first building, Morrill Hall. Its completion the following year marked the beginning of a university that would come to earn its reputation for being big enough to challenge its students, yet small enough to care about them.

As the campus grew into the Jeffer-

▲ The statue of John Mackay, one of the early benefactors of the University of Nevada, Reno, overlooks the historic Jeffersonian Quadrangle and Morrill Hall. Photo by Vance Fox

◀ Morrill Hall, the University of Nevada, Reno's, first building, dates back to 1886.

sonian academic village that benefactors such as John Mackay envisioned, the University of Nevada, Reno's, faculty, educational, and research offerings expanded with it. From a one-building campus, the university has grown into an institution with approximately 3 million square feet of floor space on its 200-acre main campus, and 12,500 acres of field laboratories and research areas statewide.

Most of the older buildings have undergone renovation, and more renovation is under way. An example is the $10-million three-phase restoration of the historic Mackay School of Mines building. New campus construction includes the $10.5-million engineering laboratory, as well as a $3.2-million renovation of student housing and $10 million for new housing and a strengthening of campus residential life. Getchell Library, the state's largest, is the hub of a six-branch system and a testament to the forethought of early Nevadans such as John Mackay.

The University of Nevada, Reno, Quadrangle is listed on the National Register of Historic Places because of its styling, age, and beauty. However, Nevada's first university is recognized

for more than its physical beauty. The quality, reasonable price, and variety of its education offerings are lauded in *How to Get An Ivy League Education at a State University*. Indeed, the university offers more than 70 bachelor's degree programs, more than 60 master's degrees, 23 doctoral degrees, the M.D., and M.D./Ph.D. According to information in the *1987 Higher Education Directory,* the University of Nevada, Reno, is one of only two schools in the nation with enrollments of less than 19,000 students offering a variety of academic programs in the schools of arts and science, medicine, engineering, business, and agriculture. There are 11

▲ Manzanita Lake is a centerpiece of the university's 200-acre main campus, in the shadows of nearby downtown Reno. Photo by Clovis Photographics

schools and colleges and a Division of Continuing Education on the campus.

The National Judicial College and the National Council of Juvenile and Family Court Judges, offering continuing education to judges and other court officers from around the world, are located on campus and cooperate with the university in offering to judges the unique Master of Judicial Studies degree.

The University of Nevada School of

Medicine has been called one of the best small medical schools in the country by the Liaison Committee on Graduate Medical Education—high accolades for a school so young. In only two decades the medical school has fulfilled goals of becoming a statewide institution that offers medical education to Nevada's young people, helping alleviate the shortage of family doctors in rural communities and providing continuing education for the state's medical community.

▼ Part of a talented and dedicated faculty, Roger Lewis, Ph.D., works with students in the biochemistry laboratory.

▼ The School of Medicine, a statewide institution, occupies five buildings on the University of Nevada, Reno, campus. Photo by Clovis Photographics

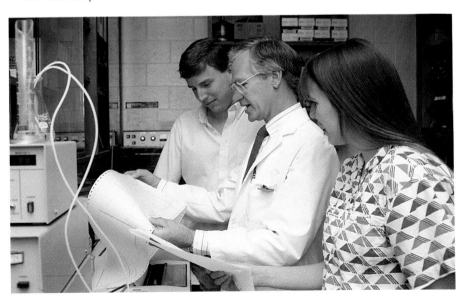

Bolstered by high-quality professional degree programs such as those offered by the School of Medicine and the National Judicial College, the University of Nevada, Reno's, reputation for excellence is growing. The Northwest Association of Schools and Colleges' 1988 reaccreditation report says, "The University of Nevada, Reno, is an impressive institution with an attractive and well-maintained campus, a talented and dedicated faculty, an energetic administration, a loyal staff, and a student body characterized by pride in their institution and general satisfaction in their educational experience."

The university's concentration on quality has prompted growing numbers of top high school scholars to remain in the state for their higher education. They recognize that the Reno campus has educational and cultural offerings that rival those of much larger institutions while maintaining accessibility of its first-rate faculty. At the University of Nevada, Reno, students receive an education that challenges their talents. The newly strengthened honors program is a way for students to test the limits of their abilities. All undergraduates are

◀ Getchell Library, the state's largest, is the hub of a six-branch system.

▼ Richard Simmonds, D.V.M., oversees animal care throughout the University of Nevada System.

◀ At the National Judicial College, judges from throughout the United States gather for continuing education courses.

▶ Fruit trees bring springtime beauty to campus with the round lecture building and the physics building in the background.

required to enroll in a 36-credit core curriculum designed to produce well-rounded, cultured graduates prepared to contribute fully to society.

The University of Nevada, Reno's, 11,000 students come from all 50 states and more than 60 foreign countries. They receive high-quality education from professors eager to share their knowledge—a good portion of which has been derived from their own research activities—with their students and their community. The university is proud of its faculty and of the level of research being conducted both on and off campus. Research funds doubled during the late 1980s alone as a result of successful faculty efforts. Because of its relatively small size, graduate students at the University of Nevada, Reno, work directly with researchers who are on the leading edge in their respective fields. This rewarding experience creates an enthusiasm in these scholars encouraging them to continue seeking better solutions to important problems.

As Nevada's land-grant university, the University of Nevada, Reno's, three-fold mission is to provide not only teaching and research, but public service as well. Whether testing contaminated soil for a distraught farmer, safety checking bridges for stress loads, seeking cures for colon diseases, assisting children with learning disabilities, or helping small business owners to succeed, the University of Nevada, Reno, is involved.

The university and its faculty are committed to bettering the community. Unlike large metropolitan areas where instructors may commute hours each day traveling to work, most University of Nevada, Reno, faculty reside in the Truckee Meadows, many in neighborhoods adjacent to the attractive hillside campus. They care about the university's

▲ The University of Nevada, Reno, Quadrangle is listed on the National Register of Historic Places for its style, age, and beauty. Photo by Vance Fox

involvement with the community because it is their home.

The University of Nevada, Reno, also serves northern Nevada as a cultural catalyst. The university sponsors hundreds of concerts, lectures, films, presentations, exhibits, and special events open to the public. The Church Fine Arts Complex boasts two theaters, several art galleries, and the Nightingale Concert Hall, which has hosted everything from Beethoven concertos performed by a faculty trio, jazz festivals, and noon-time recitals, to concerts by the Vienna Boys Choir and other international luminaries. Lawlor Events Center attracts big-name performers from Lucianno Pavarotti to Sting.

The University of Nevada, Reno, Choir has participated in concerts as far away as Spain and is featured regularly on CBS Radio's annual "Cavalcade of Christmas Music." Musicals produced by the theater department have toured U.S. military bases worldwide. The Speakers Bureau provides informative and entertaining speakers for local civic, professional, and educational organizations.

Athletics are not forgotten either. University of Nevada, Reno, athletes have come to be known as fierce competitors, providing loyal Wolf Pack fans with dramatic sporting events. Wolf Pack teams often rank nationally and compete regularly in intercollegiate championship tournaments.

As the University of Nevada, Reno, prepares for the advent of the twenty-first century, an air of confidence surrounds the student body, faculty, and staff. It is a dynamic university, prepared to offer the most up-to-date educational opportunities, beneficial research, and public service in a picturesque, historic setting.

When spring arrives on the University of Nevada, Reno, campus, visitors bask in the beauty and serenity of the historic quadrangle. The statue of John Mackay gazes over the quad, a look of determination upon his bronze face. It's as if he knows the best is yet to come.

UNIVERSITY OF NEVADA, LAS VEGAS

● Located on a 335-acre campus, the University of Nevada, Las Vegas, is an oasis just south of the Las Vegas metropolitan area. The grounds have been designated a Nevada state arboretum.

The University of Nevada, Las Vegas, is rapidly maturing into one of the nation's leading comprehensive universities. This public institution was serving an enrollment of 16,000 students by the end of the 1980s, and campus planners believe the student body will reach 20,000 within the next four years.

Known for years as a commuter school, the university began developing a more traditional campus atmosphere in the late 1980s with the addition of new student residential halls. Four new dormitories opened in 1988, and more are on the way.

More than 500 faculty members, approximately 75 percent of whom hold doctoral degrees, offer instruction in more than 100 undergraduate and graduate programs. Although many students fall into the traditional 18- to-22-year-old age group, a large group of older students attend UNLV. Most work while continuing their educations. An extensive evening program accommodates the schedules of working students.

Recognizing that the population of retired persons is becoming a significant portion of the Las Vegas community, UNLV initiated a Senior Citizens Program, which allows persons 62 years of age and older to attend tuition-free classes on campus. Several hundred seniors are enrolled in this popular program at any given time; some are working toward degrees, while others take classes for personal enrichment.

UNLV has endeavored to keep Nevada's brightest high school graduates in the state by offering incentives to top students. The Early Studies Program introduces qualified high school juniors and seniors to university-level academic work by allowing them to take classes for credit while they finish their high school graduation requirements. The Elardi Nevada Scholars Program makes a $10,000 scholarship available to valedictorians from all of the state's 53 high schools. Preprofessional programs prepare students for advanced study in health sciences.

More than 18,000 students had received degrees from UNLV by 1989. Although most have stayed in Nevada to pursue careers and start families, UNLV alumni are scattered throughout the United States and in 20 countries worldwide.

The large campus, south of Las Vegas, is one of the Las Vegas Valley's greenest areas, designated a state arboretum. Only 30 years ago the campus consisted of little more than sand and tumbleweed.

The first college-level classes in southern Nevada started in 1951 in a

diversification of Nevada. As a result, the Howard R. Hughes School of Engineering was established. A director, Dr. William R. Wells, was hired to lead the school, and ground was broken in 1987 for the 101,000-square-foot Thomas T. Beam Engineering Complex. The $14.7-million facility was formally dedicated in April 1989.

The engineering school became the university's newest college. Its civil, mechanical, and electrical engineering

◀ Mechanical engineering students in UNLV's Howard R. Hughes College of Engineering adjust a robotic arm, in a grant-supported project that involves faculty and students from the college's mechanical, electrical, and civil engineering and computer science departments.

▼ Some 16,000 students are enrolled in UNLV's eight colleges' undergraduate and graduate programs.

spare room at Las Vegas High School. Dr. James R. Dickinson (for whom the campus library is named) was the only full-time faculty member, and the student body totaled 12.

Six years later the university was founded as the Southern Regional Division of the University of Nevada by the state's single higher education governing body, the Board of Regents. In 1957 the new campus opened its first classroom and administration building—Maude Frazier Hall—on its present site.

Twenty-nine students received degrees at the university's first commencement ceremonies in 1964. The following year the Nevada Legislature named the school Nevada Southern University, and the Board of Regents hired the campus' first president, Dr. Donald C. Moyer, for whom the student union is named.

In 1968 the university was granted autonomy under Nevada's newly created University of Nevada System, giving it equal status with the University of Nevada, Reno. The Board of Regents approved the new name—University of Nevada, Las Vegas—in January 1969.

In 1989 the university had eight colleges: Arts and Letters, Business and Economics, Education, Health Sciences,

the William F. Harrah College of Hotel Administration, Science and Mathematics, the Graduate College, and the Howard R. Hughes College of Engineering. The School of Health, Physical Education, and Recreation is part of the Education College. Major gifts to university academics have created seven distinguished chairs among the colleges.

Several years ago university and community leaders agreed that the institution must play a leading role in the economic

programs have received national accreditation. The college also offers a strong program in computer science and a popular architecture program.

UNLV's scientific, social science, and business programs attract millions of dollars in research grants annually. These grants have funded research in robotics, molecular ions, environmental monitoring, environmental biology, and regional economics. And they have enabled the university to develop research centers such as the Center for Nuclear Waste Transportation Research and the Center for Survey Research.

Innovative educational and research programs exist in the College of Business and Economics. The First Interstate Bank Institute for Business Leadership coordinates all faculty and student research in the college. The institute applies the college's research capabilities to problems faced by Nevada businesses.

The Center for Business and Economic Research is a conduit through which the skills and education of UNLV faculty members are made available to the local community to conduct marketing research, socioeconomic impact analyses, and other studies benefiting private business and government agencies.

The Center for Economic Education, part of a network of 20 centers at colleges nationwide, increases economic literacy by working directly with public school students statewide.

The Desert Biology Research Center, a division of the biological science department, focuses its efforts primarily on deserts of the Southwest, with some national and international involvement as well.

The Center for Survey Research conducts sample surveys of the Nevada population on a wide range of topics. It serves the research needs of faculty and graduate students while providing valuable information for governmental agencies and private clients.

UNLV's Environmental Research Center, part of the Museum of Natural History, contains five research divisions: Anthropological Studies, the Division of Earth Sciences, the Division of Environmental Resources, the Lake Mead

Limnological Research Center, and the Quality Assurance Laboratory.

The Lake Mead Limnological Research Center is of particular interest. Its scientists and students study the vast Colorado River system, which includes Lake Mead, one of the largest man-made lakes in the world. Its programs include studies of salinity in the lake, water quality, and fisheries production. It conducts many projects related to sport fishing, and its water-quality work is of vital interest to the government agencies responsible for protecting southern Nevada's water supply.

The university also reaches several important segments of the adult community, including the men and women stationed at nearby Nellis Air Force Base. Nellis personnel, their depen-

▲ The multimillion-dollar, 101,000-square-foot Thomas T. Beam Engineering Complex was dedicated in April 1989.

dents, and employees of military contractors take university courses at the base.

UNLV also offers more than 600 classes through its Division of Continuing Education to some 16,000 adult area residents each year.

Much of the UNLV's phenomenal expansion in the 1970s and 1980s is due to support from the Nevada Legislature and the state's taxpayers. But private donors have played an important role as well. During president Robert C. Maxson's first five years at UNLV (1984-1989), the university received approxi-

▲ A student takes advantage of the quiet surroundings of the Xeriscape, an outdoor exhibit of drought-tolerant plants from the great deserts of the world.

mately $50 million in gifts and pledges. These gifts support new facilities and programs, and continue to provide scholarship incentives attracting Nevada's best and brightest students to UNLV. Some $113 million in gifts, pledges, grants, and contracts was generated by the institution during the latter half of the 1980s.

The university is the cultural hub of southern Nevada. Thousands of visitors come to the campus every year to attend athletic events, art exhibits, public lectures, concerts, and dance and theater performances.

A member of NCAA's Division I and the Big West Conference, UNLV is the home of the Runnin' Rebels basketball team. University men also compete in baseball, football, golf, soccer, swimming and diving, and tennis. Intercollegiate women's teams include basketball, cross country, track, softball, swimming and diving, and tennis.

The Charles Vanda Master Series brings world-class orchestras and soloists to the Artemus W. Ham Concert Hall on campus. The Las Vegas Symphony and Nevada Dance Theatre are resident at UNLV and join a host of university musical organizations that feature faculty and student performers. Another resident group, the Nevada School of the Arts, provides lessons and performance opportunities for school-age children.

The Nevada Institute for Contemporary Art, associated with the university, hosts art shows in the Donna Beam Art Gallery and the Museum of Natural History, which also present faculty and student exhibits.

One of the first things visitors to the campus notice is *The Flashlight,* a 35-foot-tall, 40,000-pound steel sculpture by internationally famous artists Claes Oldenburg and Coosje van Bruggen. This huge, black work stands on the patio between Artemus W. Ham Concert Hall and Judy Bayley

Theatre. It looks like a huge flashlight that has been placed with lens down on a table top. Its base is circled by a ring of lights set into the patio and covered with milky plastic. At night *The Flashlight* appears to stand in a pool of its own light.

Many visitors come to UNLV to visit the Museum of Natural History and the adjoining Demonstration Garden. In addition to exhibits that explain the biology, geology, and archaeology of the Southwest, the museum houses a large collection of desert animals. Traveling exhibits are often displayed in the museum, which attracts tourists and local schoolchildren by the thousands each year.

The Demonstration Garden is an outdoor exhibit of drought-tolerant plants from the great deserts of the world. A pleasant spot, with benches, decorative lights, and foot bridges over a dry wash, the desert garden is as attractive as it is instructional. One of its primary purposes is to offer examples of vegetation that will thrive in Las Vegas' climate.

The University of Nevada, Las Vegas, a relatively young institution, has grown from the dusty little campus of 30 years ago into a major university that is committed to teaching, research, and service to its community.

▼ Moonlight illuminates *The Flashlight,* a 35-foot-tall steel sculpture by internationally famous artists Claes Oldenburg and Coosje van Bruggen. It stands on the patio between Artemus W. Ham Concert Hall and Judy Bayley Theatre.

THE DESERT RESEARCH INSTITUTE

Water resources and air quality, global climatic change and the turbulent physics of the earth's atmosphere, humanity's prehistoric struggle to adapt to harsh environments and the search for the technology of the next century—these fundamental issues underlie research programs in progress at Desert Research Institute. DRI is a statewide division of the University of Nevada System, conducting full-time, professional research and development on environmental challenges and related technology.

Pursuing programs of basic and applied research on an international scale, 280 scientists, technicians, and support personnel conduct more than 100 research projects annually from DRI's offices and labs located throughout the Silver State. In Las Vegas and Laughlin in southern Nevada, at Stead (a former military base, north of Reno), and the Dandini Research Park in the Reno area, Nevada's natural resources are the primary focus of researchers. Managing

▲ The Desert Research Institute's Southern Nevada Science Center, under construction in Las Vegas, will open its first phase in early 1992. The expected completion date is January 1992.

and preserving the Great Basin's resources challenge researchers to produce new knowledge. Often that new information gained from DRI studies proves useful not only to Nevadans but to persons concerned about arid environments worldwide.

Given the high value of this new knowledge developed by DRI, its faculty has become internationally renowned in a number of areas. An added benefit for Nevada is that researchers provide technological support essential to Nevada's efforts to diversify its economy.

DRI's research efforts have involved locations ranging from the earth's polar regions to every continent, and to 45 of the 50 states. Diverse topics such as the atmosphere of Venus, the possibility of life forms on Mars, and the potential for growing crystalline materials in space have been examined. In an enhancement of DRI's range of

ground-based environmental research capabilities, the institute has added satellite remote sensing techniques.

DRI's research activities are carried out within its five research centers. The Water Resources Center (WRC), DRI's largest and oldest, has been the nucleus for the institute's other four centers. The WRC's research concerns the chemical, engineering, economic, and legal aspects of water resources. Computer simulation models have been developed for use in planning, managing, and evaluating groundwater flow, geothermal resources, and hydroelectric applications. The center features a strong water-quality program examining the effects of radionuclide transport at the Nevada Nuclear Test Site, located in southern Nevada. In a related program on water pollution, WRC researchers seek new techniques for detecting, identifying, and containing hazardous waste in groundwater supplies.

The center's facilities include an EPA-certified water quality laboratory, an isotope laboratory involved with groundwater recharge investigations, ex-

▼ A DRI Sierra Nevada cloud seeding generator, west of Lake Tahoe, undergoes routine maintenance between winter storms.

▲ The stable isotope mass spectrometry preparation line analyzes hydrogen and oxygen isotopes in groundwater. It is used in experimental development of techniques for estimating recharge of Nevada's groundwater systems.

tensive computer facilities, field analytical equipment, and a technical library.

The Energy and Environmental Engineering Center (EEEC) has assumed a prominent national role in research on air quality conditions in arid urban and rural regions. The center has recently developed source receptor techniques, allowing scientists to identify pollutants contributed by different types of emission sources. First applied to characterize air-quality conditions in Las Vegas and Reno, this new technology has found subsequent application in Denver, Phoenix, Santa Barbara, and the San Joaquin Valley in California.

Based on the sophisticated technology DRI has developed to identify the sources and composition of air pollution, its scientists are involved in and lead a California research program examining acid rain. Another major EEEC research area involves a ground-breaking effort to investigate the impact of pollutants moving from metropolitan areas into the relatively pristine air of vast open desert and mountain regions of the Southwest.

The Atmospheric Sciences Center's (ASC) international reputation in the areas of cloud physics, air motions, and weather modification makes it one of the largest, most comprehensive atmospheric research groups in the world. How do hurricanes form on the Gulf Coast and the Atlantic Ocean? DRI is studying that matter. Its experts study ways to suppress hail in the high plains. And through aerial cloud seeding during storms in the Sierra Nevada, winter snowpack is augmented in drought-prone Nevada. Because of its success, weather modification scientists now assist neighboring Utah and several foreign nations in similar research efforts.

Pioneering basic research is also under way to examine how ice crystals, clouds, and air turbulence are created in the earth's atmosphere, as well as how the atmosphere undergoes self-cleaning. Operating the federally funded Western Regional Climate Center, ASC provides 11 western states with valuable information about climate. Again, the tools developed by DRI's experts are in demand by researchers worldwide.

The Quaternary Sciences Center (QSC) focuses on the natural record of climatic change in the western United States during the past 1.8 million years (quaternary epoch), and the more recent development of human cultures in arid land. Using an anthropological approach, scientists are studying technological change of Native Americans from hunter gatherers to farmers. QSC is also involved in studies in the Middle East involving recent discoveries of ancient cultural development in Jordan and Cyprus.

The Biological Sciences Center is DRI's smallest and fastest-growing research group. The center's scientists have initiated an important new program in environmental remote-sensing technology emphasizing the manner in which the impacts of global climate change might first be observed in the sensitive ecologies of the great basin and similar arid environments. The center studies the earth's biosphere to learn more about the interaction within environmental systems. With the planned development of an advanced controlled-environment research greenhouse, the center will expand experiments involving environmental simulation and modeling in cooperation with other DRI centers.

▼ A TBX transmission densitometer analysis shows how much light is absorbed by urban air-pollutant particles collected in a DRI sampling filter.

SAINT MARY'S REGIONAL MEDICAL CENTER

20 to 25 minutes to do.

Keeping pace with the latest in heart care is one of Saint Mary's priorities, with capabilities ranging from cardiac catheterization and noninvasive vascular imaging to cardiac intensive care, cardiovascular surgery, and cardiac rehabilitation programs. These programs help get the recovering heart patient back on the road to normal living again.

Sleeping problems, such as insomnia and excessive daytime sleeping, are diagnosed at Saint Mary's Sleep Disorders Center, the only such facility in Nevada.

◄ **Dusk brings a peaceful Reno night to Saint Mary's Regional Medical Center.**

▼ **Equipped with the latest intensive-care equipment, Saint Mary's Maternity Center ensures the health and safety of infants.**

Founded in 1908 by the Dominican Sisters of San Rafael, California, this well-known part of Nevada's history has seen a lot of changes in eight decades, incorporating facilities and services that reflect the dynamics of medical care and patient needs.

Part of Saint Mary's regional system is the services that it provides to the far-reaching counties of Nevada and eastern California, including a regional system of emergency care for severely ill and injured patients.

Trauma care services include the state of the art in emergency/trauma room capabilities, life-saving surgical services, intensive care units for both adults and children, and emergency transport services to outlying areas, including Care Flight emergency helicopter service and ground ambulance through REMSA, the Regional Emergency Medical Services Authority.

At Saint Mary's Regional Medical Center, medical and surgical care units provide neurology, cancer care, and rehabilitation services. And facilities were recently expanded to accommodate the growing trend of performing surgery on an outpatient basis.

For ultrafast body imaging diagnostic capabilities, Saint Mary's offers the Imatron, which can do in 75 seconds what a conventional CT scanner takes

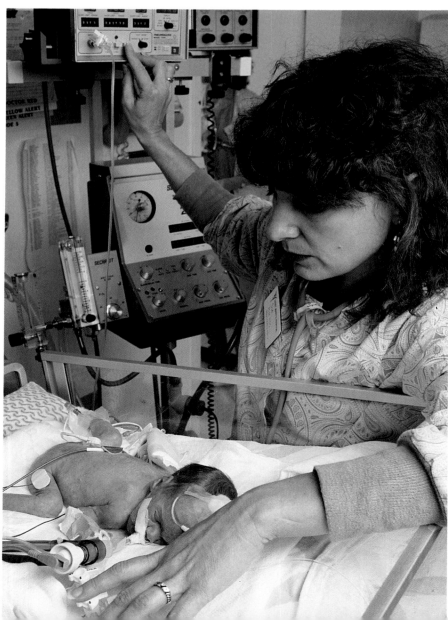

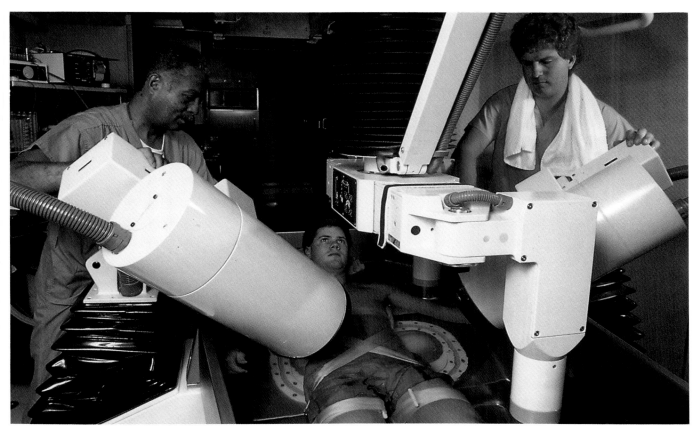

▲ Removing kidney stones without surgery is now possible through the use of high-intensity acoustical shock wave treatment (lithotripsy).

◀ Saint Mary's was the second hospital in the West to incorporate Imatron, reducing CT scanning diagnostic time from 20 minutes to 75 seconds. Photo by Bob Davis

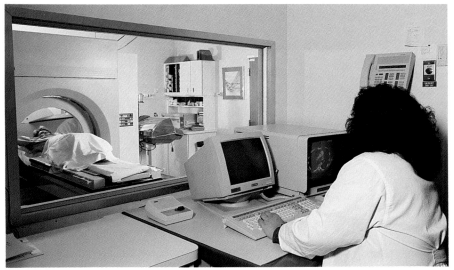

Chemical dependency programs for adolescents and adults are available as both inpatient and outpatient sessions. And programs for stress management, weight control, and smoking cessation are also part of Saint Mary's efforts to help people cope with and manage lifestyle problems.

Saint Mary's also recognizes that there are problems that business and industry must cope with to give their employees the best health care programs at the lowest costs. Therefore, Saint Mary's occupational health and wellness programs and contract arrangements to provide preferred provider care at a savings to employers have become a well-known part of the Reno business community.

Saint Mary's medical services extend throughout the Truckee Meadows and beyond. HealthCare Plus, an urgent care center, is located in south Reno. Saint Mary's Industrial Medical Clinic is a Sparks clinic specializing in treating work-related injuries and employee health problems.

And, of course, there is the facility that introduced more than 80,000 babies into the world in the past 80 years—a regional maternity center offering traditional birthing options, a family birthing center, a regional intensive care nursery, and high-risk obstetrics care and emergency transport.

Saint Mary's Regional Medical Center is located in the heart of downtown Reno, south of I-80 at the corner of Arlington Avenue and Sixth Street.

SIERRA HEALTH SERVICES

America's aging population, increased use of drugs, the battle against AIDS, and overused medical tests and procedures all contribute to the runaway cost of medical care in the United States.

Las Vegas-based Sierra Health Services is fighting to contain those costs. While making sure the people of southern Nevada have access to affordable health care, Sierra works hard to keep them healthier in the bargain.

Health care expenditures in the United States exceed $500 billion per year—three times the budget for national defense and more than 11 percent of the gross national product, according to Dr. Anthony M. Marlon, founder of Sierra Health Services and currently chairman, president, and chief executive officer. "Even more alarming are the estimates that predict this figure will almost double to $999 billion by 1995," he adds.

In Nevada, staying in a hospital costs almost $1,500 per day. The bill is picked up mostly by two groups: by employers with employee-benefit programs and by taxpayers through federal government programs, such as Medicare.

The trend cannot continue, Dr. Marlon believes. "Something is wrong," he says. "We are, quite simply, not getting what we're paying for. Perhaps just as onerous, we're paying for an awful lot of things we don't need."

His solution is managed health care such as that encouraged by Sierra Health Services and its six subsidiary companies: Health Plan of Nevada, Sierra Health and Life Insurance Co., Inc., Southwest Medical Associates, Family Health Care Services, Family Home Hospice, and Sierra Health Care Options.

Since 1972, first as a practicing cardiologist and then as a health care executive, Dr. Marlon has made it his mission to bring top-quality, affordable health care to Las Vegas. With that goal, he founded Southwest Heart Associates in the early 1970s and, in 1977, expanded that group to include other medical specialties, under the name of Southwest Medical Associates.

By 1980 the idea of health maintenance organizations (HMOs), already

▲ Anthony M. Marlon, M.D., chairman, president, and chief executive officer of Sierra Health Services.

successful in other areas of the country, was gaining support in Nevada. Dr. Marlon realized there was no other way for employers to offer employees total health care packages at a reasonable cost. To do that he formed HPN in 1982. Four years later Sierra Health and Life was launched under the Sierra Health Services umbrella.

Health Plan of Nevada (HPN) is the state's oldest and largest health maintenance organization, with more than 70,000 members. HPN members include Clark County schoolteachers, other county, state, and federal employees, and employees of most of the southern Nevada hotel/casino properties.

An HMO is a type of medical insurance based on the objective of keeping its members healthy, as well as paying for their illnesses. For the most part, an HMO is a benefit employers provide to their employees. An HMO can use the

leverage of its large member base to contract for health services with physicians, clinics, and hospitals at rates much lower than individuals would have to pay.

For a fixed premium often paid by their employers, HMO members and their families receive complete medical services at little cost. HMOs differ from traditional insurance plans by getting directly involved in the delivery of health care rather than merely reimbursing patients for services delivered by others.

HMOs place strong emphasis on preventive care, since their philosophy is that it is more cost effective to treat a member before illness strikes. Only nominal fees are charged for doctor vis-

Sierra Health Services

its. Generally there are no deductibles to meet and few claim forms to fill out.

To get the added benefits of secure, low-cost health care, HMO members agree to receive all their nonemergency care from doctors and other providers who contract with the HMO. HPN offers members two choices: to receive their medical care from physicians in a group practice or from specific individual physicians who practice from their own offices.

Though HPN can send patients to almost any hospital in southern Nevada, a contract with Humana Hospital Sunrise, HPN's primary provider, ensures that members get top-notch care when the need arises. In addition to its group

▲ **Sierra Health Services' Las Vegas corporate headquarters.**

program, HPN has launched a Medicare HMO program called Senior Dimensions, under which senior citizens can get medical care at modest cost.

Federally sponsored Medicare pays participating plans such as Senior Dimensions 95 percent of the average cost of medical services in a specific geographical area. In exchange, the HMO assumes total risk for the cost of arranging the patient's care. The plan significantly reduces the member's out-of-pocket costs and paperwork, eliminates the need for supplemental coverage, and

increases the level of benefits. It helps stem the rising costs to the government, because the HMO monitors the system. It benefits the HMO by providing an ever-increasing patient base.

But mostly, Senior Dimensions provides total, worry-free health care to those over 65: hospitalization, skilled nursing facility care, hospice care for the terminally ill, doctor visits, surgery, home health care, emergency care, mental health, substance abuse, and preventive dental care. The total premium cost to seniors, depending on the level of services desired, ranges from $15 to $40 per month.

HPN offers the Senior Dimensions program to seniors throughout Clark

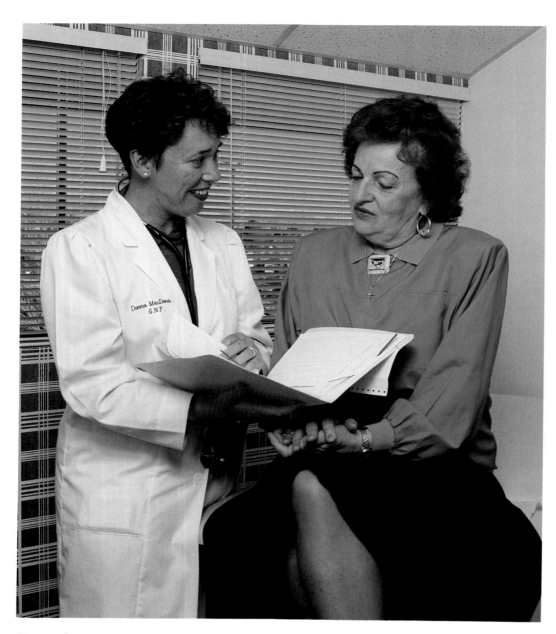

▲ Donna MacDonald, a nurse practitioner who specializes in gerontology, assists a patient in the Senior Dimensions program, a major offering from Health Plan of Nevada.

County; the Amargosa Valley; Nye County towns of Beatty, Mercury, Pahrump, and Lathrop Wells; and Sandy Valley.

Sierra Health and Life Insurance Company, Inc. (SHL), has a more conventional health insurance plan, called Gemini, sold exclusively to the group market in Nevada, New Mexico, Colorado, and Arizona.

In addition to a standard payment option, Gemini also offers a preferred-provider option that includes financial incentives for members to use designated physicians and hospitals. Members can choose to receive health care under either option at any time. Members can, for example, use their own specialist for a specific health problem, while sending their family to a designated provider for flu shots or a routine checkup.

Gemini is offered to many employers as part of a package that includes dental, vision, group-term life, and accidental death insurance, all of which are covered by SHL. A new SHL product offered to employers is the Diamond Plan. Like Gemini, the Diamond Plan offers financial incentives to insureds who utilize a select group of providers; it also provides the employer with several different coverage levels to choose from. More than 30,000 members are covered by SHL.

Southwest Medical Associates (SMA), the largest multispecialty medical group practice in Nevada, operates six medical centers in the Las Vegas area with more than 70 doctors, optometrists, and other health care specialists. SMA provides services in anesthesiology, cardiology, endocrinology, family practice, infectious diseases, internal medicine, mental health, neurology, nutrition, oncology/hematology, pathology, pediatrics, rheumatology, and urology.

SMA also has a same-day surgery center, a 24-hour physician-staffed urgent care center, an occupational/preventive medicine department, phys- ical therapy, and comprehensive laboratory, radiology, and diagnostic testing capabilities. Contracted specialists in two of the centers provide ophthalmologic care. SMA constantly recruits new physicians for its clinics to increase even further the range of medical services it offers.

Family Health Care Services (FHS) is a home health care agency licensed to operate in Nevada. FHS, which is certified by both Medicare and Medicaid, provides services to members of HPN and Sierra Health and Life Insurance.

The professional staff of nurses, therapists, medical social workers, and home health aides provides skilled care to patients at their homes under the direction of physicians. FHS provides care to patients who are recovering from surgery, to disabled persons and those recovering from accidents, to chronically or terminally ill patients, and to elderly patients who, due to illness or injury, are unable to care for themselves. In addition to routine medical care, professionals of FHS design special rehabilitation programs, develop therapy routines, and conduct outpatient-surgery follow-up visits.

FHS's home services permit patients to leave hospitals sooner and still receive high-quality care, thus cutting costs and enabling patients to recover in familiar environments. Studies indicate that patients recover more rapidly and comfortably under home health care than acute hospital care. Individual care provided by FHS is available 24 hours per day, seven days per week

A special service Family Home Hospice, another subsidiary of Sierra Health Services, is the care it provides to terminally ill patients. The goal is to maximize the quality of time remaining for patients and allow them to live as full a life as possible before dying. In addition to taking care of the patient's needs, staff members involved in this program also work with the family to provide support and counseling. Often, involvement with the family continues after the death of a patient.

Sierra's newest subsidiary, Sierra Healthcare Options, provides administrative and benefit consulting services to self-funded employer groups.

Sierra Health Services tries hard to ensure that members receive first-rate medical treatment at minimal cost with a quality assurance program, under which a panel of specialists constantly evaluates appropriateness of treatments, diagnostic tests, hospital usage, and other factors. In addition, Sierra seeks feedback from members and former members on the quality of their treatment.

Dr. Marlon says health-delivery systems such as those offered by Sierra

Health Services are the best way to control health care costs in America. "As I see it, there are only three possible solutions to our looming health care crisis," he says. "We can all learn to live with indefinite increases in the cost of our health care, we can switch to a national health care system, or we can further the development and acceptance of managed health care programs.

"The latter alternative is not only the most realistic and economical solution, but I feel it is also the one that will provide our nation with the highest level of care."

Dr. Marlon says the issue will be decided in the 1990s: "I am convinced that managed health care systems, such as Sierra Health Services—especially HMOs—will become the way an ever-increasing number of Americans will receive their health care."

▼ Southwest Medical Associates provides care in more than 15 different medical specialties. Myra Davis-Alson of SMA's Oncology Department is pictured here preparing chemotherapy for a cancer patient.

BLUE CROSS AND BLUE SHIELD OF NEVADA

◀ Blue Cross and Blue Shield of Nevada's Corporate Pointe Headquarters in Reno.

Blue Cross and Blue Shield has been helping Americans manage the cost of medical care for more than 50 years.

In 1969 the company began operating in Nevada as administrator for the state's Medicaid program. Today it provides health care coverage to thousands of Nevadans and offers a wide range of health insurance plans.

Nationally, the Blue Cross and Blue Shield organization provides health care coverage to more than 75 million people. It also manages a program to insure employees of the federal government and administers the Medicare and Medicaid programs in many states.

Nevada's rapid growth has brought great challenges to the health care industry. As the state's population has increased rapidly, so has the cost of medical care, challenging Blue Cross and Blue Shield of Nevada (BCBSN) to create new and innovative ways to control the cost of care to its subscribers. The move to preferred-provider ar-

rangements and managed care was an easy transition since the Blue Cross and Blue Shield organization has been involved in contracting with hospitals and physicians from its inception.

BCBSN significantly improved its capabilities by joining the Rocky Mountain Health Care Corporation (RMHCC) of

Denver in 1987. RMHCC is a management company that has consolidated many of the operations of a family of Blue Cross and Blue Shield plans, allowing them to pool resources and costs while improving service.

For example, through its affiliation with the Rocky Mountain group, BCBSN has acquired state-of-the-art computer technology, resulting in faster claims processing and improved customer service. While benefiting from combined resources, BCBSN maintains a strong local presence in the community, processes claims locally, and is able to respond to customers at a local level.

The company, with offices in Reno and Las Vegas, works with a network of more than 600 independent brokers and agents statewide to better service customers and distribute its products.

BCBSN's largest market is group health, dental, and vision insurance. Life and disability coverages are also offered through affiliated companies. In addition, BCBSN offers health plans to individuals, including Medicare supplemental plans for seniors.

As the oldest Nevada-based health insurance company, operating in the state for more than 20 years, BCBSN provides strength and stability so important to customers in today's rapidly changing health care insurance environment. Blue Cross and Blue Shield of Nevada will continue to hold an important position in Nevada's health care insurance marketplace because of its stability, its emphasis on value and quality, and its innovative managed care programs and provider contracting arrangements.

▶ BCBSN service representatives assist members using an on-line computer system.

LAURA SPITZER

When Bach and Beethoven ring out over Nevada's mining settlements and dusty basin-and-range towns, chances are it will be concert pianist Laura Spitzer at work.

With music degrees from the Mozarteum in Salzburg and the Peabody Institute, Spitzer introduces the world's greatest music to audiences sometimes no bigger than 50 to 75 folks in unlikely places such as Pioche, Goldfield, and Round Mountain. She drives her own truck and often moves her own piano.

"I know the location of every grand piano in the state," says Spitzer. "Outside of Reno and Las Vegas, there are only about five you can play on. It gets down to either forgetting about the concert tour or bringing my own."

From her tours of rural Nevada, Spitzer has learned that appreciation of classical music has less to do with education than with feeling. And her audiences are appreciative.

"In Minden, the audience waded through blackjack tables and slot machines to get to the concert," Spitzer recalls. "At the Caliente homecoming, a yearly reunion for all present and past inhabitants, guests strolled nonchalantly from the 1 p.m. pig-wrestling contest, boots and clothes mud-spattered, to the 2 p.m. piano recital across the street at the old railroad depot. In Yerington, I performed in the Autotorium, a car garage converted into a performing arts center. And in Goldfield . . . it was the Santa Fe Saloon."

Spitzer's recent programs have mixed Bach, Ravel, Chopin, and Liszt with

▲ Laura Spitzer brings a classical piano repertoire—and with it, a great time—to the often remote locations that comprise Nevada's mining community.

twentieth-century American works by Gottschalk, Gershwin, and Joplin—many of the same pieces she performed in her 1985 New York debut in Merkin Hall.

Sometimes she visits local schools, introducing children to the works they'll hear at the concerts, or teaching young pianists in master classes. Actually, says Spitzer, she regards the concerts themselves as a teaching experience.

"I get a feeling of mutual need with the people of these towns," Spitzer com-

ments. "In rural Nevada, even my arrival is a special event. People turn out just to watch us unload. I achieve an instant celebrity status . . . In New York, I might be the 10th pianist to perform that week. In Duckwater, I would in all likelihood be the first—ever."

Spitzer, who came to Las Vegas to teach in 1979 after earning her degrees, began the rural tours in 1983 with the help of grants from the Nevada State Council on the Arts, the loan of a truck from a local rental agency, and a piano provided by Steinway and Sons. There were also grants from companies such as Echo Bay Mines to help her keep going. Local audiences where Spitzer plays pay admissions ranging from nothing to five dollars. Since then, Spitzer has bought her own truck to carry piano and wardrobe, and has additional grants to arrange rural concerts in other states. Though her booking agent is in Las Vegas, Spitzer says she feels the truck is almost her home.

While she is asked to perform in cities such as Vancouver, Palm Springs, and San Jose, California, most of her appearances are in smaller communities—75 to 100 concerts per year, Spitzer estimates.

"I am completely hooked," says Spitzer. "In 1983 I planned to make one simple, modest tour of seven towns. Now I won't be content until I have dragged a piano into every last saloon, casino, and mineshaft in Nevada."
—This profile of Laura Spitzer is sponsored by Echo Bay Mines.

NEVADA ARTS

In the 1860s Virginia City, Nevada, was the richest and most important city between San Francisco and Denver. As such, this booming, bustling mining town with its handsome Piper's Opera House played host to such cultural lights as Shakespearean actor Edwin Booth and Jenny Lind, the Swedish Nightingale. Today concerts, some of them premiere performances of orchestral works, are still hosted in the historic Piper's each summer.

William L. Fox, executive director of the Nevada State Council on the Arts, says that it was the mining camps in the mid-1800s that provided the initial catalyst for the arts in Nevada. The mining camps brought performing arts into the state as a means to establish civic pride and to put into permanence the miners' place in history.

Even so, for the better part of a century Nevada served as a temporary stop for artists traveling from east to west. Before World War II, Fox says, Nevada boasted only one or two viable arts groups. However, by 1970, the number had grown to about 50 nonprofit cultural organizations. Today, as the

fastest-growing state, Nevada has upward of 210 state groups flourishing within its borders. As Fox puts it, "The faster you grow, the more you need the amenities of culture to stay sane."

Census figures give Nevada other key indicators of its cultural growth; it has more musicians and dancers than any other state, except New York and California, and it has more photographers than any other state—period. Fox adds that 85 percent of the artists who come to work on council programs end up moving to Nevada, "because of the cultural environment."

In the mid-1970s some 200,000 people annually attended concerts and visited museums funded by the state council; now the number is 1.2 million. The number of credible groups presenting quality artists to Nevada audiences has grown from less than a dozen to more than 50.

▲ *The Nutcracker* **brings holiday joy every year to audiences of the Nevada Dance Theatre, the state's only fully professional ballet company. Photo by Ginger Bruner**

▼ **Virko Bayley conducts the Las Vegas Symphony Orchestra, known for its exceptional performances of contemporary Eastern European and Russian music. Photo by John Aaron**

▶ The Hawkins House, which is on the National Register of Historic Places, was commissioned in 1910 by Prince Albert Hawkins, a prominent Reno attorney. Designed by renowned California architect Elmer Gray, the Hawkins House now is operated by the Sierra Nevada Museum of Art.

Some firms, such as the Union Pacific Foundation, even underwrite concert tours to rural Nevada communities.

As Fox puts it, "So if you go to Fallon, Yerington, or Panaca, you are going to find the same kinds of arts events that you are going to find in San Jose or Santa Fe. If you live in Nevada, you have access to performing arts that are far and above what you'd normally find in a town of this size, or a state of this size, and, in fact, in most western states."

Sue Clark, executive director of the Sierra Arts Foundation in Reno, emphasizes that the tremendous amount of arts activity is of excellent quality.

Patrick Gaffey, executive director of the Southern Nevada Allied Arts Council in Las Vegas, which celebrated its 25th anniversary in 1987, adds, "The one thing that can give a city that image of greatness is its culture as reflected in its art."

One such image is the earth sculpture *Double Negative,* created by Nevadan Michael Heiser when he cut into Mormon Mesa near Overton in southern Nevada and moved 240,000 tons of rhyolite and sandstone. The celebrated earthwork is owned by the Los Angeles Museum of Contemporary Art.

Another is the Art-in-Public-Places project under way at McCarran Airport in Las Vegas, where 40 airport sites have been set aside for art, and $100,000 is earmarked annually for development of the pieces to fill the spaces.

Examples of the arts image that Nevada is building are easy to find:

—A statewide cultural resource conference in Carson City that drew speakers from Washington D.C., to Los Angeles.

—The Church Fine Arts Complex, dedicated on the University of Nevada, Reno, campus in 1987, and the establishment of the University of Nevada, Las Vegas, School of Fine Arts program, which now offers master's degrees.

—A county-by-county folk art inventory that will celebrate such diverse cultural heritages as Basque music, rawhide braiding, and old-time fiddling, all traditional cultural practices usually passed informally from generation to generation.

▼ At Western Folklife Center's "Cowboy Poetry Gathering," a women's poetry session features Yula Sue Hunting, Georgie Sicking, and Kathy Lowe. Photo by Carol Edison

—The new, 15,000-square-foot E.L. Weigand Art Museum, which opened in Reno in 1989 with the "Golden Age of Painting" exhibit.

—The Las Vegas Symphony, considered one of the most important American premiere showcases for contemporary Eastern European and Russian music.

—The Cowboy Poetry Gathering in Elko that burgeoned into an international attraction in just three years.

—The choreographer for the Nevada Dance Theater—Vassili Sulich—who is the only American choreographer to have a piece accepted into the Bolshoi repertoire. The dance theater, reversing the usual Nevada arts path by exporting its skills, has toured nearly 200 American cities in the past five years.

—The nationally acclaimed pottery studio and school Dennis Parks founded in Tuscarora, north of Elko, 23 years ago.

—The Design Arts Committee that is celebrating neon as a design element by creating a Neon Art Park in Las Vegas. It is already using one square acre to store mammoth-size pieces such as the 11-foot by 16-foot Thunderbird found resting in a sign boneyard in Stockton, California.

Nevada has learned the secret of the importance of the arts to life and to business. State Senator Nick Horn, who presided over a study that recommended $120 million in new cultural funding in the next 10 years, put it into perspective when he said, "I'm asking people to have some vision, to dream some dreams. In any major city, as many people attend museums and performing arts functions as support two baseball teams. I'm not an opera fan, but the Metropolitan Opera in New York is equal to 12 World Series and two major-league baseball teams in economic impact."

15

RETAIL AND TOURISM

◆◆◆◆

*High-class retailers and distinctive
tourist attractions bring a unique
flair to Nevada's economic
landscape.*

◆◆◆◆

316

Photo by
Tom Campbell

MACY'S RENO

▲ Macy's Reno occupies two buildings: the 171,000-square-foot North Store (left), which houses women's ready-to-wear, and the 100,000-square-foot South Store (right), housing the men's and home departments.

Macy's Reno is Nevada's leading retailer. Part of Macy's California/Nevada 25-store division, the store opened its doors in 1978, bringing Macy's signature merchandising to the eastern slope of the Sierra Nevada.

Located in Meadowood Mall, Macy's Reno occupies two buildings. The 171,000-square-foot north store houses women's ready-to-wear, Macy's kids, accessories, shoes, handbags, fine and costume jewelry, cosmetics, Expressions, Clubhouse, American designer, juniors, moderate sportswear, dresses, lingerie, maternity, and petites.

The 100,000-square-foot south store, acquired from Liberty House in 1984, houses men's wear and the home store, with electronics, housewares, bed and bath, mattresses, and carpets.

The store's primary trading area is the Reno-Sparks area, with a resident population of 200,000, and Carson City, which is 30 miles to the south. It also attracts customers from the Tahoe basin, Northern California, and southern Oregon. Tourism, Nevada's number-one industry, provides an ever-changing flow of shoppers to the store.

Like Macy's stores everywhere, Macy's Reno lives by the Macy dictum that good merchandising has both content and form. Excellence in merchandising, with its hallmarks of quality, value, and service, make for an unparalleled shopping experience. Visual merchandising creates an environment that is consistent with the store's upscale

thrust. Eye-catching displays draw in the customer, and knowledgeable sales associates provide useful information about the merchandise.

The formula works well for Macy's Reno. The store merchandises to the market. There the population is young, and income level is high. The life-style is casual and active. Traditional, classical sportswear, both for women and men, is the dress of the day. Winter, with some of the world's premier skiing just minutes away, means a big skiwear business. The active labels of Thornton Bay, Timberland, Nike, and Head are as strong as the designer labels for which Macy's is renowned.

Macy's By Appointment, a personal shopper service, is stronger at the Reno store than any other in the division, reflecting Reno's on-the-go vitality. Clients from city workers to casino showroom headliners take advantage of the service daily.

Macy's Reno is more than a store. It is a good citizen. Strong support is given the United Way campaign, the Food Bank of Nevada, and the Salvation Army. Each year the store sponsors a benefit for the Nevada Women's Fund, raising money for women's scholarships to the University of Nevada. Macy's executives are active in area chambers of commerce, the Nevada Retail Association, and other community and business organizations.

Macy's Reno traces its lineage back to the California Gold Rush, when

Rowland H. Macy, a New England sea captain, first tried his hand at retailing in the gold rush town of Marysville, California, in 1850.

But doing business in a frontier town where delivery of merchandise was slow and erratic and the population was transient proved too difficult. Three months after he opened, Macy sold his store and returned to the East Coast. After two more retail failures in Boston and another in Haverhill, Massachusetts, Macy returned to New York.

In 1858 he opened R.H. Macy & Co., a four-story store on New York's Sixth Avenue. There he began innovations that would ensure his store's success. He bought goods with cash and sold them for cash, offering the identical price as advertised. These skills in merchandising, advertising, and promotion paid off. Rowland Macy's reputation as a retail genius was secure, and the foundation for what would become the world's largest department store was laid.

But Macy's was not to return to California until almost a century after the Marysville disaster. In 1945 R.H. Macy & Co. purchased O'Connor, Moffat & Co., an old San Francisco department store. Between 1945 and 1947, while

▲ The merchandise in men's active wear is geared to the outdoor Reno life-style.

continuing to operate under the O'Connor, Moffat name, Macy's completely refurbished the store and doubled its size. In October 1947 the San Francisco flagship store on Union Square was officially designated as Macy's San Francisco. Five years later the Albert's stores in San Rafael and Richmond were acquired, and, by 1954, the autonomous division became Macy's California.

The new California division began an aggressive expansion program and secured its position as the largest-volume department-store division west of the Mississippi.

To offer its sophisticated and discriminating customers unique merchandise, Macy's initiated a number of innovative retail techniques in the San Francisco store that are now standard in Macy's stores nationwide. Foremost of these are The Cellar, an arcade of housewares, gourmet food, and gifts, and the store-within-a-store concept with specialty shops filled with mer-

▲ Visual merchandising in intimate apparel is consistent with the store's upscale merchandise emphasis.

chandise gathered from worldwide.

Creative merchandising, excellent store locations, aggressive promotion and advertising, stunning display and visual merchandising, and singular dedication to customer service are just some of

what has made Macy's California an unqualified success story.

Twenty-five stores currently comprise Macy's California/Nevada: Macy's Bay Fair, Birdcage, Concord, Coddingtown, Corte Madera, Eastridge, Macy's Fairfield, Fresno, Hillsdale, Hilltop, Modesto, New Park, Oakridge, Reno, Sacramento, Serramonte, Stanford, Stockton, Stoneridge, Sunnyvale, Monterey, Valley Fair, San Rafael, Santa Rosa, and the flagship, San Francisco.

▶ The classic Waterford Crystal line is always a favorite at Macy's glassware and crystal department.

Porsche Cars North America

The mission of Reno-based Porsche Cars North America, as defined by its president, Brian Bowler, is "to create an effective corporate, marketing, and customer service style and method of operation that continually strengthens the prestige, worth, and desirability of our sports cars and other products."

It is a philosophy that fits what many consider to be the world's finest and sportiest automobile. Since 1984 PCNA has been importing, servicing, and distributing the German-built cars to the American market, where nearly half of all Porsches are sold.

From its headquarters in downtown Reno, PCNA operates a huge parts-distribution center that serves Porsche dealers nationwide from Reno-Cannon International Airport; a predelivery center in Charleston, South Carolina; four regional service training centers, including one in Reno; and a service and sales organization, which provides support for Porsche dealers throughout the United States.

To most people, the name "Porsche" (pronounced POR-sha), means essentially one thing: fast, high-quality automobiles for the road or winning cars for the racetrack.

But the Porsche heritage runs much

▼ The Parts Distribution Center in Reno stocks approximately 27,000 items and supplies more than 270 Porsche dealers nationwide.

▲ Porsche Cars North America relocated its national headquarters into its new downtown Reno building in July 1989.

deeper than just Porsche cars, the most visible product of Porsche. Porsche is also one of the world's great consulting engineering companies in automotive fields. This was true long before it began to produce cars with the Porsche name on them.

Today's sleek Porsche car traces its ancestry back before the turn of the century, when Dr. Ferdinand Porsche, a towering figure in automotive history, began designing fine cars. Porsche had more direct influence on the development of the automobile than any other person on earth, with the possible exception of Henry Ford. Curiously, all the vehicles Porsche designed were built for other companies—Daimler-Benz, Lohner, and Volkswagen—and none bore his name.

Porsche designed his first auto in 1898, when he was 23 years old, the Lohner Electric Chaise,

driven by electric motors in each front wheel hub. But, typically, it was too slow for the ambitious Porsche. So in 1900 he created the two-seat racing Lohner and won the first race in which it was entered. Always an experimenter, Porsche, over the next half-century, was a leader in automotive engineering and helped create some of Europe's best known sports cars.

In 1934 Porsche was summoned to the Chancellery in Berlin and told to design a people's car—a volkswagen. Unfortunately, he didn't live to see the wordwide success of his design. His health had deteriorated during World War II, and he died in 1951.

The first car to be called a Porsche came in 1948, introduced by Ferdinand's son, Ferdinand "Ferry" Porsche, almost as skilled an automotive designer as his father. The car began rolling out of the factory in Stuttgart in 1950, less than a year before Dr. Porsche's death. That first year 298 Porsche roadsters were sold.

Many of Porsche's engineering improvements over the years have been based on Porsche's continuous involvement in racing—both Grand Prix and endurance racing. Most of the features in today's road cars were in yesterday's endurance prototypes and Grand Prix racers—and Porsche's winning record is enviable. Porsche continues to build its string of racing victories today in the PPG Indy Car World Series.

Modern Porsche cars range from the high-performance 928 to the front-engine 944 to the racing-style 911 Carrera. These are the cars that PCNA brings to America at the rate of almost 10,000 per year.

In Reno, an 85,000-square-foot warehouse carries 27,000 different kinds of parts. From there, a part can be sent to

any Porsche dealer in America in less than 24 hours. So complete is the parts inventory in Reno "that you could wander through here and select enough of the right parts to build a complete Porsche car," says Hal Williams, a Porsche public relations representative.

Dealers send their own mechanics to Porsche's week-long training school in Reno to learn how to take care of the fine automobiles the way the company wants it done.

Before 1984 Porsches were sold and serviced, along with other German cars, through a joint marketing group in Troy, Michigan. When Porsche Cars North America was formed, its then-president, John Cook, was instrumental in selecting Reno as PCNA's home to be close to California, Porsche's largest market, without having the burden of California taxes.

Under Nevada's free-port law, Porsche pays no state inventory taxes on its store of parts waiting to be shipped elsewhere. Nor does Nevada tax either corporate or personal income. "That's great for us and for our employees," says Williams. "Reno is just an ideal place for a company our size to do business."

▲ Mainstays of the Porsche line, the classic 911 Cabriolet, Targa, and Coupe, are now available with either two-wheel or four-wheel drive.

Porsche runs its operation from a new landmark headquarters building in Reno's financial district near downtown, work place for more than 230 employees of the company's total work force of almost 400 people. And in both of its big Reno facilities there is much room to expand.

Porsche Cars North America expects to need that room as it grows into its rightful market niche. As Bowler says, the company's goal is to continue nurturing a strong and stable dealer network and to earn the favor and loyalty of its customers.

▼ Porsche has been tremendously successful in racing. Competition provides a high-intensity laboratory for testing and development.

THE WILLIAM F. HARRAH FOUNDATION NATIONAL AUTOMOBILE MUSEUM

▲ **The 1913 Mercer Raceabout, Series J, Type 35—an excellent example of a sports racing vehicle of this vintage.**

The story of The William F. Harrah Foundation National Automobile Museum is the story of the automobile in America and its contents are already considered to be one of America's national treasures.

When the Harrah National Museum opened its modern building on the banks of the Truckee River in downtown Reno, it established a new standard for the world's automobile exhibits.

Auto collections in the past have been judged only by the number and quality of their cars. In most museums, visitors wander through roped-off displays of gleaming autos, often not really understanding what they're seeing, hardly able to distinguish one grill from another—able only to put a car into personal, not historical, perspective.

Though the museum does have the largest collection of antique and classic cars on public display in the western hemisphere, the innovative new standard is in its interpretation, educating visitors about the automobile. Using ad-

vanced audiovisual techniques, huge dioramas, and unique hands-on displays, the museum tells the story of the automobile and its impact on peoples' lives. It is a museum all visitors can enjoy, even those who know little about autos or who do not appreciate elegant old cars.

"This is not just cars on display," says Benedict Dasher, chairman of the foundation since its inception in 1981. "Every individual visitor will walk out of here having learned something about the automobile. It is an important story, particularly for Americans. Autos tend to cut across lines—sociological lines, age lines, all kinds of lines."

Chuck Hilton, director of the museum, who coordinated the efforts of the team of architects and designers, calls the museum a Reno landmark. The mu-

seum's distinctive rounded exterior—the forms, colors, and materials evoke a sense of the automobile's elegance and design. The building's chrome-and-metal exterior, for example, is painted with 1957 Chevy Heather-Fire mist.

Inside more than 200 fine cars are housed on the museum's 100,000 square feet of floor space. Near the entrance is a special theatrical interpretation of the story of the automobile. "Cars ought to be seen in motion," says Ray, and the theater reflects that. In addition, real cars inside the theater are used for special effects.

Then visitors step back in time, wandering down four theme streets, each depicting a different era in the development of the auto. A unique time line reminds visitors which important events were occurring during each period. Cars of the day are parked at the curbs in front of the storefronts, typical of the time. An early Union 76 station reminds visitors what gas prices were in the 1950s. Costumed interpreters mingle with the crowds, telling the stories of the cars.

There are few crowd barriers inside the museum, and plenty of open space to photograph the cars and their backdrops. In one interpretive exhibit visitors take a "creeper" ride to see a car's underside, and another shows how engines work and how cars are built. In hands-on displays, kids can honk old horns, crank up old cars, and climb aboard.

Cars will be rotated in the displays as new acquisitions are added. Many are rebuilt in the restoration shop that museum visitors can enter to see the work in progress. For scholars, the museum maintains the world's largest collection of car biographies and photographs, as well as other research facilities. There is also a bookstore and a riverfront cafe.

Frequently the museum is thrown open in the evening to community events as well as for corporate parties and convention groups. The museum also sends cars to concours d'elegance community car shows, such as those in Hillsborough, Silverado, and Pebble

▲ A 1949 Mercury six-passenger coupe. This customized coupe was driven by James Dean in the movie classic, *Rebel Without a Cause*.

Beach, California.

The new museum was the dream of the late William F. Harrah. While gaming was Harrah's business—he founded Nevada's largest casino empire—cars were his passion. He wanted to own one model of every car ever built, and he was coming closer than any other collector to that goal before his untimely death in 1978.

For many years Harrah housed his hundreds of autos on public display in a huge warehouse complex in nearby Sparks. The green New York double-decker bus that brought visitors to the auto display from Harrah's downtown casino was a familiar sight in Reno. But Harrah knew his guests ought to see more than just 1,000 autos lined up in endless rows. Before his death he was making plans for a new museum to tell the story of the auto, much like

the one that has been built.

It took broad community support to bring the dream to reality and move the collection from that Sparks warehouse to its present gleaming housing on the river. "Ben" Dasher, a retired insurance executive who spearheaded the project, is a volunteer in the public foundation, as are eight other trustees. Many of the cars were donated to the museum by Holiday Inc., which acquired the Harrah's gaming empire in 1980. Other large gifts came from the Harrah family as well as other contributors. And the museum sits on land provided by the City of Reno.

The foundation continues to gain community support through yearly membership programs, with basic dues of $25 per year, and an Adopt-a-Car plan, which holds "wax and shine" parties and other events. Many of the cars have been adopted, and the main requirements are that members (called adoptive parents) visit their adopted cars at least 10 hours each year and help keep them in good shape.

That program, too, reflects director Hilton's philosophy that, "Cars are kind of fun things."

▼ Capable of speeds in excess of 100 miles per hour, the 1936 Mercedes-Benz 500K Special Roadster is a prime example of classic 1930s styling.

▼ The William F. Harrah Automobile Museum, shown in an artist's rendering, is among the world's most beautiful, comprehensive, and educational automobile displays.

ETHEL M CHOCOLATES, INC.

How sweet it is! A confectionery factory producing premium chocolates in the Nevada desert.

Since 1978 Ethel M Chocolates, Inc., has been creating better chocolates to meet the demand for a boxed, high-quality, American chocolate. In the decade since Ethel M was founded, the company has doubled the size of its Henderson, Nevada, manufacturing facility—from 54,000 square feet to 114,000 square feet—and grown from one retail shoppe to more than 50 in the Southwest. It also added a national mail-order operation. More than 400 employees work at the factory or in the retail shoppes.

Ethel M's success is built on a time-honored family tradition of freshness and quality that was instilled by the founder, Forrest Mars. He chose the Las Vegas area due to the box chocolate opportunity afforded by the large tourist trade. The firm is now a privately held corporation owned by Mars, Inc., of McLean, Virginia.

Some 2,000 visitors per day tour the factory and stroll through the two-acre cactus garden outside the factory's Chocolate Shoppe. In the garden they can study and photograph the ever-changing desert landscape, including more than 300 varieties of cacti, succulents, trees, and shrubs native to the Southwest and the deserts of Australia. More than 400 tons of rocks were used

▲ A taste of Las Vegas.

▼ Henderson, Nevada, is home to Ethel M's 114,000-square-foot manufacturing/tour facility.

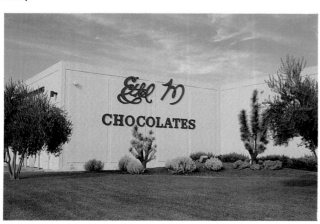

to create the stunning garden displays. Visitors can purchase similar plants and rocks at the factory's Cactus Shoppe.

Those who tour the factory see how the associates make Ethel M Chocolates in "batches." First they create batches of centers such as butter creams or caramels. Once the kitchen says the centers are ready, they are sent to the production area where they are enrobed in dark or milk chocolate. A finishing touch on each piece is a swirl of chocolate to identify the type of center. Some chocolates are molded into shapes and then filled with freshly made cherry cordials, lemon creams, or liqueur creams.

In all cases at Ethel M's it is people, not machines, who monitor the creation of the chocolates. The boxes are packed by hand. The visitor quickly understands Ethel M's devotion to quality and freshness. For those who cannot visit the factory, Ethel M's delicious chocolates are available through the nationwide mail-order system or at any one of the 50 retail shoppes. All customers, no matter where they purchase their choco-

▲ Ethel M's newest product: Derbies™ Double Decker Pecan Patties.

◄ Ethel M Chocolates are made from only the finest ingredients.

lates, will find the same freshness and quality guarantee that is apparent at the Nevada factory. Mail orders are turned around in three days and are sent in specially insulated shipping containers to protect the chocolates from damage and temperature changes. Every Ethel M Shoppe receives a fresh supply of chocolates weekly.

According to Dale Scott, retail sales manager, the first Ethel M Shoppe opened at the factory in Henderson and, as customers realized the premium quality taste of its chocolates, a natural progression of shoppe openings occurred, with more shoppes opening in Las Vegas, Reno, Tahoe, Arizona, and California.

Most Ethel M Shoppes are located in airports, hotels, and regional malls, where large numbers of customers will conveniently find friendly service and great chocolates, whether they're shopping for themselves or for someone else.

The shoppes take on holiday themes throughout the year to offer that special gift for each holiday event, such as Mother's Day, Christmas, Valentine's Day, and many others. Ted Shepherd, sales and marketing manager, says, "We direct a great deal of energy into providing the highest level of customer service at each Ethel M Chocolate Shoppe."

Ethel M's first product was its spirited, liqueur cream chocolates that feature a creamy filling blended with premium brand spirits such as

amaretto, creme de menthe, rum, or Irish Cream. Now, even with 50 different chocolates in production, Ethel M is looking to the future with its introduction of Watercolors™ Confections: nuts, butter creams, and caramels dipped in yogurt or white confectioner's coatings.

As Shepherd says of Ethel M's future, "We believe that quality really does make a difference, and it's the unwavering dedication to making the finest chocolates that has made us successful. As we look ahead, we'll continue to investigate new ways to distribute Ethel M Chocolates. We want everyone to have the chance to enjoy the taste of fresh chocolates."

▶ Ocotillo, saguaro, and Palo Verde trees are among the native southwestern species planted with Australian cacti at Ethel M's two-acre cactus garden, which delights 2,000 viewers per day.

PATRONS

The following individuals, companies, and organizations have made a valuable contribution to the quality of this publication. Windsor Publications and the State of Nevada Commission on Economic Development gratefully acknowledge their participation in *Nevada: Golden Challenge in the Silver State.*

Allison, MacKenzie, Hartman, Soumbeniotis & Russell, Ltd.*
A.G. Spanos Construction, Inc.*
American Asphalt, Inc.*
American Bank of Commerce*
American Nevada Corporation*
American Pacific Corporation*
Bally Manufacturing Corporation*
Beckley, Singleton, De Lanoy, Jemison & List, Chtd.*
Blue Cross and Blue Shield of Nevada*
The Boyd Group*
Centel*
CFA, Inc.*
Circus Circus Enterprises, Inc.*
Citibank (Nevada), National Association*
Silver Canyon
    A Division of Cosmo World of Nevada, Inc.*
Crowell, Susich, Owen & Tackes, Ltd.*
Dermody Properties*

The Desert Research Institute*
Di Loreto Construction and Development, Inc.*
Dura-Bond Bearing Co.*
Echo Bay Mines*
Economic Development Authority of Western Nevada*
Eldorado Hotel-Casino*
Ethel M Chocolates, Inc.*
First Interstate Bank of Nevada*
First Western Savings Association*
Ford Aerospace*
Harrah's*
Hunt-Spiller Manufacturing Corporation*
Investment Equity*
Jackpot Enterprises, Inc.*
JMA Architects and Engineers, Inc.*
Jones, Jones, Close & Brown*
Keefer, O'Reilly, Ferrario & Eskin*
Kerr-McGee Chemical Corp.*
Kittrell Garlock and Associates, Architects, AIA*
KRLR-Channel 21*
Lake Las Vegas*
Laura Spitzer*
Lewis Homes*
McDonald, Carano, Wilson, McCune, Bergin, Frankovich and Hicks*
Macy's Reno*
Nevada Arts*
Nevada Bell*

Nevada Development Authority*
Newmont Gold Company*
Nishika Corporation
    American 3-D Corporation*
Pioneer Chlor Alkali Company, Inc.*
Porsche Cars North America*
PriMerit Bank*
Reno Iron Works Co., Inc.*
Saint Mary's Regional Medical Center*
The Schulman Group*
SEA Consulting Engineers, Incorporated*
Sierra Health Services*
Sierra Pacific Resources*
Southwest Gas Corp.*
Summa Corporation*
Timet*
University of Nevada, Las Vegas*
University of Nevada, Reno*
Valley Bank of Nevada*
Vargas & Bartlett*
VTN Nevada*
G.C. Wallace, Inc.*
The William F. Harrah Foundation, National Automobile Museum*
Woodburn, Wedge and Jeppson*

*Particpants in Part Two: *Nevada: Golden Challenge in the Silver State.* The stories of these companies and organizations appear in Chapters 7 through 15, beginning on page 176.

BIBLIOGRAPHY

BOOKS, DOCUMENTS, AND PAMPHLETS

Amaral, Anthony. *Will James: The Last Cowboy Legend.* Reno: University of Nevada Press, 1980.

Benson, Ivan. *Mark Twain's Western Years.* Stanford University Press, 1938.

Biennial Report of Nevada State Agencies. Governor's Office of Community Services, 1989.

Big Game. Status and Hunting Season Recommendations. Nevada Department of Wildlife, 1989.

Boyer, Richard, and David Savageau. *Places Rated Almanac.* Rand McNally & Company, 1985.

———. *Places Rated Retirement Guide.* Rand McNally & Company, 1984.

City & State. The 50 States - 3rd Annual State Financial Report. Crain's Newspaper of Public Business & Finance. April 1988.

Construction of the Hoover Dam. Department of the Interior, Bureau of Reclamation, 1950.

Crampton, C. Gregory. *The Complete Las Vegas.* Salt Lake City, Utah: Peregrine Smith, Inc., 1976.

Creel, Cecil W. *A History of Nevada Agriculture.* Max C. Fleischmann College of Agriculture, University of Nevada, 1964.

Engineering and Mining Journal. March 1988.

Fletcher, F.N. *Early Nevada, The Period of Exploration, 1776-1848.* University of Nevada Press, 1972.

Georgetta, Clel. *Golden Fleece in Nevada.* Reno: Venture Publishing Co., Ltd., 1972.

Glass, Mary Ellen and Al. *Touring Nevada. A Historic and Scenic Guide.* University of Nevada Press, 1983.

Gold. Bureau of Mines Minerals Yearbook. U.S. Department of the Interior, 1986.

Hendershot, Carol. *Bing Crosby.* Northeastern Nevada Historical Society Quarterly, 1984.

Historical Agencies in North America. Directory, 13th edition. Nashville: American Association for State and Local History, 1987.

Houghton, Samuel G. *A Trace of Desert Waters.* Glendale, Calif.: Arthur H. Clark Co., 1976.

Hulse, James W. *The Nevada Adventure.* University of Nevada Press, 1972.

Information Please Almanac. Boston: Houghton Mifflin Company, 1989.

Kinsman, Clare D., and Mary Ann Tennenhouse. *Contemporary Authors.* Volumes 9-12. Detroit: Gale Research Company, 1974.

Kunitz, Stanley J., ed. *Twentieth Century Authors.* First Supplement. The H.W. Wilson Company, 1955.

Lillard, Richard G. *Desert Challenge.* Knopf, 1942.

Lincoln, Francis Church. *Mining Districts and Mineral Resources of Nevada.* Nevada Newsletter Publishing Company, 1923.

Mack, Effie Mona, Ph.D. *Nevada: A History of the State from the Earliest Times through the Civil War.* Glendale: The Arthur H. Clark Co., 1936.

Manufacturing Climates Study. Grant Thornton Management Consultants, July 1988.

McPhee, John. *Basin and Range.* Farrar-Strauss-Giroux, 1980.

Million Dollar Directory. The Dun and Bradstreet Corporation, 1988 and 1989 series.

Neil, J.M., ed. *Will James: The Spirit of the Cowboy.* Lincoln: University of Nevada Press, 1985.

Nevada. Menlo Park, Calif.: Lane Books.

Nevada: A Bicentennial History. W.W. Norton & Company, Inc., 1977.

Nevada Agricultural Statistics. Nevada Crop and Livestock Reporting Service, 1969 and 1984.

The Nevada Mineral Industry - 1985. Mackay School of Mines, University of Nevada, Reno.

Nevada Mule Deer. Status and Hunting Season Recommendations. Nevada Department of Wildlife, 1989.

The Official Museum Directory. The American Association of Museums, 1989.

Paher, Stanley W., ed. *Nevada.* Official Bicentennial Book. Las Vegas: Nevada Publications, 1976.

Payne, Albert Bigelow. *A Short Life of Mark Twain.* Harper & Brothers, 1920.

Political History of Nevada. Eighth edition. Issued by William D. Swackhamer, Secretary of State, 1986.

Reno-Sparks Convention Authority. *Marketing Report.* 1987.

Root, Phyllis, and Maxine McCormick. *Great Basin National Park.* Mankato, MN: Crestwood House, 1988.

Rowley, William D. *Reno: Hub of the Washoe Country.* Windsor Publications, Inc., 1984.

Toll, David W. *The Compleat Nevada Traveler.* Gold Hill Publishing Co., 1981.

U.S. Department of the Interior. *The Story of Boulder Dam.* Conservation Bulletin #9. Washington, D.C., 1941.

Walker, John B., and David R. Cowperthwaite. *Nevada Statistical Abstract, 1988 Edition.* Governor's Office of Community Services, 1989.

Your Competitive Edge - Mining in Nevada. Volume 5, No. 1. Nevada Employment Security Department, 1988.

PERIODICALS

Forbes magazine, November 30, 1987.

Gaming Business magazine, December 1980.

Inc. magazine, October 1988.

Nevada magazine, 1975-1988.

NEWSPAPERS

Las Vegas Review-Journal

Las Vegas Sun

Nevada Appeal

Reno Gazette-Journal

MISCELLANEOUS SOURCES

Commission on Economic Development

Commision on Tourism

Desert Research Institute

Legislative Counsel Bureau

University of Nevada, Reno

CHRONOLOGY

1827 Jedediah Smith crosses a vast stretch of territory, known today as Nevada. While crossing the area he wrote, "We frequently travel without water sometimes for two days over sandy deserts, where there was no sign of vegetation."

1844 During an expedition that includes scout Kit Carson, Captain John C. Frémont explores and names the Great Basin.

1848 Gold is discovered in California, and a year later about 30,000 Forty-Niners traverse the "Northern Mystery."

1851 The first cattle are brought to Nevada, marking the start of a successful livestock industry in the state.

1859 The Comstock Lode is discovered. After sections of the mine cave in, Philip Deidesheimer invents the "square set," a system that prevents mines from collapsing.

1863 For the first time, Samuel Clemens signs his name as Mark Twain on one of his "letters" in Virginia City's newspaper, the *Territorial Enterprise.*

1864 Nevada becomes the 36th state.

1869 The Central Pacific Railroad is completed.

1874 The University of Nevada is founded in Elko. In 1885, the university moved to Reno. Since then, the university has grown into a statewide system and includes several community colleges.

1880 The city of Reno, named after Civil War general Jesse L. Reno, has a population of 1,000. Today, 150,000 residents live in the city.

1905 Las Vegas becomes a city. It is now the biggest city in Nevada with over half a million residents.

1908 Nevada is chosen as the site for the first reclamation project in the United States; eventually the Truckee-Carson Project, now the Newlands Project, reclaimed 100,000 acres of desert.

1928 President Calvin Coolidge signs the Boulder Canyon Project Act, making way for Boulder Dam, later renamed Hoover Dam.

1931 In March, the Nevada legislature legalizes casino gambling and reduces the residency requirement for divorce from three months to six weeks.

1934 The U.S. Congress passes the Taylor Grazing Act in an attempt to solve the range wars between Nevada sheep owners and cattlemen.

1941 Military development begins in Nevada when the U.S. Army Quartermaster Corps establishes a gunnery school eight miles north of Las Vegas. Today this area is part of Nellis Air Force Base. In this same year, the U.S. Navy established a training base near Fallon, Nevada. In 1972, the base became the Fallon Naval Air Station.

1945 Robbins Cahill is appointed executive secretary of the Nevada Tax Commission. It was his job to oversee the gaming industry in Nevada, and his biggest challenges occurred while trying to control gangster activity.

1949 Edwin S. Bender convinces the Nevada state legislature to make Nevada an inland free port. This law became so important that voters added an amendment to their constitution in 1960, guaranteeing Nevada would remain a free port. As a result, the warehousing industry has grown and flourished in the state.

1953 On March 17 the first public demonstration of an atomic explosion occurs at the Nevada Test Site.

1955 The Nevada legislature establishes the Department of Economic Development. The state agency didn't become really active until the early 1980s when

Nevada's industries felt the national recession. In 1983, this agency became a division of the Commission on Economic Development. The main goal for the agency is to inform both the international and national business communities about Nevada's commercial advantages.

1959   A special act of the Nevada legislature establishes the Desert Research Institute. The institute's original purpose was to learn how Nevada could effectively manage its resources. In the meantime, the institute has become a leader in solving, or in attempting to solve, the deterioration of the environment by using the combined talents of 280 scientists, technicians, and support personnel.

1983   In this year, another state agency, the Division of Motion Pictures and Television, is formed as part of the Commission on Economic Development. Nevada uses this agency to support Hollywood film and television producers while they film productions in the state.

1986   The Great Basin National Park is established. The newest of the nation's parks, it includes 76,800 acres of valleys, mountains, and desert terrain.

1989   The Liberace Museum opens in Las Vegas.

Photo by Tom Campbell

INDEX

This book was set in Garamond Book type, 11 point on 14 point leading, and printed on 70 lb. Mead enamel.
A Varityper Graphics Text Organizer was used for layout and design.